The Translators and Editor

BENJAMIN R. FOSTER is Professor of Near Eastern Languages at Yale University. He is the author and translator of *Before the Muses: An Anthology of Akkadian Literature* and *From Distant Days: Myths, Tales, and Poetry of Ancient Mesopotamia*, as well as numerous other works in the field of Assyriology and Babylonian literature.

DOUGLAS FRAYNE is Associate Professor in the Department of Near and Middle Eastern Civilizations at the University of Toronto. He is the author of *The Early Dynastic List of Geographical Names*. He is an editor at the Royal Inscriptions of Mesopotamia Project (RIME), and is the translator and editor of three books in the RIME series: *Sargonic and Gutian Periods (2334–2113 BC)*, *Ur III Period (2112–2004 BC)*, and *Old Babylonian Period (2003–1595 BC)*.

GARY BECKMAN is Professor of Near Eastern Studies at the University of Michigan. He is the author of *Hittite Birth Rituals* and *Hittite Diplomatic Texts*. With Jack Sasson and others, he edited the encyclopedic *Civilizations of the Ancient Near East*. He is also an editor of the *Journal of Cuneiform Studies* and the *Journal of the American Oriental Society*.

A NORTON CRITICAL EDITION

THE EPIC OF GILGAMESH

A NEW TRANSLATION

ANALOGUES

CRITICISM

Translated and Edited by

BENJAMIN R. FOSTER

YALE UNIVERSITY

THE SUMERIAN
GILGAMESH POEMS

Translated by
DOUGLAS FRAYNE
UNIVERSITY OF TORONTO

THE HITTITE
GILGAMESH

Translated by
GARY BECKMAN
UNIVERSITY OF MICHIGAN

W • W • NORTON & COMPANY • *New York* • *London*

The text of this book is composed in Electra
with the display set in Bernhard Modern.
Composition by PennSet, Inc.
Manufacturing by Maple-Vail Book Group.
Book design by Antonina Krass.
Cover design by Karen Polinger Foster.

Library of Congress Cataloging-in-Publication Data
Gilgamesh. English.
The epic of Gilgamesh : a new translation, analogues, criticism / translated
and edited by Benjamin R. Foster. The Sumerian Gilgamesh poems / translated
by Douglas Frayne. The Hittite Gilgamesh / translated by Gary Beckman.
p. cm. — (A Norton critical edition)
Includes bibliographical references.

ISBN 0-393-97516-9 (pbk.)

1. Epic poetry, Assyro-Babylonian — Translations into English. I. Foster,
Benjamin R. (Benjamin Read). II. Frayne, Douglas. III. Beckman,
Gary M. IV. Title: Sumerian Gilgamesh poems. V. Title: Hittite
Gilgamesh. VI. Title. VII. Series.

PJ3771.G5 E5 2000
892'.1 — dc21   00-038035

W. W. Norton & Company, Inc., 500 Fifth Avenue, New York, N.Y. 10110
www.wwnorton.com
W. W. Norton & Company Ltd., 10 Coptic Street, London WC1A 1PU

1 2 3 4 5 6 7 8 9 0

Contents

Illustrations

Figures 1 and 5 drawn by Karen Polinger Foster and reproduced with permission.

Figures 2, 4, 6–10 reproduced with the permission of the Trustees of the British Museum. © Copyright of the Trustees of the British Museum.

Figure 4 also reproduced with the permission of William W. Hallo, Curator of the Yale Babylonian Collection.

Figure 11 reproduced with the permission of the Musée du Louvre.

Acknowledgments

I thank Andrew George (University of London) for his extraordinary generosity in allowing me to consult his manuscript edition of the standard version of the epic. I was therefore able to benefit from numerous readings, corrections, and substantial new material first deciphered and translated by him in his book *The Epic of Gilgamesh, A New Translation* (1999), in advance of his new edition of the original manuscripts. In addition, I was able to incorporate here important interpretations original with him, especially his interpretation of the episode of Gilgamesh's race with the sun, although I have here and there understood details somewhat differently. George's work on Gilgamesh is a turning point in the history of this complicated text, removing generations of conflicting proposals on difficult passages and bringing order to the known manuscripts for the first time. I am deeply grateful to him for allowing me to make so many improvements to my own work directly from his.

For access to original manuscripts of the epic, I thank William W. Hallo (Yale Babylonian Collection), Åke Sjöberg (University Museum, University of Pennsylvania), and Christopher Walker and the late Edmond Sollberger (British Museum). I thank Aage Westenholz (University of Copenhagen) for permission to use his unpublished copies and collations of various manuscripts of the epic and A. Cavigneaux (CNRS, Paris) for access to his unpublished studies of the Sumerian Gilgamesh poems.

For permission to reuse, in revised form, my translation of portions of Tablet XI, published in *The Context of Scripture,* ed. Hallo and Younger (1997), I thank E. J. Brill, NV, Leiden. For permission to reprint my translation of "The Gilgamesh Letter," I thank Mark Cohen, CDL Press.

My particular thanks go to Karen Polinger Foster for her assistance with cover design and illustrations and for her repeated careful readings of this work in conjunction with the original Akkadian and with the best modern translations, and for discussing it with me line by line. She greatly improved the English expression and readability of the translation.

For errors or shortcomings that remain, I alone am responsible.

B.R.F.

Introduction

This four-thousand-year-old tale of love, death, and adventure is the world's oldest epic masterpiece. Over a millennium before the *Iliad* and the *Odyssey*, Mesopotamian poets wrote of Gilgamesh, hero-king of the Sumerian city of Uruk. The story has four main sections: first, Gilgamesh's abuse of his subjects, the creation of his rival—the wild man Enkidu—and their eventual friendship; second, the pair's heroic quest to the forest of cedars to slay a monster and bring back a gigantic tree, thus winning immortal fame for Gilgamesh; third, the death of Enkidu, which leaves Gilgamesh terrified at the prospect of his own death; and finally, Gilgamesh's arduous search for the secret of eternal life.

Who Was Gilgamesh?

According to Mesopotamian tradition, Gilgamesh was a long-ago king of Uruk, builder of its famous city walls, traces of which are still visible today. These walls were nearly ten kilometers long and had more than nine hundred towers. Archaeologists date one phase of these immense walls to about 2700 B.C.E., so if Gilgamesh was a historical person, he may have ruled Uruk at that time. Anam, a king of Uruk during the nineteenth century B.C.E., mentions Gilgamesh as builder of the walls of his city in an inscription commemorating his own work on them, thereby comparing himself to his royal predecessor. Further, the walls of Uruk are the setting for the beginning and end of *The Epic of Gilgamesh*.

A list of ancient Mesopotamian kings, compiled in the early second millennium B.C.E., names Gilgamesh in the following passage, where he, like other kings of his era, is given a fabulously long reign: "The god Lugalbanda, a shepherd, reigned for 1200 years. The god Dumuzi, a fisherman(?), whose city was Ku'ara, reigned for 100 years. The god Gilgamesh, whose father was a phantom, lord of the city Kulaba, reigned for 126 years." *The Epic of Gilgamesh* and Sumerian poems about Gilgamesh give the name of his father as Lugalbanda, king of Uruk. They also identify his mother as the goddess Ninsun, a deified wild cow. The puzzle of Gilgamesh's parentage is reflected in the epic, where he is described as two-thirds divine and one-third human. As for the name Gilgamesh, it may mean "Old-Man-Who-Became-a-Young-Man," although this is not certain. If this understanding is correct, his name may provide a clue, beyond the great walls of Uruk, as to why Gilgamesh was remembered as a famous figure of the past, inspiring epics and poems: he sought to escape death.

Stories about the adventures of Gilgamesh were first written in Sumerian around 2100 B.C.E. These have been translated here in "The Sumerian Gilgamesh Poems" by Douglas Frayne. The kings ruling in Sumer at that time, the Third Dynasty of the city of Ur, claimed that they were descended from the ancient royal house of Gilgamesh of Uruk. One king of Ur even called Gilgamesh his "brother." The kings of Ur may well have originated at Uruk, but their claim of kinship with such a remote figure of the past was perhaps little more than a bid for prestige and antiquity for their family. They may also have wanted to avoid referring to their more recent past, when Uruk and Ur had been ruled by a dynasty not related to them. Whatever the reason, Sumerian poets of the Third Dynasty of Ur extolled the life and deeds of Gilgamesh, as well as those of his father, Lugalbanda, and composed narrative poems about them, which were enjoyed at the royal court.

A document studied in Sumerian schools of the early second millennium B.C.E., supposed to be a copy of an ancient inscription, names Gilgamesh as builder of a structure known as the Tummal, perhaps a temple treasury, at the Sumerian city of Nippur. This "ancient" inscription is probably not genuine but fabricated to make the treasury sound more venerable. In any case, the document certainly does not date to the time of Gilgamesh.

In the first millennium B.C.E., Gilgamesh was worshipped as a netherworld deity and was invoked in funerary rites. A prayer to him found on tablets from Assyria dating to the first millennium B.C.E. reads, in part, as follows:

O Gilgamesh, perfect king, judge of the netherworld gods,
Deliberative prince, neckstock of the peoples,[1]
Who examines all corners of the earth,
Administrator of the netherworld,
You are the judge and you examine as only a god can!
When you are in session in the netherworld,
You give the final verdict,
Your verdict cannot be altered nor can your sentence be commuted.
The Sun has entrusted to you his powers of judgment and verdict.
Kings, governors, and princes kneel before you,
You examine the omens that pertain to them,
You render their verdicts.

---

1. A neckstock was a device of wood used to restrain prisoners, here used to signify Gilgamesh's control over the human race.

Aelian, a Roman author of the third century C.E., perhaps quoting indirectly a Babylonian writer, tells a story of the birth of Gilgamesh (translated below, p. 154). This does not correspond to anything in the extant epic and therefore may not represent an authentic Mesopotamian tradition. Gilgamesh is also mentioned in the "Book of Giants" in the Dead Sea Scrolls, so memory of him outlasted Mesopotamian civilization.

What Is The Epic of Gilgamesh?

The Sumerian narrative poems of the late third millennium B.C.E. provided materials for narrative poems written in the Babylonian language around 1700 B.C.E., called here the "old versions" of The Epic of Gilgamesh. The longest and most original of these took episodes from the Sumerian poems and recast them into a new, cohesive plot showing how an arrogant and overbearing king was chastened by the knowledge that he too had to die, like everybody else. Pieces of various old versions have survived. These were the source for the Babylonian epic tradition about Gilgamesh, which was to last more than fifteen hundred years. Fragments of many different versions of the epic have been recovered on clay tablets from Mesopotamia, Syria, the Levant, and Anatolia, attesting to its wide distribution in ancient times.

Manuscripts of The Epic of Gilgamesh dating to the period 1500–1000 B.C.E. are referred to as the "middle versions." These preserve only scattered episodes. The longest surviving version, known from a group of manuscripts dating from the seventh century B.C.E., is referred to here as the "standard version." The term "late versions" refers to manuscripts later than the seventh century B.C.E.

Portions of The Epic of Gilgamesh were translated into non-Mesopotamian languages such as Hittite and Hurrian. The Hittite versions of the epic have been translated here in "The Hittite Gilgamesh" by Gary Beckman. The Hurrian versions are too broken and poorly understood to translate. The "Elamite version" found in some translations is actually a misunderstanding of two tablets that have nothing to do with Gilgamesh. "The Gilgamesh Letter" is an ancient parody of the epic.

When Babylonian and Sumerian tablets were rediscovered and deciphered in modern times, the story of Gilgamesh and his friend Enkidu was gradually pieced together from numerous fragmentary manuscripts. Though certain pieces are still missing, enough of the text has been found to enable modern readers to read a coherent, extended narrative poem.

Form, Authorship, and Audience of The Epic of Gilgamesh

The Mesopotamians had no word corresponding to "epic" or "myth" in their languages. Ancient scholars of Mesopotamian literature referred to the epic as the "Gilgamesh Series," that is, a lengthy work on more than one tablet, each corresponding to a "book" or "canto" in modern literature, twelve in the case of *The Epic of Gilgamesh*. Eleven of these tablets form a continuous narrative poem. The twelfth is a partial translation of a Sumerian poem about Gilgamesh appended to the narrative, perhaps during the first millennium B.C.E., because it seemed germane. This has been omitted here in preference to the more complete Sumerian original translated by Douglas Frayne for this Norton Critical Edition. No one knows how many tablets comprised the old versions, but there were probably far fewer than eleven.

The Mesopotamians knew nothing of the original author of *The Epic of Gilgamesh* but associated the eleven-tablet version with Sin-leqe-unninni, a scholar who lived in the second half of the second millennium B.C.E., centuries after the old versions were written. Nothing further is known of this man except that long after his death he was claimed as an ancestor by certain distinguished families in Babylonia.

One common assumption about ancient epics, such as the *Iliad* or the *Odyssey*, is that their written form was based on oral tradition. This does not seem to be true of *The Epic of Gilgamesh*. There is no evidence that *The Epic of Gilgamesh* began as an oral narrative performed by bards or reciters and coalesced into a written text only later. In fact, the poem as we now have it shows many signs of having been a formal, written, literary work composed and perhaps performed for well-educated people, especially scholars and members of a royal court. Rather than being popular or folkloric literature, the story of Gilgamesh may have been mostly of interest to a small circle of people who belonged to the social and economic elite of their day. A short excerpt of Tablet II, found on a student's exercise tablet from Babylon and dating from the late first millennium B.C.E., shows that the epic was studied in ancient schools.

Translating The Epic of Gilgamesh

Western literary tradition since classical antiquity has transmitted ancient works, such as the epics of Homer or the plays of Sophocles, as single unified texts with only minor "variants." This term refers to changes in wording for the same passage from one manuscript to another, or to important passages omitted in some manuscripts but included in others. For the most part, however, there are no substantive deviations among manuscripts of the same classical work, even those from centuries apart. Furthermore, ancient classical literature that survives only in fragments or quotations, such as the poetry of Sappho, has little chance of ever being pieced together into its original form, because it was written on perishable materials.

The situation for ancient Mesopotamian texts is quite different. For *The Epic of Gilgamesh*, there are numerous ancient manuscripts on durable clay tablets, some more than a thousand years older than others, from many places. When these deal with the same episodes, they show fascinating and significant variations in wording and content. This allows us to see what was added, subtracted, changed, and reinterpreted over the centuries, but it complicates presentation of the text to a modern reader. Since no single version of *The Epic of Gilgamesh* has survived intact from antiquity, any translator has to make difficult decisions about how to treat the material. The method followed here has been to take as the basic text the "standard version." These are later copies of the eleven-tablet edition associated with Sin-leqe-unninni. Where lines, sections, or episodes are missing or omitted from this version, I have supplied them where possible from other versions, both earlier and later. There is no consistent line numbering for any original text of *The Epic of Gilgamesh*. The line numbers used here refer to lines of the translation only.

Even when all versions are consulted, there are still major gaps in the narrative, as well as in individual lines or passages. Editors and translators have guessed about what the missing elements might have been; new discoveries often prove these guesses wrong. In this translation, important words or phrases not found in any ancient manuscript and not restorable from surviving traces or parallel passages are enclosed in square brackets, meaning that these are only modern interpretive surmises. Where such inferences are not possible, square brackets enclose ellipses. Question marks within parentheses following words or phrases indicate particularly uncertain restorations that might have a significant impact upon the meaning of the passage. Words or phrases in parentheses indicate explanatory additions by the translator. Ellipses without brackets indicate signs or words of unknown meaning.

It is important to remember that the ancient languages in which *The Epic of Gilgamesh* was written or translated, including Akkadian, Sumerian, and Hittite, are not so well understood as other ancient languages, such as Greek and Latin. This means that translators frequently disagree among themselves as to what a given word or phrase could mean. While this translation is based on study of the ancient manuscripts, consultation of the extensive scholarly literature about the epic, and comparison with the best modern translations, it remains a more individual product than a translation of a work by Homer or Virgil is likely to be. The goal has been to produce a readable text well grounded in the ancient sources. New discoveries constantly enlarge our understanding of the epic, whose genius and power can still move the modern reader four thousand years after it was written.

Reading The Epic of Gilgamesh

DIRECT SPEECH

The Epic of Gilgamesh contains considerable direct speech by the characters, normally introduced by the formula, "X made ready to speak, saying to Y." But in situations in which the narrator wishes to convey a sense of urgency, abruptness, anger, or excitement, this formula is often omitted (I, 94, 180, 224; VI, 7–21, contrast 24–79; VI, 84–86, contrast 87–88; VI, 154–55; VII, 141, 169; IX, 3; XI, 178, 206–8).[2] The story opens and closes using the same words, addressed by an omniscient narrator to the audience in the beginning and addressed by Gilgamesh to the exiled boatman at the end. The poem also contains first-person discourse by individual characters describing their past (XI, 9–209) or present (IX, 3–12) actions. In general, there is more direct speech by the characters than narration of their actions.

The narrative is sometimes rapid, sometimes slow. Suspense is built up by repetition (I, 113–66) or lengthy speeches at climactic moments (V, 64–116). Passage of time may be conveyed by serial repetition of lines (VII, 174–80; IX, 82–109). Description of particularly dramatic moments or speeches of great emotion may be given in full twice, as if pausing for effect (II, 66–68, 100–104). Action is presented in short episodes, often with direct speech, such as instructions, assertions, or statements of will, setting the stage for action to follow (X, 196–205). The second half of the poem makes extensive use of retrospective speech concerning events already narrated or that took place before the time of the poem, climaxing in the long speech of Utanapishtim narrating the story of the flood (XI, 9–209). While these speeches are progressively more important for Gilgamesh's broadening understanding, their effect is to slow the action in the second half of the poem, though the denouement is surprisingly rapid.

PARALLELISM

In Mesopotamian poetry, each line usually consists of a complete sentence or thought. Lines often divide into two, three, or more parts with roughly the same number of words in each part, usually two to four, though there are many variations on this pattern. There is no strict meter in Mesopotamian poetry, but the symmetry of poetic lines can give the poetry a kind of rhythm or beat that may be varied for artistic

2. References are to tablet and line of the translation.

reasons. For example, rapid rhythms may be used for a fight scene (II, 96–108), slow rhythms for an anxious mother's prayer (III, 46–85).

Lines of poetry often come in pairs, which can be related to each other in sound, rhythm, and meaning. Meaning is developed in part of a line, a whole line, in pairs of lines, or in groups of lines by use of parallelism; that is, repeated formulation of the same message such that subsequent statements may restate, expand, complete, contrast, render more specific, or carry further the first message. The following two-line example illustrates this:

> He anointed himself with oil, turned into a man,
> He put on clothing, became like a warrior.
> (II, 43–44)

In this case, the first half of each line gives complementary, sequential actions that describe Enkidu's progress in grooming himself into civilization. The second half of each line proclaims his progress from becoming a human being to becoming a leader among men.

The following example is in five lines:

> The whole of Uruk was standing beside him,
> The people formed a crowd around him,
> A throng was jostling towards him,
> Young men were mobbed around him,
> Infantile, they groveled before him.
> (II, 85 89)

This describes the street scene as Enkidu enters Uruk to challenge Gilgamesh. Activity increases as the scene focuses on the hero at the center: the outer limits are standing in a crowd, some within are jostling each other for position, the nearer ones are piling up on each other's shoulders, those closest are collapsing at his feet in awe. This quickening of action is paralleled by ever greater specification of the people involved: the whole land, a rabble or mob, the young men of the city. One senses, too, increasing derogation by the narrator, for he seems to be contemptuous of the shoving crowd of gawking, fawning men and youngsters.

NARRATIVE CONTRASTS

The reader will observe that another favored literary device of the standard version of the epic is the use of contrasts or symbols that can be redefined or even reversed in meaning between the beginning and the end of the poem. For instance, in the beginning, Gilgamesh stays up all night roistering and abusing his subjects; at the end, he cannot stay awake more than a few minutes. Gilgamesh, the king, at the apex of society, is supposed to act as shepherd of his subjects, but instead mistreats them; Enkidu, the uncivilized man, watches all night over the shepherds' flocks. Enkidu begins as a wild man roaming the steppe and saving wild beasts from the hunter; Gilgamesh becomes a wild man who kills wild beasts.

FIGURES OF SPEECH

Mesopotamian literature makes extensive use of figures of speech familiar to the modern reader, for example, a variety of similes. Some are simple comparisons: "like a lioness whose cubs are in a pitfall, he paced to and fro" (VIII, 60–61), or an attacker springs back "like a swing rope" (VII, 137). Some similes are developed further or form part of a wider set of associations: "like a guardian deity she (the harlot) led him" (II, 22). This evokes an image, familiar to Babylonians from their document seals, of a personal intercessor deity leading the seal owner into the presence of a more important deity. Yet once Enkidu has become civilized, he walks in front of the harlot to Uruk (II, 74), and later in the poem, the elders of Uruk, Gilgamesh, and Enkidu have much to say about who is to walk first as they set forth on their quest (III, 5–7, 170, etc.). So here an apparently simple simile opens a series of related images that recur throughout the poem. Some similes seem enhanced with irony: "Roof her over like the watery depths" (XI, 31), for example, is a striking way to describe the ark under construction just before the flood. The Mesopotamians considered the watery depths below the earth to have a surface over them to hold them in. This the poet compares to the roof of the ark, which is supposed to keep the waters out.

Metaphors, or implied comparisons, include such examples as "Whatever they attempt is a puff of air" (II, 187) and "his breath (of life) is death" (II, 153). They may also be refurbished and expanded, as with some of the similes. In Tablet I, line 31, for example, Gilgamesh as king is compared to a charging wild bull, an image common enough when used in praise of Mesopotamian royalty, but the image gains richness a few lines later by reference to his mother, Ninsun, as a wild cow (I, 37): Gilgamesh is a wild bull by birth, so to speak, as well as by behavior. Later in the poem, Enkidu dreams that he is trampled down by a monster "like a wild bull" (VII, 139), perhaps symbolic of Gilgamesh's role in his friend's impending doom. Likewise, the metaphor of Gilgamesh as shepherd of Uruk, contrasted to Enkidu as an actual shepherd, is an example of the refurbishment of what was nearly a "dead metaphor" elsewhere: the king as shepherd of his people.

WORDPLAY

The Epic of Gilgamesh abounds in wordplay, that is, suggestion of one word through use of another with the same or similar sound. In modern

Western literature, this technique is usually used as a game or joke, but in Mesopotamian literature wordplays were used in serious and solemn literary contexts as well as for humor. Three or more wordplays in the narration of Gilgamesh's dreams (I, 246–86), for example, provide a clear reference to homosexual love: "axe" (I, 279) can suggest "female impersonator," "force" (I, 248) can suggest "male wearing his hair in a distinctive manner to suggest prostitution," and in a three-way wordplay, "commanded" or "something evoked by" (I, 96) may also suggest "male" and "sequestered man as if in a harem." An equally complicated wordplay, intended to deceive the human race about the true nature of the events presaged by construction of the ark, apparently depends on "cakes" suggesting "darkness," "grains" suggesting something like "grievous," and "rains" suggesting "provide for," though the whole passage is difficult and its meaning in dispute (XI, 43–47). Enkidu's curse and blessing of the prostitute (VII, 67–95, 115–25) contain numerous wordplays, some with sexual overtones: "best clothes" suggests "lap" (a euphemism for genitalia). Likewise in Humbaba's curse of Gilgamesh and Enkidu (V, 113), there seem to be elaborate wordplays that mean at the same time "May they not cross water safely to the opposite bank" and "May they not find a friend to rely on," where "cross" sounds like "friend" and "bank" has an ominous echo of the word for "grave," although this example remains obscure. In the gardener's rejection of Ishtar's advances (VI, 71–74), his choice of the word "reed" (elpet) echoes harshly Ishtar's use of "touch" (luput) (VI, 69); and in line 77, "garden patch" suggests "suffering." In Tablet XI, line 227, there is a wordplay on "day" and "make known." In this translation, a few of the most important wordplays are explained, the wording is altered to suggest the tone or ambiguity, or comparable English puns and expressions are used. Others have of necessity been left aside.

USE OF FANTASTIC NUMBERS

Of all ancient Mesopotamian literary works, *The Epic of Gilgamesh* makes the most frequent use of fantastic numbers: quantity, size, weight, time, and distance. Sometimes the unit counted is not expressed but left to the reader's imagination, as in Tablet XI, line 66, "thrice thirty-six hundred measures of pitch I poured in the oven." The precise numbers may vary among different versions of the poem. In some instances, the figures do not seem to add up (II, 205–11) or simply defy calculation (X, 211–17). Some of these figures may have been mathematical jokes intended for people with a Mesopotamian mathematical education, while others may simply be exaggerations in folkloric or epic style. Among the most celebrated riddles in the poem is Gilgamesh's genealogy: two-thirds god, one-third human, for which various explanations have been offered. The fraction two-thirds appears again in the name of the boatman, Ur-Shanabi, "Servant of Two-Thirds," and in connection with launching or loading the ark (XI, 80).

PECULIARITIES OF SPEECH

Tone and usage in such an ancient text are hazardous topics for discussion, but *The Epic of Gilgamesh* contains clear differentiations in the speech of individual characters, including style, diction, grammar, and even pronounciation. Utanapishtim, for example, expresses himself in the elevated, obscure style suitable for an antediluvian sage but has a curious mannerism of rolling or doubling consonants (*sharru* for *sharu*, *shaqqa* for *shaqa*, *ushaznannu* for *ushaznanu*, *niqqu* for *niqu*). This may have suggested to an ancient audience some social or personal distinction now no longer apparent. Shamhat, the harlot, is eloquent and persuasive (I, 224–44), whereas Ishtar, the goddess, apparently speaks like a person of little education, perhaps a streetwalker (VI, 94–100, 151). The elders of Uruk are pompous and long-winded, causing Gilgamesh to laugh (II, 275); Humbaba is mincing and bombastic, and Ishullanu, the gardener, uses a nonstandard form in Tablet VI, line 72 (this could be translated either as archaic and proverbial: "Hath my mother not baked?" or as a colloquialism: "Hain't my mother baked?"). Although deliberate distortion of normal poetic language to reflect distinctive speech may occur elsewhere in Mesopotamian literature, no other work develops the device to the same extent as this poem.

COMPOUND EXPRESSIONS

A minor but distinctive motif of *The Epic of Gilgamesh* is the formation of compounds with the word "man," such as "trapping-man" or "entrapping-man" (I, 113; VII, 59), "mightiness-man" (I, 139), "joy-woe man" (I, 234), "yokel-man" (V, 27), "human-man" (I, 178), and "circumspect-man" (IV, 223). The most elaborate of these is the name of the old man who is supposed to test the plant of rejuvenation: "Old Man Has Become Young-Again-Man" (XI, 303). This type of formation is very rare outside of this poem, so may be considered a special feature of its style, though the tone or intent is no longer perceivable.

THEMES

To a Mesopotamian audience, certain themes of the poem would have been familiar from other popular literary works. The portrayal of human mortality as a consequence of divine selfishness, for example, was well known to them. They also recognized a hero as a man striving towards greater accomplishments than those of ordinary people, in spite of the limitations imposed by chance and destiny. The Mesopotamians preferred literary works set in ancient times, involving kings and gods, narrating events largely outside of everyday experience. Yet the divine and human heroes often display imperfections and personal limitations, as if remoteness of time and empirical background were no obstacles to projecting inglorious human weakness onto long-ago heroes. The theme of the partiality of divine justice was familiar to Babylonian readers as well: they would not have been surprised at the unfair condemnation of Enkidu nor at the intervention of the sun god, Shamash, to the crucial advantage of the heroes.

In the epic, the Mesopotamian audience would have recognized passages that occur in other literary works. For example, in Tablet VII, lines 147–52, Enkidu uses lines found also in the poem called "Ishtar's Descent to the Netherworld"[3] in describing his own descent to hell. Furthermore, Ishtar's threat to release the dead, in Tablet VI, lines 99–100, is also found in "Ishtar's Descent to the Netherworld." Mesopotamian readers might have relished the contrast between how this passage was used in the epic and how it was used in the other poem. In the epic, Ishtar makes these threats after going up to heaven, whereas in "Ishtar's Descent to the Netherworld," she makes the same threats at the gates of hell. They would also have noticed that in threatening to break down the tavern keeper's door (X, 22) Gilgamesh uses the same words that Ishtar uses in the other poem when threatening to break down the doors of hell, and perhaps they thought that a humorous touch. Nor is this the only instance of wording from another poem used in the Gilgamesh epic to mean something quite different. In Tablet VII, lines 83 and 85, Enkidu curses the female prostitute using the same terms with which the queen of the netherworld curses the male impersonator of women in "Ishtar's Descent to the Netherworld." These and other allusions to Mesopotamian intellectual tradition suggest that the anticipated audience included people of formal education appreciative of the adroit reuse of stock phraseology.

Mesopotamians expected their literature to stress the importance of knowledge. The significance of Gilgamesh's story lay not so much in the deeds themselves as in the lesson his experience offered to future generations. The Mesopotamians believed that highest knowledge came to sages of the remote past directly from the gods or through extraordinary events not likely to recur. For their own times, they thought that highest knowledge came from study of written works of the past.

The modern reader may well find other themes of the poem of special interest. Women, for example, are more active in this narrative than in many Mesopotamian literary works. In fact, Gilgamesh's success in his quest is largely owed to the intervention of women: his mother's with the sun god, leading to his defeat of Humbaba; the wife of the

3. Translated in *Muses*, pp. 402–9.

scorpion monster's with her husband, probably leading to his entrance into the mountain tunnel. Siduri, the tavern keeper, tells him how to get over the sea. The wife of Utanapishtim persuades her dour husband to give Gilgamesh a gift, which turns out to be the plant of rejuvenation. While Mesopotamians were familiar with a literary convention according to which women were more susceptible and approachable than men, *The Epic of Gilgamesh*'s development of this convention into a major theme has no clear ancient parallel.

To the modern reader, satirical and humorous elements of the poem may seem surprising, as a canon of Western culture is that epic is supposed to be serious and exalted. Such passages include Enkidu's replacement of his irreversible curse with a magnanimous blessing, his denunciation of an insensate door, the sun god's hollow promise to him of a fine funeral, the pedantic speech of the scorpion monster's wife, and Gilgamesh's brutal denunciation of Ishtar. There are fleeting but memorable images, such as the worm dropping out of Enkidu's nose, or the boatbuilders' purloining materials from the ark project, to which ancient parallels will not be readily found. Taken with the quantitative exaggerations of the story, such as Gilgamesh's extraordinary journey, his race with the sun, the topographical consequences of his struggle with Humbaba, and the monstrous cubic ark, such passages may betoken a complex intent that blended humor and a sophisticated pleasure in the ridiculous with a serious message about love and death. No one can say for sure.

Abbreviations

Harps: Thorkild Jacobsen, *The Harps That Once . . . Sumerian Poetry in Translation* (New Haven: Yale UP, 1987)

Muses: Benjamin R. Foster, *Before the Muses,* 2nd ed. (Bethesda, MD: CDL Press, 1996)

The Text of
THE EPIC
OF GILGAMESH

Tablet I

[*The prologue introduces Gilgamesh as a man who gained knowledge through exceptional trials. The narrator invites us to read Gilgamesh's account of his hardships and to admire the city walls and treasury for the goddess Ishtar, his architectural legacy in Uruk.*]

He who saw the wellspring, the foundations of the land,
Who knew [. . .], was wise in all things,
Gilgamesh, who saw the wellspring, the foundations of the land,
Who knew [. . .], was wise in all things,
[He . . .] throughout,   5
Full understanding of it all he gained,
He saw what was secret and revealed what was hidden,
He brought back tidings from before the flood,
From a distant journey came home, weary, at peace,
Engraved all his hardships on a monument of stone,   10
He built the walls of ramparted Uruk,
The lustrous treasury of hallowed Eanna!
See its upper wall, whose facing gleams like copper,
Gaze at the lower course, which nothing will equal,
Mount the stone stairway, there from days of old,   15
Approach Eanna, the dwelling of Ishtar,
Which no future king, no human being will equal.
Go up, pace out the walls of Uruk,
Study the foundation terrace and examine the brickwork.
Is not its masonry of kiln-fired brick?   20
And did not seven masters lay its foundations?
One square mile of city, one square mile of gardens,
One square mile of clay pits, a half square mile of Ishtar's
    dwelling,
Three and a half square miles is the measure of Uruk!
[Search out] the foundation box of copper,   25
[Release] its lock of bronze,
Raise the lid upon its hidden contents,
Take up and read from the lapis tablet
Of him, Gilgamesh, who underwent many hardships.

[*The narrator tells of the extraordinary characteristics of Gilgamesh. An old version of the epic began here.*]

3

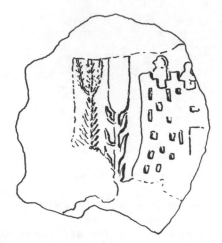

1. *Go up, pace out the walls of Uruk.* Seal impression from the end of the fourth millennium B.C.E. depicting people atop the walls of Uruk.

Surpassing all kings, for his stature renowned,   30
Heroic offspring of Uruk, a charging wild bull,
He leads the way in the vanguard,
He marches at the rear, defender of his comrades.
Mighty floodwall, protector of his troops,
Furious flood-wave smashing walls of stone,   35
Wild calf of Lugalbanda, Gilgamesh is perfect in strength,
Suckling of the sublime wild cow, the woman Ninsun,
Towering Gilgamesh is uncannily perfect.
Opening passes in the mountains,
Digging wells at the highlands' verge,   40
Traversing the ocean, the vast sea, to the sun's rising,
Exploring the furthest reaches of the earth,
Seeking everywhere for eternal life,
Reaching in his might Utanapishtim the Distant One,
Restorer of holy places that the deluge had destroyed,   45
Founder of rites for the teeming peoples,
Who could be his like for kingly virtue?[1]
And who, like Gilgamesh, can proclaim, "I am king!"
Gilgamesh was singled out from the day of his birth,

1. Mesopotamian rulers sometimes boasted of restoring ancient temples that had been destroyed and forgotten long ago. In line 45, the poet suggests that Gilgamesh became a dutiful king of this kind. Mesopotamian rulers also sometimes boasted of endowing temples with new offerings. This pair of lines (45–46) sums up religious duties expected of a good king by citing two extremes of benefactions: those from the remote past and those beginning in his own reign.

Two-thirds of him was divine, one-third of him was human! 50
The Lady of Birth drew his body's image,
The God of Wisdom brought his stature to perfection.[2]

[gap]

[. . .] stately in feature,
[. . .] in body, lofty [. . .]
His foot was a triple cubit, his leg six times twelve, 55
His stride was six times twelve cubits,
His thumb was [. . .] cubits.
His cheeks had a beard like [. . .]
The locks of his hair grew thick as a grainfield.
He was perfection in height, 60
Ideally handsome [. . .]

[Gilgamesh, in his arrogance and superior strength, abuses his subjects, apparently through some strenuous athletic competition at which he excelled. At the complaint of the citizenry, the gods create a wild man, Enkidu, as a fitting rival for Gilgamesh.]

In the enclosure of Uruk he strode back and forth,
Lording it like a wild bull, his head thrust high.
The onslaught of his weapons had no equal.
His teammates stood forth by his game stick, 65
He was harrying the young men of Uruk beyond reason.
Gilgamesh would leave no son to his father,
Day and night he would rampage fiercely.
Gilgamesh [. . .]
This was the shepherd of ramparted Uruk, 70
This was the people's shepherd,
Bold, superb, accomplished, and mature!
Gilgamesh would leave no girl to her [mother]!
The warrior's daughter, the young man's spouse,
Goddesses kept hearing their plaints.[3] 75
The gods of heaven, the lords who command,
[Said to Anu]:

You created this headstrong wild bull in ramparted Uruk,
The onslaught of his weapons has no equal.

2. According to one Mesopotamian tradition, the first human being was created by Mami, goddess of birth, whom the gods thereupon rewarded with the title "Mistress of All the Gods," and Enki, god of wisdom, working together. Subsequent human beings were born naturally. This passage means that Gilgamesh was physically a perfect human being, so much so that he resembled the first human created by the gods more than the product of a normal birth.
3. Certain goddesses were believed to pay particular attention to prayers of women. In this case, they are moved by the constant complaints of the women of Uruk that Gilgamesh was mistreating the women and men of the city.

His teammates stand forth by his game stick,   80
He is harrying the young men of Uruk beyond reason.
Gilgamesh leaves no son to his father!
Day and night he rampages fiercely.
This is the shepherd of ramparted Uruk,
This is the people's shepherd,   85
Bold, superb, accomplished, and mature!
Gilgamesh leaves no girl to her [mother]!

The warrior's daughter, the young man's spouse,
Anu(?)[4] kept hearing their plaints.

[Anu speaks.]

Let them summon [Aruru], the great one,   90
[She created] the boundless human race.
[Let her create a partner for Gilgamesh], mighty in strength,
[Let them contend with each other], that Uruk may have
     peace.

They summoned the birth goddess, Aruru:

You, Aruru, created [the boundless human race],   95
Now, create what Anu commanded,
To his stormy heart, let that one be equal,
Let them contend with each other, that Uruk may have
     peace.

When Aruru heard this,
She conceived within her what Anu commanded.   100
Aruru wet her hands,
She pinched off clay, she tossed it upon the steppe,
She created valiant Enkidu in the steppe,
Offspring of potter's clay(?), with the force of the hero Ninurta.
Shaggy with hair was his whole body,   105
He was made lush with head hair, like a woman,
The locks of his hair grew thick as a grainfield.
He knew neither people nor inhabited land,
He dressed as animals do.
He fed on grass with gazelles,   110
With beasts he jostled at the water hole,
With wildlife he drank his fill of water.

---

4. This important restoration is particularly uncertain.

[*A distraught hunter seeks his father's advice as to how to stop Enkidu's interference with his trapping. The father counsels him to go to Gilgamesh, who will give him a woman to seduce Enkidu from his untamed way of life.*]

A hunter, a trapping-man,
Encountered him at the edge of the water hole.
One day, a second, and a third he encountered him at the edge
   of the water hole.   115
When he saw him, the hunter stood stock-still with terror,
As for Enkidu, he went home with his beasts.
Aghast, struck dumb,
His heart in a turmoil, his face drawn,
With woe in his vitals,   120
His face like a traveler's from afar,
The hunter made ready to speak, saying to his father:

    My father, there is a certain fellow who has come
      [from the uplands],
    He is the mightiest in the land, strength is his,
    Like the force of heaven, so mighty is his strength.   125
    He constantly ranges over the uplands,
    Constantly feeding on grass with beasts,
    Constantly making his way to the edge of the water hole.
    I am too frightened to approach him.
    He has filled in the pits I dug,   130
    He has torn out my traps I set,
    He has helped the beasts, wildlife of the steppe, slip
      from my hands,
    He will not let me work the steppe.

His father made ready to speak, saying to the hunter:

    My son, in Uruk [dwells] Gilgamesh,   135
    [There is no one more mighty] than he.
    Like the force of heaven, so mighty is his strength.
    Take the road, set off [towards Uruk],
    [Tell Gilgamesh of] the mightiness-man.
    [He will give you Shamhat the harlot], take her with you,   140
    [Let her prevail over him], instead of a mighty man.
    When the wild beasts draw near the water hole,
    Let her strip off her clothing, laying bare her charms.
    When he sees her, he will approach her.
    His beasts that grew up with him on the steppe will deny
      him.   145

[Giving heed] to the advice of his father,
  The hunter went forth [. . .].

He took the road, set off towards Uruk,
To [the king], Gilgamesh, [he said these words]:

> There is a certain fellow [who has come from the uplands],   150
> He is mightiest in the land, strength is his,
> Like the force of heaven, so mighty is his strength.
> He constantly ranges over the uplands,
> Constantly feeding on grass with his beasts,
> Constantly making his way to the edge of the water hole.   155
> I am too frightened to approach him.
> He has filled in the pits I dug,
> He has torn out my traps I set,
> He has helped the beasts, wildlife of the steppe, slip
>   from my hands,
> He will not allow me to work the steppe.   160

Gilgamesh said to him, to the hunter:

> Go, hunter, take with you Shamhat the harlot,
> When the wild beasts draw near the water hole,
> Let her strip off her clothing, laying bare her charms.
> When he sees her, he will approach her,   165
> His beasts that grew up with him on the steppe will deny
>   him.

Forth went the hunter, taking with him Shamhat the harlot,
They took the road, going straight on their way.
On the third day they arrived at the appointed place.
Hunter and harlot sat down to wait.   170
One day, a second day, they sat by the edge of the water hole,
The beasts came to the water hole to drink,
The wildlife came to drink their fill of water.
But as for him, Enkidu, born in the uplands,
Who feeds on grass with gazelles,   175
Who drinks at the water hole with beasts,
Who, with wildlife, drinks his fill of water,
Shamhat looked upon him, a human-man,
A barbarous fellow from the midst of the steppe:

> There he is, Shamhat, open your embrace,   180
> Open your embrace, let him take your charms!
> Be not bashful, take his vitality!
> When he sees you, he will approach you,
> Toss aside your clothing, let him lie upon you,

Treat him, a human, to woman's work!   185
His wild beasts that grew up with him will deny him,
As in his ardor he caresses you!

Shamhat loosened her garments,
She exposed her loins, he took her charms.
She was not bashful, she took his vitality.   190
She tossed aside her clothing and he lay upon her,
She treated him, a human, to woman's work,
As in his ardor he caressed her.
Six days, seven nights was Enkidu aroused, flowing into Shamhat.
After he had his fill of her delights,   195
He set off towards his beasts.
When they saw him, Enkidu, the gazelles shied off,
The wild beasts of the steppe shunned his person.
Enkidu had spent himself, his body was limp,
His knees stood still, while his beasts went away.   200
Enkidu was too slow, he could not run as before,
But he had gained [reason] and expanded his understanding.

[Shamhat urges Enkidu to return with her to Uruk, artfully piquing his
interest with tales of the pleasures awaiting him there, then feigning second
thoughts as she describes Gilgamesh.]

He returned, he sat at the harlot's feet,
The harlot gazed upon his face,
While he listened to what the harlot was saying.   205
The harlot said to him, to Enkidu:

   You are handsome, Enkidu, you are become like a god,
   Why roam the steppe with wild beasts?
   Come, let me lead you to ramparted Uruk,
   To the holy temple, abode of Anu and Ishtar,   210
   The place of Gilgamesh, who is perfect in strength,
   And so, like a wild bull, he lords it over the young men.

As she was speaking to him, her words found favor,
He was yearning for one to know his heart, a friend.
Enkidu said to her, to the harlot: 215

   Come, Shamhat, escort me
   To the lustrous hallowed temple, abode of Anu and Ishtar,
   The place of Gilgamesh, who is perfect in strength,
   And so, like a wild bull, he lords it over the young men.
   I myself will challenge him, [I will speak out] boldly,   220
   [I will] raise a cry in Uruk: I am the mighty one!

[I am come forward] to alter destinies!
He who was born in the steppe [is mighty], strength is his!

[*Shamhat speaks.*]

[Come then], let him see your face,
[I will show you Gilgamesh], where he is I know full well.   225
Come then, Enkidu, to ramparted Uruk,
Where fellows are resplendent in holiday clothing,
Where every day is set for celebration,
Where harps and drums are [played].
And the harlots too, they are fairest of form,   230
Rich in beauty, full of delights,
Even the great (gods) are kept from sleeping at night![5]
Enkidu, you who [have not] learned to live,
Oh, let me show you Gilgamesh, the joy-woe man.
Look at him, gaze upon his face,   235
He is radiant with virility, manly vigor is his,
The whole of his body is seductively gorgeous.
Mightier strength has he than you,
Never resting by day or night.
O Enkidu, renounce your audacity!   240
Gilgamesh is beloved of Shamash,
Anu, Enlil, and Ea broadened his wisdom.
Ere you come down from the uplands,
Gilgamesh will dream of you in Uruk.

[*The scene shifts to Uruk, where Gilgamesh is telling his mother, Ninsun,
his dreams. She explains them to him.*]

Gilgamesh went to relate the dreams, saying to his mother: 245

Mother, I had a dream last night:
There were stars of heaven around me,
Like the force of heaven, something kept falling upon me!
I tried to carry it but it was too strong for me,
I tried to move it but I could not budge it.   250
The whole of Uruk was standing by it,
The people formed a crowd around it,
A throng was jostling towards it,
Young men were mobbed around it,
Infantile, they were groveling before it!   255
[I fell in love with it], like a woman I caressed it,

---

5. The Mesopotamians considered a small group of the gods "great" or "superior," above all the
others.

I carried it off and laid it down before you,
Then you were making it my partner.

The mother of Gilgamesh, knowing and wise,
Who understands everything, said to her son,   260
Ninsun [the wild cow], knowing and wise,
Who understands everything, said to Gilgamesh:

    The stars of heaven around you,
    Like the force of heaven, what kept falling upon you,
    Your trying to move it but not being able to budge it,   265
    Your laying it down before me,
    Then my making it your partner,
    Your falling in love with it, your caressing it like a woman,
    Means there will come to you a strong one,
    A companion who rescues a friend.   270
    He will be mighty in the land, strength will be his,
    Like the force of heaven, so mighty will be his strength.
    You will fall in love with him and caress him like a woman.
    He will be mighty and rescue you, time and again.

He had a second dream,   275
He arose and went before the goddess, his mother,
Gilgamesh said to her, to his mother:

    Mother, I had a second dream.
    An axe was thrown down in a street of ramparted Uruk,
    They were crowding around it,   280
    The whole of Uruk was standing by it,
    The people formed a crowd around it,
    A throng was jostling towards it.
    I carried it off and laid it down before you,
    I fell in love with it, like a woman I caressed it,   285
    Then you were making it my partner.

The mother of Gilgamesh, knowing and wise,
Who understands everything, said to her son,
Ninsun [the wild cow], knowing and wise,
Who understands everything, said to Gilgamesh: 290

    My son, the axe you saw is a man.
    Your loving it like a woman and caressing it,
    And my making it your partner
    Means there will come to you a strong one,

A companion who rescues a friend,   295
He will be mighty in the land, strength will be his,
Like the strength of heaven, so mighty will be his strength.

Gilgamesh said to her, to his mother:

> Let this befall according to the command of the great
>   counselor Enlil,
> I want a friend for my own counselor,   300
> For my own counselor do I want a friend!

Even while he was having his dreams,
Shamhat was telling the dreams of Gilgamesh to Enkidu,
Each was drawn by love to the other.

Tablet II

[*Shamhat begins the process of civilizing Enkidu. She takes him to an encampment of shepherds, where he learns how to eat, drink, dress, and groom himself to human standards. Whereas Gilgamesh keeps his subjects awake at night with his roistering, Enkidu stays up all night to protect the flocks. Most of this tablet is known from older versions, combined here with later ones.*]

While Enkidu was seated before her,
Each was drawn by love to the other.
Enkidu forgot the steppe where he was born,
For six days, seven nights Enkidu was aroused and flowed
    into Shamhat.
The harlot said to him, to Enkidu: 5

    You are handsome, Enkidu, you are become like a god,
    Why roam the steppe with wild beasts?
    Come, let me lead you to ramparted Uruk,
    To the holy temple, abode of Anu,
    Let me lead you to ramparted Uruk,   10
    To hallowed Eanna, abode of Ishtar,
    The place of Gilgamesh, who is perfect in strength,
    And so, like a wild bull, he lords it over the people.
    You [are just like him],
    You will love him like your own self.   15
    Come away from this desolation, bereft even of shepherds.

He heard what she said, accepted her words,
He was yearning for one to know his heart, a friend.
The counsel of Shamhat touched his heart.
She took off her clothing, with one piece she dressed him,   20
The second she herself put on.
Clasping his hand, like a guardian deity she led him,[1]
To the shepherds' huts, where a sheepfold was,
The shepherds crowded around him,
They murmured their opinions among themselves: 25

---

1. In Mesopotamian art, an individual guardian deity, often female, is shown leading a person into the presence of a great god. The poet has this imagery in mind.

13

This fellow, how like Gilgamesh in stature,
In stature tall, proud as a battlement.
No doubt he was born in the steppe,
Like the force of heaven, mighty is his strength.

They set bread before him,   30
They set beer before him.
He looked uncertainly, then stared,
Enkidu did not know to eat bread,
Nor had he ever learned to drink beer!
The harlot made ready to speak, saying to Enkidu: 35

    Eat the bread, Enkidu, the staff of life,
    Drink the beer, the custom of the land.

Enkidu ate the bread until he was sated,
He drank seven juglets of the beer.
His mood became relaxed, he was singing joyously,   40
He felt lighthearted and his features glowed.
He treated his hairy body with water,
He anointed himself with oil, turned into a man,
He put on clothing, became like a warrior.
He took his weapon, hunted lions,   45
The shepherds lay down to rest at night.
He slew wolves, defeated lions,
The herdsmen, the great gods, lay down to sleep.
Enkidu was their watchman, a wakeful man,
He was [. . .] tall.   50

                              [gap]

[A *passerby on his way to a wedding feast tells Enkidu of Gilgamesh's abuse
of marriage: he is the first to have the bride. Enkidu, aghast, strides off to
Uruk. Whereas before Shamhat had led him, like a guardian deity, now he
walks in front like a challenger.*]

He was making love with Shamhat.
He lifted his eyes, he saw a man.
He said to the harlot:

    Shamhat, bring that man here!
    Why has he come?   55
    I will ask him to account for himself.

The harlot summoned the man,
He came over, Enkidu said to him:

Fellow, where are you rushing?
What is this, your burdensome errand?   60

The man made ready to speak, said to Enkidu:

They have invited me to a wedding,
Is it not people's custom to get married?
I have heaped high on the festival tray
The fancy dishes for the wedding.   65
People's loins are open for the taking.
For Gilgamesh, king of ramparted Uruk,
People's loins are open for the taking!
He mates with the lawful wife,
He first, the groom after.   70
By divine decree pronounced,
From the cutting of his umbilical cord, she is his due.[2]

At the man's account, his face went pale.

[gap]

Enkidu was walking in front, with Shamhat behind him.

[As foretold in Gilgamesh's dream, a crowd gathers around Enkidu as he enters Uruk. He has arrived in time for a wedding ceremony, but this may have been the yearly religious ritual wherein the king joined with a representative of a goddess to ensure universal fertility and engender a royal heir, so not in fact the abuse of power described by the man with the tray, above.]

When he entered the street of ramparted Uruk,   75
A multitude crowded around him.
He stood there in the street of ramparted Uruk,
With the people crowding around him.
They said about him:

He is like Gilgamesh in build,   80
Though shorter in stature, he is stronger of frame.
[This man, where] he was born,
[Ate] the springtime [grass],
He must have nursed on the milk of wild beasts.

The whole of Uruk was standing beside him,   85
The people formed a crowd around him,
A throng was jostling towards him,

2. This means that by his birthright Gilgamesh can take brides first on their wedding nights, then leave them to their wedded husbands.

Young men were mobbed around him,
Infantile, they groveled before him.

In Uruk at this time sacrifices were underway,   90
Young men were celebrating.
The hero stood ready for the upright young man,
For Gilgamesh, as for a god, the partner was ready.
For the goddess of lovemaking, the bed was made,
Gilgamesh was to join with the girl that night.   95

[*Enkidu blocks the king's way to the ceremony. They wrestle in the street.*
Gilgamesh wins by pinning Enkidu over his shoulders while keeping one foot
and the other knee on the ground. He turns away to indicate cessation of
the match. Enkidu praises his superiority and royal birth.]

Enkidu approached him,
They met in the public street.
Enkidu blocked the door to the wedding with his foot,
Not allowing Gilgamesh to enter.
They grappled each other, holding fast like wrestlers,   100
They shattered the doorpost, the wall shook.
Gilgamesh and Enkidu grappled each other,
Holding fast like wrestlers,
They shattered the doorpost, the wall shook!
They grappled each other at the door to the wedding,   105
They fought in the street, the public square.
It was Gilgamesh who knelt for the pin, his foot on the ground.
His fury abated, he turned away.
After he turned away,
Enkidu said to him, to Gilgamesh: 110

      As one unique did your mother bear you,
      The wild cow of the ramparts, Ninsun,
      Exalted you above the most valorous of men!
      Enlil has granted you kingship over the people.

                          [*gap*]

They kissed each other and made friends.   115

                          [*gap*]

[*As foretold in the dream, Gilgamesh goes off to his mother, Ninsun, perhaps*
seeking her blessing on his friendship with Enkidu.]

2. *It was Gilgamesh who knelt for the pin, his foot on the ground.* This seal image shows a triumphant hero immobilizing a lion with what may have been the same gesture described here.

He is mighty in the land, strength is his,
Like the force of heaven, mighty is his strength.
His tall stature [. . .]

The mother of Gilgamesh made ready to speak,
Said to Gilgamesh,   120
Ninsun, the wild cow made ready to speak,
Said to Gilgamesh:

My son, [. . .]
Bitterly [. . .]

[*gap*]

[*In a second speech, Gilgamesh describes Enkidu's friendless state.*]

Enkidu has neither [father nor mother],   125
His hair was growing freely [. . .]
He was born in the steppe, no one [. . .]

Enkidu stood still, [listening to what he said],
He shuddered and [sat down . . .]

Tears filled his eyes,   130
He was listless, his strength turned to weakness.
They clasped each other [. . .],
They joined hands like [. . .].

Gilgamesh made ready to speak,
Saying to Enkidu: 135

> Why are your eyes full of tears,
> Why are you listless, your strength turned to weakness?

Enkidu said to him, to Gilgamesh:

> Cries of sorrow, my friend, have cramped my muscles,
> Woe has entered my heart [. . .]   140

[*Gilgamesh proposes a quest to kill a monster named Humbaba, in order to cut a giant cedar tree in the forest Humbaba guards. Felling evergreen trees on distant mountains was a well-known demonstration of kingly power in early Mesopotamia. Enkidu, horrified, tries vainly to dissuade him.*]

Gilgamesh made ready to speak,
Saying to Enkidu:

> There dwells in the forest the fierce monster Humbaba,
> [You and I shall] kill [him]
> [And] wipe out [something evil from the land].   145

[gap]

Enkidu made ready to speak,
Saying to Gilgamesh:

> My friend, I knew that country
> When I roamed with the wild beasts.
> The forest is . . . sixty double leagues in every direction,   150
> Who can go into it?
> Humbaba's cry is the roar of a deluge,
> His maw is fire, his breath is death.
> Why do you want to do this?
> The haunt of Humbaba is a hopeless quest.   155

Gilgamesh made ready to speak,
Saying to Enkidu:

I must go up the mountain [. . .] forest,
I must cut [a cedar tree . . .]
That cedar must be [big] enough   160
[To make] whirlwinds [when it falls]

[gap]

Enkidu made ready to speak,
Saying to Gilgamesh:

How shall the likes of us go to the forest of cedars, my friend?
In order to safeguard the forest of cedars,   165
Enlil has appointed him to terrify the people,
Enlil has destined him seven fearsome glories.[3]
That journey is not to be undertaken,
That creature is not to be looked upon.
The guardian of [. . .], the forest of cedars,   170
Humbaba's cry is the roar of a deluge,
His maw is fire, his breath is death.
He can hear rustling in the forest for sixty double leagues.
Who can go into his forest?
Adad is first and Humbaba is second.   175
Who, even among the gods, could attack him?
In order to safeguard the forest of cedars,
Enlil has appointed him to terrify the people,
Enlil has destined him seven fearsome glories.
Besides, whosoever enters his forest is struck down by disease. 180

Gilgamesh made ready to speak,
Saying to Enkidu:

Why, my friend, do you raise such unworthy objections?
Who, my friend, can go up to heaven?
The gods dwell forever in the sun,   185
People's days are numbered,
Whatever they attempt is a puff of air.
Here you are, even you, afraid of death,
What has become of your bravery's might?
I will go before you,   190
You can call out to me, "Go on, be not afraid!"
If I fall on the way, I'll establish my name:
"Gilgamesh, who joined battle with fierce Humbaba"
      (they'll say).

3. The Mesopotamians believed that divine beings were surrounded by a blinding, awe-inspiring
   radiance. In the old versions of The Epic of Gilgamesh, this radiance, called here "glories,"
   was considered removable, like garments or jewelry.

You were born and grew up on the steppe,
When a lion sprang at you, you knew what to do.   195
Young men fled before you

[gap]

You speak unworthily,
How you pule! You make me ill.
I must set [my hand to cutting] a cedar tree,
I must establish eternal fame.   200
Come, my friend, let's both be off to the foundry,
Let them cast axes such as we'll need.

[After supervising the casting of enormous axes and weapons, Gilgamesh
informs the citizenry of Uruk of his planned campaign. First he addresses
the elders, speaking of his desire for eternal fame, next the young men, appealing to their sense of adventure. He promises to return in time to celebrate
the springtime festival of the new year. Enkidu and the elders attempt un-
successfully to dissuade him.]

Off they went to the craftsmen,
The craftsmen, seated around, discussed the matter.
They cast great axes,   205
Axe blades weighing 180 pounds each they cast.
They cast great daggers,
Their blades were 120 pounds each,
The cross guards of their handles thirty pounds each.
They carried daggers worked with thirty pounds of gold,   210
Gilgamesh and Enkidu bore ten times sixty pounds each.

He bolted the seven gates of Uruk,
[. . .] listened, the multitude convened.
[. . .] turned out in the street of ramparted Uruk,
Gilgamesh [. . .] his throne,   215
[. . . in the street] of ramparted Uruk,
[Enkidu] sat before him.
[Gilgamesh spoke to the elders of ramparted Uruk]:

[Hear me, O elders of ramparted Uruk],
The one of whom they speak   220
I, Gilgamesh, would see!
The one whose name resounds across the whole world,
I will hunt him down in the forest of cedars.
I will make the land hear
How mighty is the scion of Uruk.   225
I will set my hand to cutting a cedar,
An eternal name I will make for myself!

[Gilgamesh turns to the young men of the city. In an old version of this episode, the elders respond at this point, see below, lines 257–73: the standard version apparently expanded this incident to include parallel speeches to both the elders and the young men.]

Hear me, O young men [of ramparted Uruk],
Young men of Uruk who understand this cause!
I have taken on a noble quest,   230
I travel a distant road, to where Humbaba is.
I face a battle unknown,
I mount a campaign unknown.
Give me your blessing, that I may go on my journey,
[That I may indeed see] your faces [safely again],   235
That I may indeed reenter joyfully the gate of ramparted
    Uruk,
That I may indeed return to hold the festival for the new year,
That I may indeed celebrate the festival for the new year
    twice over.
May that festival be held in my presence, the fanfare sound!
May the drums resound before [you]!   240

Enkidu pressed advice upon the elders,
Upon the young men of Uruk who understood this cause:

Tell him he must not go to the forest of cedars,
That journey is not to be undertaken,
That creature is not to be looked upon.   245
The guardian of the forest of cedars [. . .]
Humbaba's cry is the roar of a deluge,
His maw is fire, his breath is death,
He can hear rustling in the forest for sixty double leagues.
Who can go into his forest?   250
Adad is first and Humbaba is second.
Who, even among the gods, could attack him?
In order to safeguard the forest of cedars,
Enlil has appointed him to terrify the people,
Enlil has destined him seven fearsome glories.   255
Besides, whosoever enters his forest is struck down by disease.

The elders of ramparted Uruk arose,
They responded to Gilgamesh with their advice:

You are young, Gilgamesh, your feelings carry you away,
You are ignorant of what you speak, flightiness has taken you, 260
You do not know what you are attempting.
We have heard of Humbaba, his features are grotesque,

Who is there who could face his weaponry?
He can hear rustling in the forest for sixty double leagues.
Who can go into it?   265
Humbaba's cry is the roar of a deluge,
His maw is fire, his breath is death.
Adad is first and Humbaba is second.
Who, even among the gods, could attack him?
In order to safeguard the forest of cedars,   270
Enlil has appointed him to terrify the people,
Enlil has destined him seven fearsome glories.
Besides, whosoever enters his forest is struck down by disease.

When Gilgamesh heard the speech of his counselors,
He looked at his friend and laughed: 275

Now then, my friend, [do you say the same?]:
"I am afraid [to die]"?

[gap]

Tablet III

[*The elders offer advice to Gilgamesh for the quest. They entrust his safety to Enkidu. Line 11 contains a wordplay on the Babylonian words for "brides" and "interments," portending Enkidu's fate.*]

The elders spoke to him, saying to Gilgamesh:

> [Come back safely to] Uruk's haven,
> Trust not, Gilgamesh, in your strength alone,
> Let your eyes see all, make your blow strike home.
> He who goes in front saves his companion,   5
> He who knows the path protects his friend.
> Let Enkidu walk before you,
> He knows the way to the forest of cedars,
> He has seen battle, been exposed to combat.
> Enkidu will protect his friend, safeguard his companion,   10
> Let him return, to be a grave husband.
> We in our assembly entrust the king to you,
> On your return, entrust the king again to us.

[*Gilgamesh and Enkidu go off to the temple of Ninsun, to ask her blessing.*]

Gilgamesh made ready to speak,
Saying to Enkidu: 15

> Come, my friend, let us go the sublime temple,
> To go before Ninsun, the great queen.
> Ninsun the wise, who is versed in all knowledge,
> Will send us on our way with good advice.

Clasping each other, hand in hand,   20
Gilgamesh and Enkidu went to the sublime temple,
To go before Ninsun, the great queen.
Gilgamesh came forward and entered before her:

> O Ninsun, I have taken on a noble quest,
> I travel a distant road, to where Humbaba is,   25
> To face a battle unknown,

23

To mount a campaign unknown.
Give me your blessing, that I may go on my journey,
[That I may indeed see] your face [safely again],
That I may indeed reenter joyfully the gate of ramparted
    Uruk,   30
That I may indeed return to hold the festival for the new year,
That I may indeed celebrate the festival for the new year
    twice over.
May that festival be held in my presence, the fanfare sound!
May their drums resound before [you]!

[Ninsun prays to Shamash to help her son on his quest.]

Ninsun the [wild cow] heard them out with sadness,   35
The speeches of Gilgamesh, her son, and Enkidu.
Ninsun entered the bathhouse seven times,
She bathed herself in water with tamarisk and soapwort.[1]
[She put on] a garment as beseemed her body,
[She put on] an ornament as beseemed her breast,   40
She set [. . .] and donned her tiara.
[. . .] harlots [. . .] the ground,
She climbed [the stairs], mounted to the roof terrace,
She set up an incense offering to Shamash.
She made the offering, to Shamash she raised her hands in prayer: 45

Why did you endow my son Gilgamesh with a restless heart?
Now you have moved him to travel
A distant road, to where Humbaba is,
To face a battle unknown,
To mount an expedition unknown.   50
Until he goes and returns,
Until he reaches the forest of cedars,
Until he has slain fierce Humbaba,
And wipes out from the land the evil thing you hate,
In the day, [when you traverse the sky],   55
May Aya, your bride, not fear to remind you,
"Entrust him to the watchmen of the night."

[gap]

O [Shamash], you opened [. . .] for the beasts of the
    steppe,
You came out for the land to [. . .],
The mountains [glow], the heavens [brighten],   60
The beasts of the steppe [behold] your fierce radiance.

1. A medicinal plant used in cleansing and magic.

At your light's rising, [. . .] assembles,
The great gods stand in attendance [upon your glow],
May [Aya, your bride], not fear to remind you,
"Entrust him to the watchmen of the night."   65

[*gap*]

While Gilgamesh journeys to the forest of cedars,
May the days be long, may the nights be short,
May his loins be girded, his arms [strong]!
At night, let him make a camp for sleeping,
[Let him make a shelter] to fall asleep in.   70
May Aya, your bride, not fear to remind you,
When Gilgamesh, Enkidu, and Humbaba meet,
Raise up for his sake, O Shamash, great winds against
    Humbaba,
South wind, north wind, east wind, west wind, moaning wind,
Blasting wind, lashing wind, contrary wind, dust storm,   75
Demon wind, freezing wind, storm wind, whirlwind:
Raise up thirteen winds to blot out Humbaba's face,
So he cannot charge forward, cannot retreat,
Then let Gilgamesh's weapons defeat Humbaba.
As soon as your own [radiance] flares forth,   80
At that very moment heed the man who reveres you.
May your swift mules [. . .] you,
A comfortable seat, a [. . .] bed is laid for you,
May the gods, your brethren, serve you your [favorite] foods,
May Aya, the great bride, dab your face with the fringe
    of her spotless garment.   85

Ninsun the wild cow made a second plea to Shamash:

O Shamash, will not Gilgamesh [. . .] the gods for you?
Will he not share heaven with you?
Will he not share tiara and scepter with the moon?
Will he not act in wisdom with Ea in the depths?   90
Will he not rule the human race with Irnina?
Will he not dwell with Ningishzida in the Land of No Return?

[*gap*]

[*Ninsun apparently inducts Enkidu into the staff of her temple.*]

After Ninsun the wild cow had made her plea,
Ninsun the wild cow, knowing and wise, who understands
    everything,

[. . .] Gilgamesh [. . .].   95
She extinguished the incense, [she came down from the roof
   terrace],
She summoned Enkidu to impart her message:

> Mighty Enkidu, though you are no issue of my womb,
> Your little ones shall be among the devotees of Gilgamesh,
> The priestesses, votaries, cult women of the temple.   100

She placed a token around Enkidu's neck:

> As the priestesses take in a foundling,
> And the daughters of the gods bring up an adopted child,
> I herewith take Enkidu, whom [. . .], as my adopted son,
> Enkidu for [. . .], may Gilgamesh treat him well.   105

[gap]

> While you journey [. . .] to the forest of cedars,
> May the days be long, may the nights be short,
> May your loins be girded, your arms [strong].
> At night make a camp for sleeping,
> Let [. . .] watch over [. . .]   110

[Enkidu promises Ninsun that he will bring Gilgamesh back safely.]

> Until he has gone and returned,
> Until he has reached the forest of cedars

[gap]

*[The following episodes are taken from an old version, which arranged the
material differently from the standard version. Gilgamesh takes an oracle to
determine the prognosis for his quest. Divination, often by slaughtering a
sheep or goat and looking for certain marks or formations on the liver or
entrails, was normal practice in Mesopotamia to predict the outcome of important undertakings or crises, such as illness. The result of Gilgamesh's
divination is apparently unfavorable, so he tries to change the prognosis by
offering various blandishments to Shamash, god of oracles.]*

Gilgamesh knelt before [Shamash],
The speech he made [. . .]:

> I am going, O Shamash, with my hands [raised in prayer],   115
> Afar off may my life be safe.
> Return me [in safety to ramparted Uruk],
> Place your protection [upon me].

Gilgamesh summoned [the diviners],
His oracle [. . .]   120
To the [. . .] temple.
Tears poured down Gilgamesh's [face]:

> My god, the road [. . .]
> [. . .] and his ways, my god, I do not know.
> [If] I come out safely,   125
> [I will . . .] you to your heart's content,
> [I will build] a house for your delight,
> [I will seat you] on thrones.

[*In the large gap in the text that occurs here, Gilgamesh and Enkidu are
still in Uruk, perhaps carrying out various rites and drawing up plans for a
great door to be made from the cedar tree they plan to cut down. Next
Gilgamesh gives instructions for the city in his absence. The town officials
wish him well. The two friends begin final preparations for departure, with
the blessing of the elders and the young men. Enkidu at last gives up his
objections.*]

> The young men should not form a crowd in the
>   street [. . .],
> Judge the lawsuit of the weak, call the strong to account,[2]   130
> While in a trice we attain our desire,
> And set up our [. . .] at Humbaba's gate.

His dignitaries stood by, wishing him well,
In a crowd, the young men of Uruk ran along behind him,
While his dignitaries made obeisance to him: 135

> Come back safely to Uruk's haven!
> Trust not, Gilgamesh, in your strength alone,
> Let your eyes see all, make your blow strike home.
> He who goes in front saves his companion,
> He who knows the path protects his friend.   140
> Let Enkidu walk before you,
> He knows the way to the forest of cedars.
> He has seen battle, been exposed to combat.
> [. . .] at the mountain passes.
> Enkidu will protect his friend, safeguard his companion, 145
> Let him return, to be a grave husband.
> We in our assembly entrust the king to you,
> On your return, entrust the king again to us.

---

2. Mesopotamian rulers were supposed to ensure that poor and defenseless people received the
   same legal process as the rich and powerful.

Enkidu made ready to speak, saying to Gilgamesh:

> Turn back, my friend, [. . .]   150
> You must not [. . .] this journey!

[gap]

[. . .] his equipment,
[. . .] the great daggers,
[The bow] and the quiver
[. . .] in their hands.   155
He took up the axes,
[. . .] his quiver, the Elamite bow,[3]
[He set] his dagger at his belt.
[The elders] made way for him,
[The young men] sent him on his way: 160

> Gilgamesh, [how long] till you return to the city [. . .]?

The elders [hailed him],
Counseled Gilgamesh for the journey:

> Trust not, Gilgamesh, in your own strength,
> Let your vision be clear, take care of yourself.   165
> Let Enkidu go ahead of you,
> He has seen the road, has traveled the way.
> He knows the ways into the forest
> And all the tricks of Humbaba.
> He who goes first safeguards his companion,   170
> His vision is clear, [he protects himself].
> May Shamash help you to your goal,
> May he disclose to you what your words propose,
> May he open for you the barred road,
> Make straight the pathway to your tread,   175
> Make straight the upland to your feet.
> May nightfall bring you good tidings,
> May Lugalbanda stand by you in your cause.
> In a trice accomplish what you desire,
> Wash your feet in the river of Humbaba whom you seek.   180
> When you stop for the night, dig a well,
> May there always be pure water in your waterskin.[4]
> You should libate cool water to Shamash
> And be mindful of Lugalbanda.

---

3. Elam was a country in southwestern Iran, apparently known for its fine bows.
4. Mesopotamian travelers carried drinking water in leather bags.

Enkidu made ready to speak, saying to Gilgamesh: 185

> [As] you insist, make the journey.
> Do not be afraid, watch me.
> [. . .] who made his dwelling in the forest,
> The [. . .], where Humbaba goes.

[gap]

> [. . .] who goes with me,   190
> [I will bring him safe] to you,
> [. . .] in joy!

Upon hearing this speech,
The young men acclaimed him:

> Go, Gilgamesh, may [. . .]   195
> May your god go [by your side],
> May he disclose to you [your heart's desire].
> May [. . .] advise you,
> He who knows [. . .]

[In the gap that follows, the two friends set out on their quest.]

Tablet IV

[*Gilgamesh and Enkidu go on their journey. As they camp each night, Enkidu makes Gilgamesh a shelter and lays out a magic circle for him to sleep in. This may be a circle of flour as known from Mesopotamian sorcery and oath-taking. Gilgamesh prays for a dream to portend the outcome of the expedition. He dreams three times of mountains. The first falls upon him, the second holds him fast, and the third erupts. In each case, he barely escapes the mountain's fury. Enkidu explains that the mountain is Humbaba, who will make a terrifying attack but will collapse and die. Next he dreams of a lion-headed monster-bird and then a bull attacking him. Since the text is very damaged here and various versions exist, the number, sequence, and contents of the dreams are most uncertain.*]

At twenty double leagues they took a bite to eat,
At thirty double leagues they made their camp,
Fifty double leagues they went in a single day,
A journey of a month and a half in three days.
They approached Mount Lebanon.   5
Towards sunset they dug a well,
Filled [their waterskin with water].
Gilgamesh went up onto the mountain,
He poured out flour for an [offering, saying]:

> O mountain, bring me a propitious dream!   10

Enkidu made Gilgamesh a shelter for receiving dreams,
A gust was blowing, he fastened the door.
He had him lie down in a circle of [flour],
And spreading out like a net, Enkidu lay down in the doorway.
Gilgamesh sat there, chin on his knee.   15
Sleep, which usually steals over people, fell upon him.
In the middle of the night he awoke,
Got up and said to his friend:

> My friend, did you not call me? Why am I awake?
> Did you not touch me? Why am I disturbed?   20
> Did a god not pass by? Why does my flesh tingle?
> My friend, I had a dream,
> And the dream I had was very disturbing.

30

[We . . .] on the flanks of a mountain,
The mountain fell [upon us],   25
We [. . .] like flies!

The one born in the steppe [. . .],
Enkidu explained the dream to his friend:

    My friend, your dream is favorable,
    The dream is very precious [as an omen].   30
    My friend, the mountain you saw is [Humbaba],
    We will catch Humbaba and [kill him],
    Then we will throw down his corpse on the field of battle.
    Further, at dawn the word of Shamash will be in our favor.

At twenty double leagues they took a bite to eat,   35
At thirty double leagues they made their camp,
Fifty double leagues they went in a single day,
A journey of a month and a half in three days.
They approached Mount Lebanon.
Towards sunset they dug a well,   40
They filled [their waterskin with water].
Gilgamesh went up onto the mountain,
He poured out flour for [an offering, saying]:

    O mountain, bring me a propitious dream!

Enkidu made Gilgamesh a shelter for receiving dreams,   45
A gust was blowing, he fastened the door.
He had him lie down in a circle of [flour],
And spreading out like a net, Enkidu lay down in the doorway.
Gilgamesh sat there, chin on his knee.
Sleep, which usually steals over people, fell upon him.   50
In the middle of the night he awoke,
Got up and said to his friend:

    My friend, did you not call me? Why am I awake?
    Did you not touch me? Why am I disturbed?
    Did a god not pass by? Why does my flesh tingle?   55
    My friend, I had a second dream,
    And the dream I had was very disturbing.
    A mountain was in my dream, [. . . an enemy].
    It threw me down, pinning my feet [. . .],
    A fearsome glare grew ever more intense.   60
    A certain young man, handsomest in the world, truly
        handsome he was,

He pulled me out from the base of the mountain [. . .],
He gave me water to drink and eased my fear,
He set my feet on the ground again.

The one born in the steppe [. . .],   65
Enkidu explained the dream to his friend:

My friend, your dream is favorable,
The dream is very precious [as an omen].
My friend, we will go [. . .]
The strange thing [was] Humbaba,   70
Was not the mountain, the strange thing, Humbaba?
Come then, banish your fear,
[. . .]
As for the man you saw [. . .]

[gap]

[Enkidu's explanation presumably was that the man was Shamash or Lugalbanda coming to help them, but only scattered words of the explanation are
preserved.]

At twenty double leagues they took a bite to eat,   75
At thirty double leagues they made their camp,
Fifty double leagues they went in a single day,
A journey of a month and a half in three days.
They approached Mount Lebanon.
Towards sunset they dug a well,   80
They filled [their waterskin with water].
Gilgamesh went up onto the mountain,
He poured out flour as [an offering, saying]:

O mountain, bring me a propitious dream!

Enkidu made Gilgamesh a shelter for receiving dreams,   85
A gust was blowing, he fastened the door.
He had him lie down in a circle of [flour],
And spreading out like a net, Enkidu lay down in the doorway.
Gilgamesh sat there, chin on his knee.
Sleep, which usually steals over people, fell upon him.   90
In the middle of the night he awoke,
Got up and said to his friend:

My friend, did you not call me? Why am I awake?
Did you not touch me? Why am I disturbed?

Did a god not pass by? Why does my flesh tingle? 95
My friend, I had a third dream,
And the dream I had was very disturbing.
The heavens cried out, the earth was thundering,
Daylight faded, darkness fell,
Lightning flashed, fire shot up, 100
The [flames] burgeoned, spewing death.
Then the glow was dimmed, the fire was extinguished,
The [burning coals] that were falling turned to ashes.
You who were born in the steppe, let us discuss it.

Enkidu [explained], helped him accept his dream, 105
Saying to Gilgamesh:

[gap]

[Enkidu's explanation is mostly lost, but perhaps it was that the volcanolike
explosion was Humbaba, who flared up, then died.]

Humbaba, like a god [. . .]
[. . .] the light flaring [. . .]
We will be [victorious] over him.
Humbaba aroused our fury [. . .] 110
[. . .] we will prevail over him.
Further, at dawn the word of Shamash will be in our favor.

At twenty double leagues they took a bite to eat,
A thirty double leagues they made their camp.
Fifty double leagues they went in a single day, 115
A journey of a month and a half in three days.
They approached Mount Lebanon.
Towards sunset they dug a well,
They filled [their waterskin with water].
Gilgamesh went up onto the mountain, 120
He poured out flour as [an offering, saying]:

O mountain, bring me a propitious dream!

Enkidu made Gilgamesh a shelter for receiving dreams,
A gust was blowing, he fastened the door.
He had him lie down in a circle of [flour], 125
And spreading out like a net, Enkidu lay down in the doorway.
Gilgamesh sat there, chin on his knee.
Sleep, which usually steals over people, fell upon him.
In the middle of the night he awoke,

My friend, did you not call me? Why am I awake?   130
Did you not touch me? Why am I disturbed?
Did a god not pass by? Why does my flesh tingle?
My friend, I had a [fourth] dream,
The dream I had was very disturbing.
My friend, I saw a fourth dream,   135
More terrible than the other three.
I saw the lion-headed monster-bird Anzu in the sky.
He began to descend upon us, like a cloud.
He was terrifying, his appearance was horrible!
His maw was fire, his breath death.   140
A young man [. . .] a way to go across(?),
[. . .] he was standing by me in my dream.
[He . . .] its wings, he seized its arms,
Then he threw it [to the ground].

[gap]

[Enkidu explains the fourth dream.]

The lion-headed monster-bird Anzu who descended
          upon us, like a cloud,   145
Who was terrifying, whose appearance was horrible,
Whose maw was fire, whose breath was death,
Whose dreadful aura frightens you,
I will . . . its foot, I will lift you up(?).
The young man you saw was mighty Shamash   150

[gap]

At twenty double leagues they took a bite to eat,
At thirty double leagues they made their camp,
Fifty double leagues they went in a single day,
A journey of a month and a half in three days.
They approached Mount Lebanon.   155
Towards sunset they dug a well,
Filled [their waterskin with water].
Gilgamesh went up onto the mountain,
He poured out flour for an [offering, saying]:

O mountain, bring me a propitious dream!   160

Enkidu made him a shelter for receiving dreams,
A gust was blowing, he fastened the door.
He had him lie down in a circle of [flour],
And spreading out like a net, Enkidu lay down in the doorway.

Gilgamesh sat there, chin on his knee.   165
Sleep, which usually steals over people, fell upon him.
In the middle of the night he awoke,
Got up and said to his friend:

> My friend, did you not call me? Why am I awake?
> Did you not touch me? Why am I disturbed?   170
> Did a god not pass by? Why does my flesh tingle?
> My friend, I had a dream,
> And the dream I had was very disturbing.

[It is not clear how many dreams there were in all though one version refers
to five. A poorly preserved manuscript of an old version includes the following
dream that could be inserted here, as portions of it are fulfilled in Tablet VI.]

> I was grasping a wild bull of the steppe!
> As it bellowed, it split the earth,   175
> It raised clouds of dust, blotting out the sky.
> I crouched down before it,
> It seized my hands [. . .], pinioned my arms.
> (Someone) pulled me out [. . .]
> He stroked my cheeks, he gave me to drink from his waterskin.   180

[gap]

[Enkidu explains the dream.]

> It is the god, my friend, to whom we go,
> The wild bull was no enemy at all,
> The wild bull you saw is Shamash, the protector,
> He will take our hands in need.
> The one who gave you water to drink from his waterskin   185
> Is your god who proclaims your glory, Lugalbanda.
> We should rely on one another,
> We will accomplish together a deed unheard of in the land.

[gap]

[Something has happened to discourage Gilgamesh, perhaps an unfavorable
oracle. Shamash comes to their aid with timely advice, just before they hear
Humbaba's cry.]

[Before Shamash his tears flowed down]:

> [What . . .] said [in Uruk . . .],   190
> Remember, stand by me, hear [my prayer],
> Gilgamesh, scion of [ramparted Uruk]!

Shamash heard what he said,
From afar a warning voice called to him from the sky:

> Hurry, confront him, do not let him go off [into the forest],   195
> Do not let him enter the thicket nor [. . .]!
> He has not donned [all] of his seven fearsome glories,
> One he has on, six he has left off!

They [. . .]
They charged forward like wild bulls.   200
He let out a single bloodcurdling cry,
The guardian of the forest shrieked aloud,
[. . .]
Humbaba was roaring like thunder.

Gilgamesh made ready to speak,   205
Said to Enkidu:

> Humbaba [. . .]
> We cannot confront him separately.

[gap]

[In the broken section here, the two friends, exchanging terms of encouragement, reach the edge of the forest.]

Gilgamesh spoke to him, said to Enkidu:

> My friend, why do we raise such unworthy objections?   210
> Have we not crossed all [the mountains . . .]?
> [The end of the quest] is before us.
> Before we [. . .]
> My friend knows battle,
> One who [. . .] combat,   215
> You rubbed on [herbs], you did not fear [death],[1]
> [. . .], like a street hawker(?),
> Your battle cry should be dinning like a drum!
> Let the paralysis leave your arm, let weakness quit your
>   [knees],
> Take my hand, my friend, let us [walk on] together!   220
> Your heart should be urging you to battle.
> Forget about death, [. . .] life!
> [. . .], the circumspect-man,

---

1. The meaning of this line is very uncertain. It may refer to some protective magical procedure. In the Mesopotamian "Epic of Creation," for example, the hero god carries vegetable antidotes to counteract magic spells cast by the enemy.

He who marches [first], protects himself,
Let him keep his comrade safe!   225
Those two will have established fame down through the ages.

The pair reached [the edge of the forest],
They stopped their talk and stood there.

Tablet V

[The friends are found admiring the wondrous forest and the paths of Humbaba, its guardian.]

They stood at the edge of the forest,
They gazed at the height of the cedars,
They gazed at the way into the forest.
Where Humbaba would walk, a path was made,
Straight were the ways and easy the going.   5
They saw the cedar mountain, dwelling of the gods, sacred to
    the goddess Irnina.
On the slopes of that mountain, the cedar bears its abundance,
Agreeable is its shade, full of pleasures.
The undergrowth is tangled, the [thicket] interwoven.
Near the cedar [. . .] the balsam tree   10

[gap]

[Weapons at the ready, the two friends advance, encouraging each other.]

From afar off the swords [. . .]
And after the scabbards were [. . .]
Axes touched with [the whetstone],
Daggers and swords [. . .]
One by one [. . .]   15
They crept forward [. . .]
Humbaba [. . .]

[gap]

Enkidu made ready to speak, saying to Gilgamesh:

> Humbaba [. . .]
> One by one [. . .].   20
> [Two] garments [. . .]
> On the treacherous pathway [we can go together],
> Two [. . .]

38

3. *They gazed at the height of the cedars.* This wall relief suggests how the poet may
have visualized the cedar mountain.

> A three-strand rope does not [. . .],
> Two cubs are [stronger] than a mighty lion.   25

[gap]

[*In older versions, they begin to cut trees and Humbaba hears the noise. In
the standard version, they meet Humbaba first. He proves to be something
of a snob, disdaining the steppe-born Enkidu, whom he ridicules as a midget
and a reptile. Gilgamesh then has second thoughts.*]

Humbaba made ready to speak, saying to Gilgamesh:

> How well-advised they are, the fool Gilgamesh and the yokel-
>   man!
> Why have you come here to me?
> Come now, Enkidu, small-fry, who does not know his father,
> Spawn of a turtle or tortoise, who sucked no mother's milk!   30
> I used to see you when you were younger but would not go
>   near you.
> [Had I killed the likes of] you, would I have filled my belly?
> [. . .] you have brought Gilgamesh before me,
> [. . .] you stand there, a barbarian foe!
> I should [cut off your head], Gilgamesh, throat and neck,   35
> I should let cawing buzzard, screaming eagle, and vulture
>   feed on your flesh.

Gilgamesh made ready to speak, saying to Enkidu:

> My friend, Humbaba's features have grown more grotesque,
> We strode up like heroes towards [. . .] to vanquish him,
> Yet my heart [. . .] right away.   40

[*Enkidu urges him on, quoting his brave words at Uruk and seeking to stiffen
his resolve.*]

Enkidu made ready to speak, saying to Gilgamesh:

Why, my friend, do you raise such unworthy objections?
How you pule! You make me ill.
Now, my friend, this has dragged on long enough.
The time has come to pour the copper into the mold.   45
Will you take another hour to blow the bellows,
An hour more to let it cool?
To launch the flood weapon, to wield the lash,
Retreat not a foot, you must not turn back,
[Let your eyes see all], let your blow strike home!   50

[gap]

[In the combat with Humbaba, the rift valley of Lebanon is formed by their circling feet.]

He struck the ground and [. . .] to confront him.
At their heels the earth split apart,
As they circled, the ranges of Lebanon were sundered!
The white clouds turned black,
Death rained down like fog upon them.   55
Shamash raised the great winds against Humbaba,
South wind, north wind, east wind, west wind, moaning wind,
Blasting wind, lashing wind, contrary wind, dust storm,
Demon wind, freezing wind, storm wind, whirlwind:
The thirteen winds blotted out Humbaba's face,   60
He could not charge forward, he could not retreat.
Then Gilgamesh's weapons defeated Humbaba.

[Humbaba begs for his life. Gilgamesh wavers but Enkidu is adamant. Humbaba calls him a beast and a boor, appealing to Gilgamesh's superior sensibilities. Gilgamesh is willing to spare Humbaba, with no further mention of the alleged evil that Shamash hates, but Enkidu urges him to the deed.]

Humbaba begged for life, saying to Gilgamesh:

You were once a child, Gilgamesh, you had a mother who
    bore you,
You are the offspring [of Ninsun the wild cow].   65
[You grew up to fulfill] the oracle of Shamash, lord of the
    mountain:
"Gilgamesh, scion of Uruk, is to be king."

[gap]

O Gilgamesh, a dead man cannot [. . .],
[. . .] a living being can [. . .] his master.

4. *My friend, Humbaba's features have grown more grotesque.* These demonic faces show how Mesopotamians imagined Humbaba.

> O Gilgamesh, spare my life!   70
> Let me dwell here for you [as your . . .],
> Say however many trees you [require . . .],
> For you I will guard the myrtle wood [. . .]
> Trees, the pride of [your . . .] palace.

Enkidu made ready to speak, saying to Gilgamesh: 75

> My friend! Do not listen to what Humbaba [says],
> [Do not heed] his entreaties!

                        [*gap*]

[*Humbaba is speaking to Enkidu.*]

You know the lore of my forest, the lore of [. . .],
And you understand all I have to say.
I might have lifted you up, dangled you from a twig at the
    entrance to my forest,   80
I might have let cawing buzzard, screaming eagle, and vulture
    feed on your flesh.
Now then, Enkidu, [mercy] is up to you [. . .],
Tell Gilgamesh to spare my life!

Enkidu made ready to speak, saying to Gilgamesh:

    My friend! Humbaba is guardian of the forest [of cedars],   85
    Finish him off for the kill, put him out of existence.
    Humbaba is guardian of the forest [of cedars],
    Finish him off for the kill, put him out of existence,
    Before Enlil the foremost one hears of this!
    [The great] gods will become angry with us,   90
    Enlil in Nippur, Shamash [in Larsa . . .].
    Establish [your reputation] for all time:
    "Gilgamesh, who slew Humbaba."

When Humbaba heard [. . .]
Humbaba [raised] his head [. . .]   95

                 [*gap*]

[*Humbaba continues to plead with Enkidu.*]

    You sit like a shepherd before [. . .]
    And like a hired man you [. . .]
    Now is the time, Enkidu, [. . .]
    Tell Gilgamesh to spare my life!

Enkidu made ready to speak, saying to Gilgamesh: 100

    My friend, Humbaba is guardian of the forest [of cedars],
    Finish him off for the kill, put him out of existence.
    Humbaba is guardian of the forest [of cedars],
    Finish him off for the kill, put him out of existence,
    Before [Enlil] the foremost one hears of this!   105
    The great gods will become angry with us,
    Enlil in Nippur, Shamash [in Larsa . . .].
    Establish your reputation for all time:
    "Gilgamesh, who slew Humbaba."

When Humbaba heard [. . .]   110

[gap]

[Realizing he is doomed, Humbaba curses them, concluding with an elaborate wordplay.]

> May they never [. . .]
> May the pair of them never reach old age!
> May Gilgamesh and Enkidu come across no graver friend
>   to bank on!

Enkidu made ready to speak, saying to Gilgamesh:

> My friend, I speak to you, but you do not heed me [. . .]   115
> Until the curse [. . .]

[gap]

[An old version contains the following exchange between Gilgamesh and Enkidu concerning the seven fearsome glories of Humbaba.]

Gilgamesh said to Enkidu:

> Now, [my friend], let us go on to victory!
> The glories will be lost in the confusion,
> The glories will be lost and the brightness will [. . .].   120

Enkidu said to him, to Gilgamesh:

> My friend, catch the bird and where will its chicks go?
> Let us search out the glories later,
> They will run around in the grass like chicks.
> Strike him again, then kill his retinue [. . .]   125

[Gilgamesh kills Humbaba. In some versions he has to strike multiple blows before the monster falls.]

Gilgamesh heeded his friend's command,
He raised the axe at his side,
He drew the sword at his belt.
Gilgamesh struck him on the neck,
Enkidu, his friend, [. . .].   130
They pulled out [. . .] as far as the lungs,
He tore out the [. . .],
He forced the head into a cauldron.
[. . .] in abundance fell on the mountain,

5. *He struck him, Humbaba the guardian, down to the ground.* This scene from a
bronze bowl shows this episode.

[. . .] in abundance fell on the mountain,   135
[. . .]
He struck him, Humbaba the guardian, down to the ground.
His blood [. . .]
For two leagues the cedars [. . .].
He killed the [glories] with him.   140
The forest [. . .].
He slew the monster, guardian of the forest,
At whose cry the mountains of Lebanon [trembled],
At whose cry all the mountains [quaked].
He slew the monster, guardian of the forest,   145
[He trampled on] the broken [. . .],
He struck down the seven [glories].
The battle net [. . .], the sword weighing eight times sixty
    pounds,
He took the weight of ten times sixty pounds upon him,
He forced his way into the forest,   150
He opened the secret dwelling of the supreme gods.

[gap]

[*They cut cedars, then Enkidu builds a gigantic door that they float down
the Euphrates as a gift to Enlil. Enkidu, not anticipating the consequences,
hopes that Enlil will be grateful to Gilgamesh for the door.*]

[. . .] the cedars that they cut, one after another.
[. . .] the flying chips,

Gilgamesh cut down the trees,
Enkidu chose the timbers.   155
Enkidu made ready to speak, said to Gilgamesh:

>You killed the guardian by your strength,
>Who else could cut through this forest of trees?
>My friend, we have felled the lofty cedar,
>Whose crown once pierced the sky.   160
>I will make a door six times twelve cubits high, two times
>   twelve cubits wide,
>One cubit shall be its thickness,
>Its hinge pole, ferrule, and pivot box shall be unique.[1]
>Let no stranger approach it, may only a god go through.
>Let the Euphrates bring it to Nippur,   165
>Nippur, the sanctuary of Enlil.
>May Enlil be delighted with you,
>May Enlil rejoice over it!

[. . .]
They lashed together a raft [. . .]   170
Enkidu embarked [. . .]
And Gilgamesh [. . .] the head of Humbaba.

---

1. Mesopotamian doors did not use hinges but were often made of a panel attached to a post. It was this post, or "hinge pole," that rotated when the door was opened or closed, sometimes on a piece of metal, or "ferrule," at the bottom. The top of the post was cased or enclosed so the door post would not slip off its pivot point.

Tablet VI

[*Gilgamesh strips to put on fresh garments after the expedition. Ishtar, goddess of love and sex, is attracted to him and proposes marriage, offering him majesty and wealth.*]

He washed his matted locks, cleaned his head strap,[1]
He shook his hair down over his shoulders.
He threw off his filthy clothes, he put on clean ones,
Wrapping himself in a cloak, he tied on his sash,
Gilgamesh put on his kingly diadem.   5
The princess Ishtar coveted Gilgamesh's beauty:

> Come, Gilgamesh, you shall be my bridegroom!
> Give, oh give me of your lusciousness!
> You shall be my husband and I shall be your wife.
> I will ready for you a chariot of lapis and gold,   10
> With golden wheels and fittings of gemstones,
> You shall harness storm demons as if they were giant mules.
> Enter our house amidst fragrance of cedar,
> When you enter our house,
> The splendid exotic doorsill shall do you homage,   15
> Kings, nobles, and princes shall kneel before you,
> They shall bring you gifts of mountain and lowland as tribute.
> Your goats shall bear triplets, your ewes twins,
> Your pack-laden donkey shall overtake the mule,
> Your horses shall run proud before the wagon,   20
> Your ox in the yoke shall have none to compare!

[*Gilgamesh spurns Ishtar's proposal, heaping scorn upon her. He enumerates her past lovers, all of whom she doomed to a cruel destiny.*]

Gilgamesh made ready to speak,
Saying to the princess Ishtar:

---

1. This may refer to a band of cloth that held up Gilgamesh's long hair. When it was released, the hair fell free over the shoulders, a sign of undress in Mesopotamia. Such a band is visible behind the ear of Gilgamesh in figure 5.

[What shall I give you] if I take you to wife?
[Shall I give you] a headdress(?) for your person, or clothing?   25
[Shall I give you] bread or drink?
[Shall I give you] food, worthy of divinity?
[Shall I give you] drink, worthy of queenship?
Shall I bind [. . .]?
Shall I heap up [. . .]?   30
[. . .] for a garment.
[What would I get] if I marry you?
[You are a brazier that goes out] when it freezes,
A flimsy door that keeps out neither wind nor draught,
A palace [that crushes] a warrior,   35
A mouse(?) that [gnaws through] its housing,
Tar that [smears] its bearer,
Waterskin that [soaks] its bearer,
Weak stone that undermines a wall,
Battering ram that destroys the wall for an enemy,   40
Shoe that pinches its wearer!
Which of your lovers [lasted] forever?
Which of your heroes went up [to heaven]?
Come, I call you to account for your lovers:
He who had [jugs of cream] on his shoulders and [. . .]
    on his arm,   45
For Dumuzi, your girlhood lover,
You ordained year after year of weeping.
You fell in love with the brightly colored roller bird,
Then you struck him and broke his wing.
In the woods he sits crying "My-wing!"   50
You fell in love with the lion, perfect in strength,
Then you dug for him ambush pits, seven times seven.
You fell in love with the wild stallion, eager for the fray,
Whip, goad, and lash you ordained for him,
Seven double leagues of galloping you ordained for him,   55
You ordained that he muddy his water when he drinks,
You ordained perpetual weeping for his mother, divine Silili.
You fell in love with the shepherd, keeper of herds,
Who always set out cakes baked in embers for you,
Slaughtered kids for you every day.   60
You struck him and turned him into a wolf,
His own shepherd boys harry him off,
And his own hounds snap at his heels!
You fell in love with Ishullanu, your father's gardener,
Who always brought you baskets of dates,   65
Who daily made your table splendid.
You wanted him, so you sidled up to him:
"My Ishullanu, let's have a taste of your vigor!

Bring out your member, touch our sweet spot!"
Ishullanu said to you,   70
"Me? What do you want of me?
Hath my mother not baked? Have I not eaten?
Shall what I taste for food be insults and curses?
In the cold, is my cover to be the touch of a reed?"
When you heard what he said,   75
You struck him and turned him into a scarecrow(?),
You left him stuck in his own garden patch,
His well sweep goes up no longer, his bucket does not
     descend.
As for me, now that you've fallen in love with me, you will
     treat me like them!

[*Ishtar rushes off to her parents in a passion and sobs out her indigna-
tion. Her speech is noteworthy for its jarring colloquialisms. Her father,
Anu, the sky god, attempts mildly to pacify her, but Ishtar will have punishment at any price. She demands her father's bull to let loose against the
heroes. She gets her way after threatening to release the dead. She also promises to garner food against the seven years of famine that will follow the
attack of the bull.*]

When Ishtar heard this,   80
Ishtar was furious and went up to heaven,
Ishtar went sobbing before Anu, her father,
Before Antum, her mother, her tears flowed down:

     Father, Gilgamesh has said outrageous things about me,
     Gilgamesh's been spouting insults about me,   85
     Insults and curses against me!

Anu made ready to speak,
Saying to the princess Ishtar:

     Well now, did you not provoke the king, Gilgamesh,
     And so Gilgamesh spouted insults about you,   90
     Insults and curses against you?

Ishtar made ready to speak,
Saying to Anu, her father:

     Well then, Father, pretty please, the Bull of Heaven,
     So I can kill Gilgamesh on his home ground.   95
     If you don't give me the Bull of Heaven,
     I'll strike [. . .] to its foundation,
     I'll [. . .],

I'll raise up the dead to devour the living,
The dead shall outnumber the living! 100

Anu made ready to speak,
Saying to the princess Ishtar:

If you insist on the Bull of Heaven from me,
Let the widow of Uruk gather seven years of chaff,
[Let the farmer of Uruk] raise [seven years of hay]. 105

Ishtar made ready to speak,
Saying to Anu, her father:

[. . .] I stored up,
[. . .] I provided,
[The widow of Uruk has] gathered seven years of chaff, 110
The farmer [of Uruk] has raised [seven years of] hay.
[With] the Bull of Heaven's [fury I will kill him]!

When Anu heard what Ishtar said,
He placed the lead rope of the Bull of Heaven in her hand,
Ishtar led the Bull of Heaven away. 115

[The bull rampages down the Euphrates, lowering its water level with great
gulps and opening up enormous pits in the ground with its snorts. Enkidu
pinions the animal, and Gilgamesh stabs it to death.]

When it reached Uruk,
It dried up the groves, reedbeds, and marshes,
It went down to the river, it lowered the river by seven cubits.
At the bull's snort, a pit opened up,
One hundred young men of Uruk fell into it. 120
At its second snort, a pit opened up,
Two hundred young men of Uruk fell into it.
At its third snort, a pit opened up,
Enkidu fell into it, up to his middle.
Enkidu jumped out and seized the bull by its horns, 125
The bull spewed its foam in his face,
Swished dung at him with the tuft of its tail.
Enkidu made ready to speak,
Saying to Gilgamesh:

My friend, we boasted of [. . .], 130
How shall we answer [. . .]?
I have seen, my friend, the strength of the Bull of
Heaven . . . ,

So knowing its strength, [I know] how to deal with it.
I will get around the strength of the Bull of Heaven,
I will circle behind the Bull of Heaven,   135
I will grab it by the tuft of its tail,
I will set my feet on its [. . .],
Then you, like a strong, skillful slaughterer,
Thrust your dagger between neck, horn, and tendon!

Enkidu circled behind the Bull of Heaven,   140
He grabbed it by the tuft of its tail,
He set his feet on its [. . .],
And Gilgamesh, like a strong, skillful slaughterer,
Thrust his dagger between neck, horn, and tendon!

[*Gilgamesh and Enkidu offer the creature's heart to Shamash with a prayer.
Ishtar is distraught, again using colloquial language. Enkidu rips off the
bull's haunch and throws it at her. He insults her, saying he would butcher
her too if he could. Ishtar convenes her cult women and sets up a lament
over the bull's haunch.*]

After they had killed the Bull of Heaven,   145
They ripped out its heart and set it before Shamash.
They stepped back and prostrated themselves before Shamash,
Then the two comrades sat down beside each other.
Ishtar went up on the wall of ramparted Uruk,
She writhed in grief, she let out a wail: 150

> That bully Gilgamesh who demeaned me, he's killed the
>   Bull of Heaven!

When Enkidu heard what Ishtar said,
He tore off the bull's haunch and flung it at her:

> If I could vanquish you, I'd turn you to this,
> I'd drape the guts beside you!   155

Ishtar convened the cult women, prostitutes, harlots,
She set up a lament over the haunch of the bull.

[*The bull's immense horns are marvels of craftsmanship. Gilgamesh hangs
them up in his bedroom as a trophy.*]

Gilgamesh summoned all the expert craftsmen,
The craftsmen marveled at the massiveness of its horns,
They were molded from thirty pounds each of lapis blue,   160
Their outer shell was two thumbs thick!

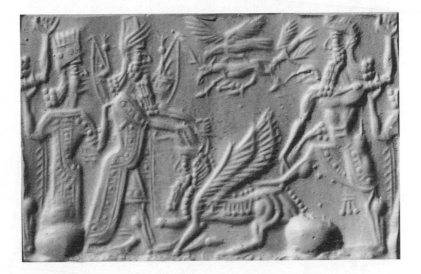

6. *And Gilgamesh, like a strong, skillful slaughterer, / Thrust his dagger between neck, horn, and tendon!* This seal image shows this episode, with Ishtar standing by in anguish.

Six times three hundred quarts of oil, the capacity of both,
He donated to anoint the statue of his god, Lugalbanda.
He brought them inside and hung them up in his master bedroom.

[*Gilgamesh and Enkidu parade in triumph. Gilgamesh makes a short speech, ending with a final condemnation of Ishtar.*]

They washed their hands in the Euphrates,   165
Clasping each other, they came away,
Paraded through the streets of Uruk.
The people of Uruk crowded to look upon them.
Gilgamesh made a speech
To the servant-women of [his palace]:   170

> Who is the handsomest of young men?
> Who is the most glorious of males?
> Gilgamesh is the handsomest of young men!
> [Gilgamesh] is the most glorious of males!
> [She at whom] we flung [the haunch] in our passion,   175
> [Ishtar], she has no one in the street to satisfy her,
> [. . .]

Gilgamesh held a celebration in his palace.
The young men slept stretched out on the couch of night.
While Enkidu slept, he had a dream.   180
Enkidu went to relate his dream,
Saying to his friend:

Tablet VII

My friend, why were the great gods in council?

[gap]

[According to a Hittite version (see p. 163) Enkidu sees the gods Anu, Enlil, Ea, and Shamash in council. Anu decrees that because Enkidu and Gilgamesh killed the bull and cut cedars, one of them must die. Enlil, perhaps grateful for the cedar door, decides that it should be Enkidu. Shamash considers this unfair, but Enlil overrules him. When the standard version resumes, Enkidu is cursing the cedar door. The concluding words of his curse parody traditional Mesopotamian inscriptions affixed to monuments, which called the wrath of the gods upon anyone who damaged, removed, or usurped the monument.]

Enkidu raised [. . .],
He spoke to the door [as if it were human]:

O bosky door, insensate,
Which lends an ear that is not there, 5
I sought your wood for twenty double leagues,
Till I beheld a lofty cedar [. . .]
No rival had your tree [in the forest . . .].
Six times twelve cubits was your height, two times twelve
cubits was your width,
One cubit was your thickness, 10
Your hinge pole, ferrule, and pivot box were unique.
I made you, I brought you to Nippur, I set you up.
Had I known, O door, how you would [requite me],
And that this your goodness [towards me . . .],
I would have raised my axe, I would have chopped you down, 15
I would have floated you as a raft to the temple of Shamash,
I would have brought you into the temple of Shamash,
I would have set up the cedar [. . . in the . . .] of the
temple of Shamash,
I would have set up the lion-headed monster-bird Anzu at
its gate,
[. . .] the way to you [. . .] 20
I would have [. . .],

53

Then in Uruk [. . .] you,
Because Shamash heard my plea . . .
He gave me the weapon to [kill Humbaba].
Now then, O door, it was I who made you, it was I who set
    you up.   25
I [. . .], I will tear you out!
May a king who shall arise after me despise you,
May [. . .] conceal you,
May he alter my inscription and put on his own!

He tore out [his hair], threw away [his clothing].   30

When he heard out this speech, swiftly, quickly his tears flowed
    down,
When Gilgamesh heard out Enkidu's speech, swiftly, quickly,
    his tears flowed down.

[*Gilgamesh comforts Enkidu by suggesting that death may be a greater bur-
den for those left behind than for the deceased. Gilgamesh promises that he
will make a magnificent funerary statue of his friend. Death is inevitable; it
is foolish to complain.*]

Gilgamesh made ready to speak, saying to Enkidu:

[. . .] superb,
My friend, you are rational but [you say] strange things,   35
Why, my friend, does your heart speak strange things?
The dream is a most precious omen, though very frightening,
Your [lips] are buzzing like flies.
[Though frightening], the dream is a precious omen.
The [gods] left mourning for the living,   40
The dream left mourning for the living,
The dream left woe for the living!
Now I shall go pray to the great gods,
I will be assiduous to [my own god], I will pray to yours,
To [Anu], father of the gods [. . .],   45
[To] Enlil, counselor of the gods, [. . .],
[. . .]
I will make your image of gold beyond measure.
You can pay no silver, no gold can you [. . .],
What Enlil commanded is not like the [. . .] of the gods,   50
What he commanded, he will not retract.
The verdict he has scrivened, he will not reverse nor erase.
My friend, he will not [. . .]
People often die before their time.

[At dawn, Enkidu prays to Shamash, god of justice and right-dealing. He calls his curse upon the two human agents whom he blames for his destiny, the hunter and the harlot. For the hunter he wishes a poor catch, for the harlot the worst of a whore's life. Lines 60–61 depend on a wordplay on the Akkadian words for "friend" and "food ration."]

At the first glimmer of dawn,   55
Enkidu lifted his head, weeping before Shamash,
Before the sun's fiery glare, his tears flowed down:

> I have turned to you, O Shamash, on account of the precious
>   days of my life,
> As for that hunter, the entrapping-man,
> Who did not let me get as much life as my friend,   60
> May that hunter not get enough to make him a living.
> Make his profit loss, cut down his take,
> May his income, his portion evaporate before you,
> Any wildlife that enters [his traps], make it go out the
>   window!

When he had cursed the hunter to his heart's content,   65
He resolved to curse the harlot Shamhat:

> Come, Shamhat, I will ordain you a destiny,
> A destiny that will never end, forever and ever!
> I will lay on you the greatest of all curses,
> Swiftly, inexorably, may my curse come upon you.   70
> May you never make a home that you can enjoy,
> May you never caress [a child] of your own,
> May you never be received among decent women.
> May [beer sludge(?)] impregnate your lap,
> May the drunkard bespatter your best clothes with vomit.   75
> [May your swain prefer] beauties,
> [May he pinch you] like potter's clay.
> May you get no [. . .] alabaster,
> [May no . . .] table to be proud of be set in your house.
> May the nook you enjoy be a doorstep,   80
> May the public crossroads be your dwelling,
> May vacant lots be your sleeping place,
> May the shade of a wall be your place of business.
> May brambles and thorns flay your feet,
> May toper and sober slap your cheek.[1]   85
> May [riffraff] of the street shove each other in your brothel,
> May there be a brawl [there . . .].

---

1. That is, may anyone hit her, drunk or not.

[When you stroll with your cronies], may they catcall
    after you.
May the builder not keep your roof in repair,
May the screech owl roost [in the ruins of your home].   90
May a feast never be held [where you live].

[gap]

May your purple finery be expropriated,
May filthy underwear be what you are given,
Because you diminished me, an innocent,
Yes me, an innocent, you wronged me(?) in my steppe.   95

[*Shamash remonstrates, asserting that friendship with Gilgamesh was worth
an untimely death and promising Enkidu a fine funeral. He also tells him
that Gilgamesh will take his place as "wild man" of the steppe, no doubt
the fullest possible observance of the loss of his friend, short of taking his
place in the netherworld.*]

When Shamash heard what he said,
From afar a warning voice called to him from the sky:

    O Enkidu, why curse Shamhat the harlot,
    Who fed you bread, fit for a god,
    Who poured you beer, fit for a king,   100
    Who dressed you in a noble garment,
    And gave you handsome Gilgamesh for a comrade?
    Now then, Gilgamesh is your friend and blood brother!
    Won't he lay you down in the ultimate resting place?
    In a perfect resting place he will surely lay you down!   105
    He will settle you in peaceful rest in that dwelling sinister,
    Rulers of the netherworld will do you homage.
    He will have the people of Uruk shed bitter tears for you,
    He will make the [pleasure-loving] people burdened down for
        you,
    And, as for him, after your death, he will let his hair grow
        matted,   110
    He will put on a lion skin and roam the steppe.

[*Enkidu, with bitter humor, immediately reverses the "destiny that will never
end" for the harlot. He now wishes her the best of a whore's life: an eager,
generous clientele from all levels of society.*]

When Enkidu heard the speech of the valiant Shamash,
His raging heart was calmed,
[. . .] his fury was calmed:

Come, Shamhat, I will ordain you a destiny,   115
My mouth that cursed you, let it bless you instead.
May governors and dignitaries fall in love with you,
May the man one double league away slap his thighs
    in excitement,
May the man two double leagues away let down his hair.
May the subordinate not hold back from you, but open
    his trousers,   120
May he give you obsidian,[2] lapis, and gold,
May ear bangles be your gift.
To the man whose wealth is secure, whose granaries are full,
May Ishtar, [. . .] of the gods, introduce you,
For your sake may the wife and mother of seven be
    abandoned.   125

Enkidu was sick at heart,
He lay there lonely.
[He told] his friend what weighed on his mind:

[*Enkidu tells Gilgamesh a dream he had the night before. The timing of this
is not clear, suggesting that the text has been assembled from different materials at this point. The dream is of dying and the afterlife. Mesopotamian
tradition was unanimous on this grim view of the netherworld, characterized
by darkness, hunger and thirst, dust, and no rewards beyond those provided
by the solicitude of one's surviving kin. A fragment discovered at Megiddo,
perhaps dating to the fourteenth century B.C.E., preserves a version of this
episode in which Enkidu may blame Gilgamesh for the killing of Humbaba,
but this is uncertain.*]

My friend, what a dream I had last night!
Heaven cried out, earth made reply,   130
I was standing between them.
There was a certain man, his face was somber,
His face was like that of the lion-headed monster-bird Anzu,
His hands were the paws of a lion,
His fingernails were the talons of an eagle.   135
He seized me by the hair, he was too strong for me,
I hit him but he sprang back like a swing rope,
He hit me and capsized me like a [raft].
Like a wild bull he trampled me,
He [. . .] my whole body with his slaver,   140
"Save me, my friend!"—[but you did not save me]!
You were afraid and did not [. . .]
You [. . .]

2. A dark, glassy imported volcanic stone, prized in Mesopotamia for making implements because it was hard and could hold a sharp edge.

[gap]

[. . .] and turned me into a dove,
He trussed my limbs like a bird's.   145
Holding me fast, he took me down to the house of
    shadows, the dwelling of hell,
To the house whence none who enters comes forth,
On the road from which there is no way back,
To the house whose dwellers are deprived of light,
Where dust is their fare and their food is clay.   150
They are dressed like birds in feather garments,
Yea, they shall see no daylight, for they abide in darkness.
[Dust lies thick] on the door [and bolt],
To the house [. . .].
When I entered that house of dust,   155
I saw crowns in a heap,
There dwelt the kings, the crowned heads who once
    ruled the land,
Who always set out roast meat for Anu and Enlil,
Who always set out baked offerings, libated cool water
    from waterskins.
In that house of dust I entered,   160
Dwelt high priests and acolytes,
Dwelt reciters of spells and ecstatics,[3]
Dwelt the anointers of the great gods,
Dwelt old King Etana and the god of the beasts,
Dwelt the queen of the netherworld, Ereshkigal.   165
Belet-seri, scribe of the netherworld, was kneeling before her,
She was holding [a tablet] and reading to her,
[She lifted] her head, she looked at me:
"Who brought this man?"

[gap]

[Whereas the two friends have interpreted or, one might say, explained away
the grim symbolism of all the dreams they have had since the beginning of
their friendship, this dream is so obvious and compelling in its portent that
no interpretation is called for.]

---

3. Mesopotamian poets often used extremes to convey totality: high priests were at the top of
the hierarchy, assistants, or "acolytes," at the bottom, so line 161 means that all ranks of the
priesthood were in the netherworld along with other people. Reciters of spells were learned
scholars while prophets, or "ecstatics," were people who spoke in a trance without having
studied their words. They were sometimes social outcasts or people without education. Line
162 therefore refers to all who communicated or made use of the words of the gods.

I who went with you through all hardships, 170
Remember me, my friend, do not forget what I have
    undergone!
My friend had a dream needing no interpretation.

[*Enkidu's final illness is conveyed by monotonous repetition of the days of
its course. This climaxes in a parting speech, little of which is now preserved.*]

The day he had the dream, [his strength] ran out.
Enkidu lay there one day, [a second day] he was ill,
Enkidu lay in his bed, [his illness grew worse]. 175
A third day, a fourth day, [Enkidu's illness grew worse].
A fifth, a sixth, a seventh,
An eighth, a ninth, [a tenth day],
[Enkidu's illness grew worse].
An eleventh, a twelfth day, 180
Enkidu lay in his bed.
He called for Gilgamesh, [roused him with his cry]:

My friend laid on me [the greatest] curse of all!
When in battle [. . .]
I feared the battle [but will die in my bed], 185
My friend, he who [falls quickly] in battle [is glorious].
I [. . .] in battle.

[*gap*]

[*Enkidu dies.*]

Tablet VIII

[*Gilgamesh laments his dead friend, Enkidu. Line 18 refers to an episode that does not appear in the extant portions of the epic.*]

At the first glimmer of dawn,
Gilgamesh [lamented] his friend:

Enkidu, my friend, your mother the gazelle,
Your father the wild ass brought you into the world,
Onagers raised you on their milk,   5
And the wild beasts taught you all the grazing places.
The pathways, O Enkidu, to the forest of cedars,
May they weep for you, without falling silent, night and day.
May the elders of the teeming city, ramparted Uruk, weep
    for you,
May the crowd who blessed our departure weep for you.   10
May the heights of highland and mountain [weep for you],
[. . .]
May the lowlands wail like your mother.
May [the forest] of balsam and cedar weep for you,
Which we slashed in our fury.   15
May bear, hyena, panther, leopard, deer, jackal,
Lion, wild bull, gazelle, ibex, the beasts and creatures
    of the steppe, weep for you.
May the sacred Ulaya River weep for you, along whose
    banks we once strode erect,
May the holy Euphrates weep for you,
Whose waters we libated from waterskins.   20
May the young men of ramparted Uruk weep for you,
Who watched us slay the Bull of Heaven in combat.
May the plowman weep for you [at his plow],
Who extolled your name in the sweet song of harvest home.[1]
May they weep for you, [. . .] of the teeming city of Uruk,   25
Who exalted your name at the first [. . .].
May the shepherd and herdsman weep for you,
Who held the milk and buttermilk to your mouth,

1. Mesopotamian literature referred to work songs sung when the crops were brought in from
   the harvest as symbols of happiness and prosperity.

60

May the [nurse] weep for you,
Who treated your rashes(?) with butter.   30
May the [. . .] weep for you,
Who held the ale to your mouth.
May the harlot weep for you,
Who massaged you with sweet-smelling oil.
May the wedding guests weep for you,   35
Who [. . .]
Like brothers may they weep for you,
Like sisters may they tear out their hair for your sake.
[. . .] Enkidu, as your father, your mother,
I weep for you bitterly, [. . .]   40

Hear me, O young men, listen to me,
Hear me, O elders of [Uruk], listen to me!
I mourn my friend Enkidu,
I howl as bitterly as a professional keener.
Oh for the axe at my side, oh for the safeguard by my hand,   45
Oh for the sword at my belt, oh for the shield before me,
Oh for my best garment, oh for the raiment that pleased me
    most!
An ill wind rose against me and snatched it away!
O my friend, swift wild donkey, mountain onager, panther
    of the steppe,
O Enkidu my friend, swift wild donkey, mountain onager,
    panther of the steppe!   50
You who stood by me when we climbed the mountain,
Seized and slew the Bull of Heaven,
Felled Humbaba who [dwelt] in the forest of cedar,
What now is this sleep that has seized you?
Come back to me! You hear me not.   55

But, as for him, he did not raise his head.
He touched his heart but it was not beating.
Then he covered his friend's face, like a bride's.
He hovered round him like an eagle,
Like a lioness whose cubs are in a pitfall,   60
He paced to and fro, back and forth,
Tearing out and hurling away the locks of his hair,
Ripping off and throwing away his fine clothes like something
    foul.

[*Gilgamesh commissions a memorial statue for Enkidu.*]

At the first glimmer of dawn,
Gilgamesh sent out a proclamation to the land: 65

Hear ye, blacksmith, lapidary, metalworker, goldsmith,
    jeweler!
Make [an image] of my friend,
[Such as no one ever] made of his friend!
The limbs of my friend [. . .]
[Your beard] of lapis, your chest of gold,   70
Your skin of [. . .]

[gap]

I will lay you down in the ultimate resting place,
In a perfect resting place I will surely lay you down.
I will settle you in peaceful rest in that dwelling sinister,
Rulers of the netherworld will do you homage.   75
I will have the people of Uruk shed bitter tears for you,
I will make the pleasure-loving people burdened down for
    you,
And, as for me, now that you are dead, I will let my hair
    grow matted,
I will put on a lion skin and roam the steppe!

[gap]

At the first glimmer of dawn, Gilgamesh arose,   80
[He . . . the storehouse],
He broke its seal, he surveyed the treasure,
[He brought out] carnelian,[2] [. . .] alabaster,
He fashioned [. . .]
He set out [. . .] for his friend.   85
[. . .]
[. . . made of] ten pounds of gold,
[. . .] pounds of gold,
[. . .] pounds of gold,
[. . .] pounds of gold,   90
[. . .]
[. . .] between them, mounted in thirty pounds of gold.

[gap]

[In the fragmentary lines that follow, there is mention of weapons and or-
naments of gold, silver, ivory, and iron.]

He slaughtered fatted [cattle] and sheep, heaped them high for
    his friend,

2. A reddish stone, prized in Mesopotamia for making beads and seals.

[. . .]
They carried off all the meat for the rulers of the netherworld.   95
[. . .] Ishtar, the great queen,
[. . . made of . . .], the sacred wood,
He displayed in the open for Ishtar, the great queen,
Saying: "May Ishtar, the great queen, accept this,
May she welcome my friend and walk at his side."   100
[. . .]
He displayed in the open for Ashimbabbar [. . .],
Saying: "May Ashimbabbar, [. . .], accept this,
May he welcome my friend and walk at his side."
A jar of lapis [. . .],   105
[. . .]
He displayed in the open for Ereshkigal, [queen of the
     netherworld],
Saying: "May Ereshkigal, [queen of the crowded netherworld],
     accept this,
May she welcome my friend and walk at his side."
A flute of carnelian [. . .],   110
He displayed in the open for Dumuzi, the shepherd, beloved of
     [Ishtar],
Saying: "May Dumuzi, the shepherd, beloved of [Ishtar],
     accept this,
May he welcome my friend and walk at his side."
A chair of lapis [. . .]
A staff of lapis [. . .]   115
He displayed in the open for Namtar, [courier of the netherworld],
Saying: "May Namtar, [courier of the crowded netherworld],
     accept this,
May he welcome my friend and walk at his side."

[gap]

A bracelet(?) of silver, a ring(?) of [. . .],
He displayed in the open for Qassa-tabat, sweeper(?)
     [of the netherworld],   120
Saying: "May Qassa-tabat, sweeper(?) [of the crowded
     netherworld], accept this,
May he welcome my friend and walk at his side.
May my friend not . . . nor lose courage."
[. . .] of alabaster, the inside inlaid with lapis and carnelian,
[. . .] of the cedar forest,   125
[. . .] inlaid with carnelian,
He displayed in the open for Ninshuluhha, housekeeper
     of the netherworld,
Saying: "May Ninshuluhha, housekeeper of the crowded
     netherworld, accept this,

7. *He filled a lapis bowl with butter.* Lapis bowl and whetstone from a grave at Ur.

May she welcome my friend and walk at his side.
May she intercede on behalf of my friend, lest he lose courage."   130
The obsidian knife with lapis fitting,
The sharpening stone pure-whetted with Euphrates water,
He displayed in the open for Bibbu, meat carver of the
    netherworld,
Saying: "May Bibbu, meat carver of the crowded netherworld,
    accept this,
Welcome my friend and walk at his side."   135
[. . .] carnelian and alabaster,
He displayed in the open for [. . .]-absu, blame-bearer
    of the netherworld,
Saying: "May [. . .]-absu, blame-bearer of the crowded
    netherworld, accept this,
Welcome my friend and walk at his side."

[*gap*]

[The lying-in-state and obsequies continue.]

At the first glimmer of dawn, Gilgamesh opened the [. . .],   140
He brought out a great table of precious wood,
He filled a carnelian bowl with honey,
He filled a lapis bowl with butter,
He adorned [. . .] and displayed it in the open.

[*gap*]

Tablet IX

[Gilgamesh, distraught, roams the steppe. He then sets forth on a quest to find Utanapishtim, the survivor of the flood.]

Gilgamesh was weeping bitterly for Enkidu, his friend,
As he roamed the steppe:

> Shall I not die too? Am I not like Enkidu?
> Oh woe has entered my vitals!
> I have grown afraid of death, so I roam the steppe.   5
> Having come this far, I will go on swiftly
> Towards Utanapishtim, son of Ubar-Tutu.
> I have reached mountain passes at night.
> I saw lions, I felt afraid,
> I looked up to pray to the moon,   10
> To the moon, beacon of the gods, my prayers went forth:
> "[. . .] keep me safe!"

[At night] he lay down, then awoke from a dream.
[. . .] moon, he rejoiced to be alive.
He raised the axe at his side,   15
He drew the sword from his belt,
He dropped among them like an arrow,
He struck [the lions], scattered, [and killed them].

[gap]

[The following episode, found in an old version, may be placed here. In an obscure passage, a god apparently tells Shamash what Gilgamesh is doing.]

> He has put on their skins, he eats their flesh.
> Gilgamesh [digs] wells where they never were before,   20
> [. . .] the water, he pursues the winds.

Shamash was distressed, bending down, he said to Gilgamesh:

> Gilgamesh, wherefore do you wander?
> The eternal life you are seeking you shall not find.

Gilgamesh spoke to him, the valiant Shamash: 25

> After my restless roaming in the steppe,
> There will be ample repose, deep in the earth.
> I have been asleep all these years!
> Now let my eyes see the sun, let me have all the light
>   I could wish for,
> Darkness is infinite, how little light there is!   30
> When may the dead see the radiance of the sun?

[As the standard version resumes, Gilgamesh approaches in awe the scorpion
monsters who guard the gateway to the sun's passage through the mountains.
The description of the scorpion monsters is so hyperbolic as to suggest humorous intent, especially when the scorpion monster's wife corrects her
husband.]

The twin peaks are called Mashum.
When he arrived at the twin peaks called Mashum,
Which daily watch over the rising [and setting of the sun],
Whose peaks thrust upward to the vault of heaven,   35
Whose flanks reach downward to hell,
Where scorpion monsters guard its gateway,
Whose appearance is dreadful, whose venom is death,
Their fear-inspiring radiance spreads over the mountains,
They watch over the sun at its rising and setting,   40
When Gilgamesh saw their fearsomeness and terror,
He covered his face.
He took hold of himself and approached them.

The scorpion monster called to his wife:

> This one who has come to us, his body is flesh of a god!   45

The wife of the scorpion monster answered him:

> Two-thirds of him is divine, one-third is human

The scorpion monster, the male one, called out,
[To Gilgamesh, scion] of the gods, he said these words:

> [Who are you] who have come this long way,   50
> [. . .] before me,
> [. . .] whose crossing is arduous,
> [. . .] I want to know,
> [The goal towards which] you are setting forth,
> [. . .] I want to know.   55

[gap]

[*When Gilgamesh explains his quest, the scorpion monster asserts that no one can traverse the tunnel through mountains. Apparently the sun crosses the sky during the twelve hours of day and passes through the tunnel during the twelve hours of night so as to return to its rising point.*]

[. . .] Utanapishtim my forefather [. . .]
Who took his place in the assembly of the gods [. . .]
Death and life [. . .]

The scorpion monster made ready to speak, spoke to him,
Saying to Gilgamesh: 60

There is no [. . .], Gilgamesh,
No one has ever [. . .] the mountain.
Its passage is twelve double hours [. . .]
Dense is the darkness, [no light is there],
To the rising of the sun [. . .]   65
To the setting of the sun [. . .]
To the setting of the sun [. . .]

[gap]

[*In the intervening gap, something persuades the scorpion monster to open the gateway to the tunnel through the mountains. To judge from the analogy of Utanapishtim and his wife, encountered later in the epic, not to mention Ninsun and the tavern keeper, also later in the epic, the scorpion monster's wife intervenes on Gilgamesh's behalf and convinces her husband to admit him.*]

Woe [in his vitals],
[His features weathered] by cold [and sun],
With sighs [. . .],   70
Now then, [show him the way to Utanapishtim].

[*The scorpion monster apparently warns Gilgamesh that he has only twelve hours to get through the sun's tunnel before the sun enters it at nightfall.*]

The scorpion monster made ready to speak, spoke to him,
Said to Gilgamesh, [scion of the gods]:

Go, Gilgamesh, [. . .]
Mount Mashum [. . .]   75
The mountain ranges [. . .]
Safely [. . .].

[He opened to him] the gateway of the mountain,
Gilgamesh [entered the mountain . . .]
[He heeded] the words of the [scorpion monster],   80
[He set out on] the way of the sun.

[*Gilgamesh races through the tunnel, a heroic run equal to the sun's journey across the sky. It is so dark that he cannot reassure himself by looking back to the light from the entrance behind him to know that the sun is still in the heavens. At the same time, he knows that if he sees light ahead of him, he is doomed.*]

When he had gone one double hour,
Dense was the darkness, no light was there,
It would not let him look behind him.
When he had gone two double hours,   85
Dense was the darkness, no light was there,
It would not let him look behind him.
When he had gone three double hours,
Dense was the darkness, no light was there,
It would not let him look behind him.   90
When he had gone four double hours,
Dense was the darkness, no light was there,
It would not let him look behind him.
When he had gone five double hours,
Dense was the darkness, no light was there,   95
It would not let him look behind him.
When he had gone six double hours,
Dense was the darkness, no light was there,
It would not let him look behind him.
When he had gone seven double hours,   100
Dense was the darkness, there was no light,
It would not let him look behind him.
When he had gone eight double hours, he rushed ahead,
Dense was the darkness, there was no light,
It would not let him look behind him.   105
When he had gone nine double hours, he felt the north wind,
[. . .] his face,
Dense was the darkness, there was no light,
It would not let him look behind him.
When he had gone ten double hours,   110
[The time for the sun's entry] was drawing near.
[When he had gone eleven double hours], just one double hour
    [was left],
[When he had gone twelve double hours], he came out ahead of
    the sun!
[He had run twelve double hours], bright light still reigned!

8. *Dense was the darkness, no light was there.* This episode was probably inspired by the Tigris tunnel, a stone passage in Armenia where the river flows under a mountain. This tunnel was several times visited by Mesopotamian kings. This relief shows men exploring it with torches.

He went forward, seeing [. . .], the trees of the gods.   115
The carnelian bore its fruit,
Like bunches of grapes dangling, lovely to see,
The lapis bore foliage,
Fruit it bore, a delight to behold.

[*The fragmentary lines that remain continue the description of the wonderful grove. Identification of most of the stones is conjectural.*]

[. . .] balsam [. . .],   120
[. . .] cedar [. . .].
Its fronds were green chlorite, [. . .] sweet dates,
Coral(?), [. . .], rubies(?),
Instead of thorns and brambles, there were [. . .] of red stone,
He took up a carob, it was [. . .] of green stone!   125
Agates, hematite, [. . .], amber(?),
Instead of [. . .] and cucumbers, there were [. . .] of yellow
    stone,
Instead of [. . .] there were [. . .] of turquoise,

The [. . .] cowrie shells.[1]
It had water to make the [. . .] delightful.   130
Gilgamesh [. . .] as he walked along,
He looked up and gazed at it.

1. Chlorite (line 122), a soft stone, was prized in Mesopotamia for making bowls and small
   containers. Carob (line 125) was a common seedpod eaten or made into juice; hence, the
   most ordinary-looking fruit turned out to be a precious stone in this garden. Cowries (line
   129), or small imported seashells, were prized for making jewelry and were sometimes used
   in burial rites.

Tablet X

[Gilgamesh approaches the tavern of Siduri, a female tavern keeper who lives at the end of the earth. This interesting personage is unknown outside this poem, nor is it clear who her clientele might be in such a remote spot. Alarmed by Gilgamesh's appearance, she locks her door. In contrast to his deference to the scorpion monster, Gilgamesh is aggressive. When he identifies himself, the tavern keeper is skeptical and wants to know why anyone so splendid as Gilgamesh appears in such condition.]

Siduri the tavern keeper, who dwells at the edge of the sea,
She sits on a [stool of . . .]
For her was wrought the cuprack,[1] for her the [brewing vat of gold],
It(?) is covered with a lid(?) [of . . .].
Gilgamesh made his way towards her [. . .],   5
He was clad in a skin, fearsomeness [. . .]
He had flesh of gods in [his body].
Woe was in his vitals,
His face was like a traveler's from afar.
The tavern keeper eyed him from a distance,   10
Speaking to herself, she said these words,
She [debated] with herself:

> This no doubt is a slaughterer of wild bulls!
> Why would he make straight for my door?

At the sight of him the tavern keeper barred her door,   15
She barred her door and mounted to the roof terrace.
But he, Gilgamesh, put his ear to the [door . . .],
He lifted his chin and [. . .].

Gilgamesh said to her, to the tavern keeper:

> Tavern keeper, when you saw me why did you bar your door,   20
> Bar your door and mount to the roof terrace?
> I will strike down your door, I will shatter [your doorbolt],

1. Some Mesopotamian drinking cups were conical, with pointed bottoms, so they were set in a wooden rack to hold them up when they were full of liquid.

9. *The tavern keeper eyed him from a distance.* Ivory head of a woman. Taverns in Mesopotamia were often kept by independent businesswomen.

[. . .] my [. . .]
[. . .] in the steppe.

[The tavern keeper said to him, to] Gilgamesh: 25

[. . .] I barred my door,
[. . . I mounted to] the roof terrace.
[. . .] I want to know.

Gilgamesh said to her, to the tavern keeper:

[. . .] 30
[I am Gilgamesh . . .], who killed the guardian,
Who seized and killed the bull that came down from heaven,
Who felled Humbaba who dwelt in the forest of cedars,
Who killed lions at the mountain passes.

The tavern keeper said to him, to Gilgamesh: 35

[If you are indeed Gilgamesh], who killed the guardian,
Who felled Humbaba who dwelt in the forest of cedars,
Who killed lions at the mountain passes,
Who seized and killed the bull that came down from heaven,
Why are your cheeks emaciated, your face cast down,   40
Your heart wretched, your features wasted,
Woe in your vitals,
Your face like a traveler's from afar,
Your features weathered by cold and sun,
Why are you clad in a lion skin, roaming the steppe?   45

Gilgamesh said to her, to the tavern keeper:

My cheeks would not be emaciated, nor my face cast down,
Nor my heart wretched nor my features wasted,
Nor would there be woe in my vitals,
Nor would my face be like a traveler's from afar,   50
Nor would my features be weathered by cold and sun,
Nor would I be clad in a lion skin, roaming the steppe,
But for my friend, swift wild donkey, mountain onager,
   panther of the steppe,
But for Enkidu, swift wild donkey, mountain onager,
   panther of the steppe,
My friend whom I so loved, who went with me
   through every hardship,   55
Enkidu, whom I so loved, who went with me
   through every hardship,
The fate of mankind has overtaken him.
Six days and seven nights I wept for him,
I would not give him up for burial,
Until a worm fell out of his nose.   60
I was frightened [. . .]
I have grown afraid of death, so I roam the steppe,
My friend's case weighs heavy upon me.
A distant road I roam over the steppe,
My friend Enkidu's case weighs heavy upon me!   65
A distant road I roam over the steppe,
How can I be silent? How can I hold my peace?
My friend whom I loved is turned into clay,
Enkidu, my friend whom I loved, is turned into clay!
Shall I too not lie down like him,   70
And never get up forever and ever?

[*An old version adds the following episode.*]

> After his death I could find no life,
> Back and forth I prowled like a bandit in the steppe.
> Now that I have seen your face, tavern keeper,
> May I not see that death I constantly fear! 75

The tavern keeper said to him, to Gilgamesh:

> Gilgamesh, wherefore do you wander?
> The eternal life you are seeking you shall not find.
> When the gods created mankind,
> They established death for mankind, 80
> And withheld eternal life for themselves.
> As for you, Gilgamesh, let your stomach be full,
> Always be happy, night and day.
> Make every day a delight,
> Night and day play and dance. 85
> Your clothes should be clean,
> Your head should be washed,
> You should bathe in water,
> Look proudly on the little one holding your hand,
> Let your mate be always blissful in your loins, 90
> This, then, is the work of mankind.

[*gap*]

Gilgamesh said to her, to the tavern keeper:

> What are you saying, tavern keeper?
> I am heartsick for my friend.
> What are you saying, tavern keeper? 95
> I am heartsick for Enkidu!

[*gap*]

[*The standard version resumes.*]

Gilgamesh said to her, to the tavern keeper:

> Now then, tavern keeper, what is the way to Utanapishtim?
> What are its signs? Give them to me.
> Give, oh give me its signs! 100

If need be, I'll cross the sea,
If not, I'll roam the steppe.

The tavern keeper said to him, to Gilgamesh:

Gilgamesh, there has never been a place to cross,
There has been no one from the dawn of time who could
     ever cross this sea.   105
The valiant Shamash alone can cross this sea,
Save for the sun, who could cross this sea?
The crossing is perilous, highly perilous the course,
And midway lie the waters of death, whose surface is
     impassable.
Suppose, Gilgamesh, you do cross the sea,   110
When you reach the waters of death, what will you do?
Yet, Gilgamesh, there is Ur-Shanabi, Utanapishtim's boatman,
He has the Stone Charms with him as he trims pine trees
     in the forest.
Go, show yourself to him,
If possible, cross with him, if not, then turn back.   115

[*Gilgamesh advances and without preamble attacks Ur-Shanabi and smashes
the Stone Charms. Ur-Shanabi tells Gilgamesh that the Stone Charms were
needed to cross the waters of death. The nature of these objects has never
been satisfactorily explained. Although some scholars suggest that they were
anchors or counterweights, the Hittite version (see p. 164) calls them "images," so they may have been magic amulets that warded off the waters of
death.*]

When Gilgamesh heard this,
He raised the axe at his side,
He drew the sword at his belt,
He crept forward, went down towards them,
Like an arrow he dropped among them,   120
His battle cry resounded in the forest.
When Ur-Shanabi saw the shining [. . .],
He raised his axe, he [trembled(?)] before him,
But he, for his part, struck his head [. . .] Gilgamesh,
He seized his arm [. . .] his chest.   125
And the Stone Charms, the [protection . . . (?)] of the boat,
Without which no one [crosses the waters] of death,
He smashed them [and threw them into] the broad sea,
Into the channel [he threw them, his own hands] foiled him,
He smashed them [and threw them] into the channel!   130
[. . .] the boat,
And he [. . .] to the bank.

[*An old version preserves the following, in which Sur-Sunabu is another form of the name Ur-Shanabi.*]

He turned back and stood before him.
Sur-Sunabu stared at him,
Sur-Sunabu said to him, to Gilgamesh: 135

    What is your name, pray tell?
    I am Sur-Sunabu, servant of Utanapishtim the Distant One.

Gilgamesh said to him, to Sur-Sunabu:

    Gilgamesh is my name.
    I am he who came from [Uruk], the abode of Anu,   140
    Who traveled here around the mountains,
    A distant road where the sun comes forth.
    Now that I have see your face, Sur-Sunabu,
    Show me Utanapishtim the Distant One.

[*The standard version resumes.*]

Ur-Shanabi said to him, to Gilgamesh: 145

    Why are your cheeks emaciated, your face cast down,
    Your heart wretched, your features wasted,
    Woe in your vitals,
    Your face like a traveler's from afar,
    Your features weathered by cold and sun,   150
    Why are you clad in a lion skin, roaming the steppe?

Gilgamesh said to him, to Ur-Shanabi:

    My cheeks would not be emaciated, nor my face cast down,
    Nor my heart wretched, nor my features wasted,
    Nor would there be woe in my vitals,   155
    Nor would my face be like a traveler's from afar,
    Nor would my features be weathered by cold and sun,
    Nor would I be clad in a lion skin, roaming the steppe,
    But for my friend, swift wild donkey, mountain onager,
        panther of the steppe,
    But for Enkidu, my friend, swift wild donkey, mountain
        onager, panther of the steppe,   160
    He who stood by me as we ascended the mountain,
    Seized and killed the bull that came down from heaven,
    Felled Humbaba who dwelt in the forest of cedars,
    Killed lions at the mountain passes,

My friend whom I so loved, who went with me through
    every hardship,   165
Enkidu, whom I so loved, who went with me through
    every hardship,
The fate of mankind has overtaken him.
Six days and seven nights I wept for him,
I would not give him up for burial,
Until a worm fell out of his nose.   170
I was frightened [. . .]
I have grown afraid of death, so I roam the steppe,
My friend's case weighs heavy upon me.
A distant road I roam over the steppe,
My friend Enkidu's case weighs heavy upon me!   175
A distant road I roam over the steppe,
How can I be silent? How can I hold my peace?
My friend whom I loved is turned into clay,
Enkidu, my friend whom I loved, is turned into clay!
Shall I too not lie down like him,   180
And never get up forever and ever?

Gilgamesh said to him, to Ur-Shanabi:

Now then, Ur-Shanabi, what is the way to Utanapishtim?
What are its signs? Give them to me,
Give, oh give me its signs!   185
If need be, I'll cross the sea,
If not, I'll roam the steppe.

Ur-Shanabi said to him, to Gilgamesh:

Your own hands have foiled you, Gilgamesh,
You have smashed the Stone Charms, you have [thrown them
    into the channel],   190
The Stone Charms are smashed [. . .]

[gap]

[An old version has the following here.]

The Stone Charms, Gilgamesh, are what carry me,
Lest I touch the waters of death.
In your fury you have smashed them,
The Stone Charms, they are what I had with me to make
    the crossing!   195

[*As the standard version resumes, Gilgamesh cuts punting poles. Then they
set out across the sea. When they reach the waters of death, Gilgamesh
pushes once with each punting pole, then lets it go, lest he touch the waters
of death. For the last part of the journey, beyond the waters of death, Gilgamesh desperately holds up his clothing as an improvised sail. The numbers
and distances in this passage have not been convincingly explained.*]

    Gilgamesh, raise the axe in your hand,
    Go down into the forest, [cut twice sixty] poles each
       five times twelve cubits long,
    Dress them, set on handguards(?),
    Bring them to me.

When Gilgamesh heard this,   200
He raised the axe at his side,
He drew the sword at his belt,
He went down into the forest, cut [twice sixty] poles each
   five times twelve cubits long,
He dressed them, set on handguards(?),
He brought them to him.   205
Gilgamesh and Ur-Shanabi embarked [in the boat],
They launched the boat, they [embarked] upon it.
A journey of a month and a half they made in three days!
Ur-Shanabi reached the waters of death,
Ur-Shanabi said to him, to Gilgamesh: 210

    Stand back, Gilgamesh! Take the first [pole],
    Your hand must not touch the waters of death [. . .],
    Take the second, the third, the fourth pole, Gilgamesh,
    Take the fifth, sixth, and seventh pole, Gilgamesh,
    Take the eight, ninth, and tenth pole, Gilgamesh,   215
    Take the eleventh and twelfth pole, Gilgamesh.

With twice sixty Gilgamesh had used up the poles.
Then he, for his part, took off his belt [. . .],
Gilgamesh tore off his clothes from his body,
Held high his arms for a mast.   220
Utanapishtim was watching him from a distance,
Speaking to himself, he said these words,
He debated to himself:

    Why have [the Stone Charms], belonging to the boat,
      been smashed,
    And one not its master embarked [thereon]?   225
    He who comes here is no man of mine,
    And at his right [. . .]?
    I look but he is no [man] of mine,

10. *Gilgamesh and Ur-Shanabi embarked* [*in the boat*]. Seal image showing two figures in a boat.

> I look but he is [. . .]
> I look but he is [. . .]   230

[gap]

[*In the fragmentary lines that follow, Gilgamesh lands at Utanapishtim's wharf and questions him.*]

Utanapishtim said to him, to Gilgamesh:

> Why are your cheeks emaciated, your face cast down,
> Your heart wretched, your features wasted,
> Woe in your vitals,
> Your face like a traveler's from afar,   235
> Your features weathered by cold and sun,
> Why are you clad in a lion skin, roaming the steppe?

[*Gilgamesh tells Utanapishtim his mission, wallowing in the luxury of self-pity on the difficulties of his quest.*]

Gilgamesh said to him, to Utanapishtim:

> My cheeks would not be emaciated, nor my face cast down,
> Nor my heart wretched, nor my features wasted,   240
> Nor would there be woe in my vitals,
> Nor would my face be like a traveler's from afar,
> Nor would my features be weathered by cold and sun,
> Nor would I be clad in a lion skin, roaming the steppe,

But for my friend, swift wild donkey, mountain onager,
    panther of the steppe,   245
But for Enkidu, my friend, swift wild donkey, mountain
    onager, panther of the steppe,
He who stood by me as we ascended the mountain,
Seized and killed the bull that came down from heaven,
Felled Humbaba who dwelt in the forest of cedars,
Killed lions at the mountain passes,   250
My friend whom I so loved, who went with me through
    every hardship,
Enkidu, whom I so loved, who went with me through
    every hardship,
The fate of mankind has overtaken him.
Six days and seven nights I wept for him,
I would not give him up for burial,   255
Until a worm fell out of his nose.
I was frightened [. . .]
I have grown afraid of death, so I roam the steppe,
My friend's case weighs heavy upon me.
A distant road I roam over the steppe,   260
My friend Enkidu's case weighs heavy upon me!
A distant path I roam over the steppe,
How can I be silent? How can I hold my peace?
My friend whom I loved is turned into clay,
Enkidu, my friend whom I loved, is turned into clay!   265
Shall I too not lie down like him,
And never get up, forever and ever?

Gilgamesh said to him, to Utanapishtim:

So it is to go find Utanapishtim, whom they call the
    "Distant One,"
I traversed all lands,   270
I came over, one after another, wearisome mountains,
Then I crossed, one after another, all the seas.
Too little sweet sleep has smoothed my countenance,
I have worn myself out in sleeplessness,
My muscles ache for misery,   275
What have I gained for my trials?
I had not reached the tavern keeper when my clothes
    were worn out,
I killed bear, hyena, lion, panther, leopard, deer, ibex,
    wild beasts of the steppe,
I ate their meat, I [. . .] their skins.
Let them close behind me the doors of woe,   280
[Let them seal them] with pitch and tar,

For my part, I [. . .] no amusement,
For me, [. . .]

[*Utanapishtim responds in a long speech, poorly known because of damage
to the manuscripts. He chides Gilgamesh for his self-pity and ostentatious
mourning, all the more unseemly because the gods had favored him. The
village idiot, he points out, wears rags and eats bad food, but no one accords
him merit for that. After a gap in the text, Utanapishtim is found discoursing
on the nature of death.*]

Utanapishtim said to him, to Gilgamesh:

Why, O Gilgamesh, did you prolong woe,   285
You who are [formed] of the flesh of gods and mankind,
You for whom [the gods] acted like fathers and mothers?
When was it, Gilgamesh, you [. . .] to a fool?
They set a throne for you in the assembly of elders [. . .]
While the fool is given beer dregs instead of butter,   290
Bran and coarse flour instead of [. . .].
He wears sacking instead of a [. . .],
But he ties it round himself like a sash of honor,
Because he has no sense [nor reason],
He has no good advice [. . .].   295
Think on him, Gilgamesh, [. . .]

[*gap*]

You strive ceaselessly, what do you gain?
When you wear out your strength in ceaseless striving,
When you torture your limbs with pain,
You hasten the distant end of your days.   300
Mankind, whose descendants are snapped off like reeds
    in a canebrake,[2]
The handsome young man, the lovely young woman,
    death [. . .]
No one sees death,
No one sees the face of death,
No one [hears] the voice of death,   305
But cruel death cuts off mankind.
Do we build a house forever?
Do we make a home forever?
Do brothers divide an inheritance forever?
Do disputes prevail [in the land] forever?   310
Do rivers rise in flood forever?

2. Mesopotamian poetry often refers to reeds to suggest something easily broken and im-
permanent.

Dragonflies drift downstream on a river,
Their faces staring at the sun,
Then, suddenly, there is nothing.
The sleeper and the dead, how alike they are!   315
They limn not death's image,
No one dead has ever greeted a human in this world.
The supreme gods, the great gods, being convened,
Mammetum, she who creates destinies, ordaining destinies
    with them,
They established death and life,   320
They did not reveal the time of death.

Tablet XI

[*Gilgamesh, whose search for Utanapishtin has been characterized by increasing violence, now finds to his astonishment that there is no battle to be fought; heroics will bring him no further. Now he needs knowledge. He asks Utanapishtim, the wisest man who ever lived, his great question: how did he alone escape the universal fate of the human race?*]

Gilgamesh said to him, to Utanapishtim the Distant One:

> As I look upon you, Utanapishtim,
> Your limbs are not different, you are just as I am.
> Indeed, you are not different at all, you are just as I am!
> Yet your heart is drained of battle spirit,   5
> You lie flat on your back, your arm [idle].
> You then, how did you join the ranks of the gods and find
>   eternal life?

[*In answer, Utanapishtim relates the story of the flood. According to Tablet I, among Gilgamesh's main achievements was bringing back to the human race this hitherto unknown history. The story as told here is abbreviated. In the fuller account, preserved in a Babylonian narrative poem called "Atrahasis,"[1] the gods sent the flood because the human race had multiplied to such an extent that their clamor was unbearable to Enlil, the chief god living on earth. After various attempts to reduce the population of the earth were thwarted by Enki (Ea), the god of wisdom and fresh water, Enlil ordered a deluge to obliterate the entire human race. At this point, Utanapishtim takes up the story. He lived at the long-vanished city of Shuruppak and was a favorite of the god Ea, who warned him of the flood, despite his oath not to reveal it. Ea circumvented this by addressing the wall of a reed enclosure Utanapishtim had built near water, perhaps as a place to receive dreams and commands from his god. Utanapishtim is ordered to build a boat. When his fellow citizens ask him what he is about, he is to reply in ambiguous language, foretelling a "shower of abundance" soon.*]

Utanapishtim said to him, to Gilgamesh:

---

1. Translated in *Muses*, pp. 160–203.

I will reveal to you, O Gilgamesh, a secret matter,
And a mystery of the gods I will tell you.   10
The city Shuruppak, a city you yourself have knowledge of,
Which once was set on the [bank] of the Euphrates,
That aforesaid city was ancient and gods once were within it.
The great gods resolved to send the deluge,
Their father Anu was sworn,   15
The counselor the valiant Enlil,
Their throne-bearer Ninurta,
Their canal-officer Ennugi,
Their leader Ea was sworn with them.
He repeated their plans to the reed fence: 20
"Reed fence, reed fence, wall, wall!
Listen, O reed fence! Pay attention, O wall!
O Man of Shuruppak, son of Ubar-Tutu,
Wreck house, build boat,
Forsake possessions and seek life,   25
Belongings reject and life save!
Take aboard the boat seed of all living things.
The boat you shall build,
Let her dimensions be measured out:
Let her width and length be equal,   30
Roof her over like the watery depths."
I understood full well, I said to Ea, my lord:
"Your command, my lord, exactly as you said it,
I shall faithfully execute.
What shall I answer the city, the populace, and the elders?"   35
Ea made ready to speak,
Saying to me, his servant
"So, you shall speak to them thus:
'No doubt Enlil dislikes me,
I shall not dwell in your city.   40
I shall not set my foot on the dry land of Enlil,
I shall descend to the watery depths and dwell with my
    lord Ea.
Upon you he shall shower down in abundance,
A windfall of birds, a surprise of fishes,
He shall pour upon you a harvest of riches,   45
In the morning cakes in spates,
In the evening grains in rains.' "

[*The entire community helps to build the boat. The hull is constructed before
the interior framing, as was customary in the ancient world, with cordage
used to sew the planks together and to truss the hull for strength. The boat
is an enormous cube. Utanapishtim, here referred to as "Atrahasis," loads on
his family, his possessions, and every type of animal, as well as skilled individuals to keep alive knowledge of arts and crafts.*]

At the first glimmer of dawn,
The land was assembling at the gate of Atrahasis:
The carpenter carried his axe,   50
The reed cutter carried his stone,
The old men brought cordage(?),
The young men ran around [. . .],
The wealthy carried the pitch,
The poor brought what was needed of [. . .].   55
In five days I had planked her hull:
One full acre was her deck space,
Ten dozen cubits, the height of each of her sides,
Ten dozen cubits square, her outer dimensions.
I laid out her structure, I planned her design: 60
I decked her in six,
I divided her in seven,
Her interior I divided in nine.
I drove the water plugs into her,[2]
I saw to the spars and laid in what was needful.   65
Thrice thirty-six hundred measures of pitch I poured
    in the oven,
Thrice thirty-six hundred measures of tar [I poured out]
    inside her.
Thrice thirty-six hundred measures basket-bearers brought
    aboard for oil,
Not counting the thirty-six hundred measures of oil that the
    offering consumed,
And the twice thirty-six hundred measures of oil that the
    boatbuilders made off with.   70
For the [builders] I slaughtered bullocks,
I killed sheep upon sheep every day,
Beer, ale, oil, and wine
[I gave out] to the workers like river water,
They made a feast as on New Year's Day,   75
[. . .] I dispensed ointment with my own hand.
By the setting of Shamash,[3] the ship was completed.
[Since boarding was(?)] very difficult,
They brought up gangplanks(?), fore and aft,
They came up her sides(?) two-thirds (of her height).   80
[Whatever I had] I loaded upon her:

2. The "water plugs" have been explained in various ways, for example, as caulking, stabilizers, depth markers, water taps, bilge drains, and drains to let out rainwater when the boat was beached. None of these suggestions is supported by Mesopotamian evidence.
3. The references to Shamash here and in line 87 suggest that in some version of this story, now lost, Shamash, rather than Enki, warned Utanapishtim of the flood and told him how much time he had to build his ship. This substitution of the one god for the other may have been suggested by Shamash's role as protector of Gilgamesh in the epic. In the oldest account of the Babylonian story of the flood, Enki sets a timing device, apparently a water clock, to tell Utanapishtim how much time he has before the coming of the deluge.

What silver I had I loaded upon her,
What gold I had I loaded upon her,
What living creatures I had I loaded upon her,
I sent up on board all my family and kin,   85
Beasts of the steppe, wild animals of the steppe, all types
    of skilled craftsmen I sent up on board.
Shamash set for me the appointed time:
"In the morning, cakes in spates,
In the evening, grains in rains,
Go into your boat and caulk the door!"   90
That appointed time arrived,
In the morning cakes in spates,
In the evening grains in rains,
I gazed upon the face of the storm,
The weather was dreadful to behold!   95
I went into the boat and caulked the door.
To the caulker of the boat, to Puzur-Amurri the boatman,
I gave over the edifice, with all it contained.

[*The flood, accompanied by thunder and a fiery glow, overwhelms the earth.
The gods are terrified by its violence and what they have done.*]

At the first glimmer of dawn,
A black cloud rose above the horizon.   100
Inside it Adad was thundering,
While the destroying gods Shullat and Hanish went in front,
Moving as an advance force over hill and plain.
Errakal tore out the mooring posts (of the world),
Ninurta came and made the dikes overflow.   105
The supreme gods held torches aloft,
Setting the land ablaze with their glow.
Adad's awesome power passed over the heavens,
Whatever was light was turned into darkness,
[He flooded] the land, he smashed it like a [clay pot]!   110
For one day the storm wind [blew],
Swiftly it blew, [the flood came forth],
It passed over the people like a battle,
No one could see the one next to him,
The people could not recognize one another in the
    downpour.   115
The gods became frightened of the deluge,
They shrank back, went up to Anu's highest heaven.
The gods cowered like dogs, crouching outside.
Ishtar screamed like a woman in childbirth,
And sweet-voiced Belet-ili wailed aloud: 120
"Would that day had come to naught,
When I spoke up for evil in the assembly of the gods!

How could I have spoken up for evil in the assembly
    of the gods,
And spoken up for battle to destroy my people?
It was I myself who brought my people into the world,   125
Now, like a school of fish, they choke up the sea!"
The supreme gods were weeping with her,
The gods sat where they were, weeping,
Their lips were parched, taking on a crust.
Six days and seven nights   130
The wind continued, the deluge and windstorm leveled
    the land.
When the seventh day arrived,
The windstorm and deluge left off their battle,
Which had struggled, like a woman in labor.
The sea grew calm, the tempest stilled, the deluge ceased. 135

[As the floodwaters recede, Utanapishtim can see land at the far horizon.
The boat is caught on a mountain.]

I looked at the weather, stillness reigned,
And the whole human race had turned into clay.
The landscape was flat as a rooftop.
I opened the hatch, sunlight fell upon my face.
Falling to my knees, I sat down weeping,   140
Tears running down my face.
I looked at the edges of the world, the borders of the sea,
At twelve times sixty double leagues the periphery emerged.
The boat had come to rest on Mount Nimush,
Mount Nimush held the boat fast, not letting it move.   145
One day, a second day Mount Nimush held the boat fast,
    not letting it move.
A third day, a fourth day Mount Nimush held the boat fast,
    not letting it move.
A fifth day, a sixth day Mount Nimush held the boat fast,
    not letting it move.

[Utanapishtim sends out three birds to see if land has emerged near the boat.
He then quits the boat and makes an offering to the gods, who crowd around
it, famished.]

When the seventh day arrived,
I brought out a dove and set it free.   150
The dove went off and returned,
No landing place came to its view, so it turned back.
I brought out a swallow and set it free,
The swallow went off and returned,
No landing place came to its view, so it turned back.   155

11. *I brought out a dove and set it free*. Detail of a wall painting from a Mesopotamian palace.

I brought out a raven and set it free,
The raven went off and saw the ebbing of the waters.
It ate, preened, left droppings, did not turn back.
I released all to the four directions,
I brought out an offering and offered it to the four directions. 160
I set up an incense offering on the summit of the mountain,
I arranged seven and seven cult vessels,
I heaped reeds, cedar, and myrtle in their bowls.[4]

4. The Mesopotamians sometimes burned various plants and branches in order to produce an attractive odor when making offerings to the gods.

The gods smelled the savor,
The gods smelled the sweet savor,   165
The gods crowded round the sacrificer like flies.

[*The mother goddess blames Enlil for the flood, saying her glittering necklace
of fly-shaped beads, which may stand for the rainbow, will memorialize the
human race drowned in the flood.*]

As soon as Belet-ili arrived,
She held up the great fly-ornaments that Anu had made
     in his ardor:
"O gods, these shall be my lapis necklace, lest I forget,
I shall be mindful of these days and not forget, not ever!   170
The gods should come to the incense offering,
But Enlil should not come to the incense offering,
For he, irrationally, brought on the flood,
And marked my people for destruction!"
As soon as Enlil arrived,   175
He saw the boat, Enlil flew into a rage,
He was filled with fury at the gods:
"Who came through alive? No man was to survive destruction!"
Ninurta made ready to speak,
Said to the valiant Enlil: 180
"Who but Ea could contrive such a thing?
For Ea alone knows every artifice."

[*Ea's speech urges future limits. Punish but do not kill; diminish but do not
annihilate. He suggests that in the future less drastic means than a flood be
used to reduce the human population. He refers to Utanapishtim as Atrahasis, his name in the independent Babylonian flood story. Enlil grants
Utanapishtim and his wife eternal life but removes them far away from the
rest of the human race.*]

Ea made ready to speak,
Said to the valiant Enlil:
"You, O valiant one, are the wisest of the gods,   185
How could you, irrationally, have brought on the flood?
Punish the wrongdoer for his wrongdoing,
Punish the transgressor for his transgression,
But be lenient, lest he be cut off,
Bear with him, lest he [. . .].   190
Instead of your bringing on a flood,
Let the lion rise up to diminish the human race!
Instead of your bringing on a flood,
Let the wolf rise up to diminish the human race!
Instead of your bringing on a flood,   195
Let famine rise up to wreak havoc in the land!

Instead of your bringing on a flood,
Let pestilence rise up to wreak havoc in the land!
It was not I who disclosed the secret of the great gods,
I made Atrahasis have a dream and so he heard the secret
    of the gods.   200
Now then, make some plan for him."
Then Enlil came up into the boat,
Leading me by the hand, he brought me up too.
He brought my wife up and had her kneel beside me.
He touched our brows, stood between us to bless us: 205
"Hitherto Utanapishtim has been a human being,
Now Utanapishtim and his wife shall become like us gods.
Utanapishtim shall dwell far distant at the source
    of the rivers."
Thus it was that they took me far distant and had me dwell
    at the source of the rivers.
Now then, who will convene the gods for your sake,   210
That you may find the eternal life you seek?
Come, come, try not to sleep for six days and seven nights.

[*Utanapishtim has challenged Gilgamesh to go without sleep for a week; if
he fails this test, how could he expect to live forever? Even as he speaks,
Gilgamesh drifts off to sleep. Thus passes from the scene the all-night rowdy
of Tablet I.*]

As he sat there on his haunches,
Sleep was swirling over him like a mist.
Utanapishtim said to her, to his wife: 215

    Behold this fellow who seeks eternal life!
    Sleep swirls over him like a mist.

[*Utanapishtim's wife, taking pity on Gilgamesh, urges her husband to
awaken him and let him go home. Utanapishtim insists on a proof of how
long he slept, lest Gilgamesh claim that he had only dozed. She is to bake
him fresh bread every day and set it beside him, marking the wall for the
day. The bread spoils progressively as Gilgamesh sleeps for seven days.*]

His wife said to him, to Utanapishtim the Distant One:

    Do touch him that the man may wake up,
    That he may return safe on the way whence he came,   220
    That through the gate he came forth he may return
        to his land.

Utanapishtim said to her, to his wife:

Since the human race is duplicitous, he'll endeavor
    to dupe you.
Come, come, bake his daily loaves, put them one after another
    by his head,
Then mark the wall for each day he has slept.   225

She baked his daily loaves for him, put them one after another
    by his head,
Then dated the wall for each day he slept.
The first loaf was dried hard,
The second was leathery, the third soggy,
The crust of the fourth turned white,   230
The fifth was gray with mold, the sixth was fresh,
The seventh was still on the coals when he touched him, the man
    woke up.

[*Gilgamesh wakes at last. Claiming at first that he has scarcely dozed a
moment, he sees the bread and realizes that he has slept for the entire time
he was supposed to remain awake for the test. He gives up in despair. What
course is left for him? Utanapishtim does not answer directly but orders the
boatman to take him home. Further, the boatman himself is never to return.
Thus access to Utanapishtim is denied the human race forever. Gilgamesh
is bathed and given clothing that will stay magically fresh until his return
to Uruk.*]

Gilgamesh said to him, to Utanapishtim the Distant One:

Scarcely had sleep stolen over me,
When straightaway you touched me and roused me.   235

Utanapishtim said to him, to Gilgamesh:

[Up with you], Gilgamesh, count your daily loaves,
[That the days you have slept] may be known to you.
The first loaf is dried hard,
The second is leathery, the third soggy,   240
The crust of the fourth has turned white,
The fifth is gray with mold,
The sixth is fresh,
The seventh was still in the coals when I touched you and
    you woke up.

Gilgamesh said to him, to Utanapishtim the Distant One: 245

What then should I do, Utanapishtim, whither should I go,
Now that the Bereaver has seized my [flesh]?[5]
Death lurks in my bedchamber,
And wherever I turn, there is death!

Utanapishtim said to him, to Ur-Shanabi the boatman: 250

Ur-Shanabi, may the harbor [offer] you no [haven],
May the crossing point reject you,
Be banished from the shore you shuttled to.
The man you brought here,
His body is matted with filthy hair,   255
Hides have marred the beauty of his flesh.
Take him away, Ur-Shanabi, bring him to the washing place.
Have him wash out his filthy hair with water, clean as snow,
Have him throw away his hides, let the sea carry them off,
Let his body be rinsed clean.   260
Let his headband be new,
Have him put on raiment worthy of him.
Until he reaches his city,
Until he completes his journey,
Let his garments stay spotless, fresh and new.   265

Ur-Shanabi took him away and brought him to the washing place.
He washed out his filthy hair with water, clean as snow,
He threw away his hides, the sea carried them off,
His body was rinsed clean.
He renewed his headband,   270
He put on raiment worthy of him.
Until he reached his city,
Until he completed his journey,
His garments would stay spotless, fresh and new.

[*Gilgamesh and Ur-Shanabi embark on their journey to Uruk. As they push
off from the shore, Utanapishtim's wife intervenes, asking her husband to
give the hero something to show for his quest. Gilgamesh brings the boat
back to shore and waits expectantly. Utanapishtim tells him of a plant of
rejuvenation. Gilgamesh dives for the plant by opening a shaft through the
earth's surface to the water below. He ties stones to his feet, a technique used
in traditional pearl diving in the Gulf. When he comes up from securing the
plant, he is on the opposite side of the ocean, where he started from.*]

Gilgamesh and Ur-Shanabi embarked on the boat,   275
They launched the boat, they embarked upon it.
His wife said to him, to Utanapishtim the Distant One:

5. "The Bereaver" is an epithet of death. It could also mean something like "kidnapper."

Gilgamesh has come here, spent with exertion,
What will you give him for his homeward journey?

At that he, Gilgamesh, lifted the pole,   280
Bringing the boat back by the shore.
Utanapishtim said to him, to Gilgamesh:

Gilgamesh, you have come here, spent with exertion,
What shall I give you for your homeward journey?
I will reveal to you, O Gilgamesh, a secret matter,   285
And a mystery of the gods I will tell you.
There is a certain plant, its stem is like a thornbush,
Its thorns, like the wild rose, will prick [your hand].
If you can secure this plant, [. . .]
[. . .]   290

No sooner had Gilgamesh heard this,
He opened a shaft, [flung away his tools].
He tied heavy stones [to his feet],
They pulled him down into the watery depths [. . .].
He took the plant though it pricked [his hand].   295
He cut the heavy stones [from his feet],
The sea cast him up on his home shore.

[*Gilgamesh resolves to take the plant to Uruk to experiment on an old man.
While Gilgamesh is bathing on the homeward journey, a snake eats the plant
and rejuvenates itself by shedding its skin. Gilgamesh gives up. Immense
quantities of water have flooded up through the shaft he dug and covered
the place. He has left behind his tools so cannot dig another shaft. He has
also lost the boat, so there is no going back.*]

Gilgamesh said to him, to Ur-Shanabi the boatman:

Ur-Shanabi, this plant is cure for heartache,
Whereby a man will regain his stamina.   300
I will take it to ramparted Uruk,
I will have an old man eat some and so test the plant.
His name shall be "Old Man Has Become Young-Again-Man."
I myself will eat it and so return to my carefree youth.

At twenty double leagues they took a bite to eat,   305
At thirty double leagues they made their camp.

Gilgamesh saw a pond whose water was cool,
He went down into it to bathe in the water.
A snake caught the scent of the plant,

[Stealthily] it came up and carried the plant away,   310
On its way back it shed its skin.

Thereupon Gilgamesh sat down weeping,
His tears flowed down his face,
He said to Ur-Shanabi the boatman:

    For whom, Ur-Shanabi, have my hands been toiling?   315
    For whom has my heart's blood been poured out?
    For myself I have obtained no benefit,
    I have done a good deed for a reptile!
    Now, floodwaters rise against me for twenty double leagues,
    When I opened the shaft, I flung away the tools.   320
    How shall I find my bearings?
    I have come much too far to go back, and I abandoned
       the boat on the shore.

[*Upon completing his journey, Gilgamesh invites Ur-Shanabi to inspect the walls of Uruk, using the same words used by the narrator in Tablet I.*]

At twenty double leagues they took a bite to eat,
At thirty double leagues they made their camp.
When they arrived in ramparted Uruk,   325
Gilgamesh said to him, to Ur-Shanabi the boatman:

    Go up, Ur-Shanabi, pace out the walls of Uruk.
    Study the foundation terrace and examine the brickwork.
    Is not its masonry of kiln-fired brick?
    And did not seven masters lay its foundations?   330
    One square mile of city, one square mile of gardens,
    One square mile of clay pits, a half square mile of Ishtar's
       dwelling,
    Three and a half square miles is the measure of Uruk!

ANALOGUES TO
THE EPIC OF GILGAMESH

The Sumerian Gilgamesh Poems

Six Sumerian epic poems dealing with the fabled king Gilgamesh have been known for roughly sixty years: "Gilgamesh and Akka," "Gilgamesh and Huwawa A," "Gilgamesh and Huwawa B," "Gilgamesh and the Bull of Heaven," "Gilgamesh, Enkidu, and the Netherworld," and "The Death of Gilgamesh." In addition, a seventh composition, "The Gudam Epic," likely belongs to this group. The compositions were known to the ancients by their first line.

The poems are known from tablet copies found in various sites in modern-day Iraq; they date, for the most part, to the Old Babylonian period, more specifically to the reigns of Kings Rim-Sin of Larsa (c. 1822–1763 B.C.E.) and Hammurabi and Samsu-iluna of Babylon (c. 1792–1712 B.C.E.). Scholars have suggested that these Sumerian Gilgamesh compositions were actually composed and set down in writing around three hundred years earlier, during the period of the Third Dynasty of Ur (c. 2094–2047 B.C.E.). In a hymn in honor of Shulgi, a king of Ur, he too is called the son of the goddess Ninsun and the god Lugalbanda (Gilgamesh's divine parents), and the king refers to himself as the brother and friend of Gilgamesh.

These translations are essentially the work of Douglas Frayne, revised and edited by Benjamin Foster for this Norton Critical Edition.

Gilgamesh and Akka

The Sumerian epic poem "Gilgamesh and Akka" is the shortest of the Sumerian Gilgamesh compositions. It describes an unsuccessful siege of Uruk by the army of King Akka of Kish. While the story of the siege of Uruk does not find a counterpart in the later Akkadian version of *The Epic of Gilgamesh*, the literary motif of Gilgamesh's seeking counsel first with the assembly of city elders and then with the assembly of able-bodied young men of the city does find an echo in Tablet II of the epic, admittedly in a different context, namely before the expedition to the Cedar Forest.

In Early Dynastic II times (c. 2650 B.C.E), to which the events narrated in this epic likely date, the rival city-states of Uruk and Kish competed for control over the land of Sumer (now the southern portion of modern-day Iraq) and Akkad (now the middle portion of modern-day Iraq). The defeat of the army of Akka narrated in this poem was perhaps but one episode in a prolonged struggle between these two powers.

[*The arrival of the emissaries from Kish.*]

The emissaries of Akka, son of Enmebaragesi,
Proceeded from Kish to Uruk, to Gilgamesh.

[*Gilgamesh seeks counsel from the assembly of city elders.*]

Before the elders of his city, Gilgamesh
Presented the question, carefully choosing his words:

> There are wells to be finished, many wells of the land
>   to be finished,[1]   5
> Many shallow wells of the land to be finished,
> Many deep wells with rope-hoists[2] to be finished,
> (Do we answer:) "We do not want to submit to the house
>   of Kish" or "We do not want to fight"?

The convened assembly of his city's elders
Replied to Gilgamesh: 10

> There are wells to be finished, many wells of the land
>   to be finished,
> Many shallow wells of the land to be finished,
> Many deep wells with rope-hoists to be finished,
> Let us submit to the house of Kish, let us not fight.

Gilgamesh, lord of Kulaba,   15
Trusted in the goddess Inanna,
And did not take to heart the words of his city's elders.

[*Gilgamesh seeks support from the assembly of the city's young men.*]

Before the able-bodied young men of his city, Gilgamesh
A second time presented the question, carefully choosing his words:

> There are wells to be finished, many wells of the land
>   to be finished,   20
> Many shallow wells of the land to be finished,
> Many deep wells with rope-hoists to be finished,

1. This means that Uruk's water supply was insufficient to stand a siege.
2. The rope-hoists were the ropes used to haul buckets of water from the wells.

(Do we answer:) "We do not want to submit to the house
   of Kish" or "We do not want to fight"?

The convened assembly of his city's able-bodied young men replied
   to Gilgamesh:

As they say: is it the ones who stand or the ones who sit,   25
The ones who ride with princes,
Or the ones who cling to their donkeys' haunches,
Which of them has the spirit for this?
You should not submit to the house of Kish, but we have
   no need to fight.[3]

[*The young men sing a hymn to the city of Uruk.*]

Uruk, the handiwork of the gods,   30
Eanna, the temple come down from heaven—
It is the great gods who made them.
Its mighty city wall is a cloud touching the earth,
Its lofty seat was established by the god An.

[*They address Gilgamesh.*]

You cared for them, O king and hero,   35
O lusty one, prince beloved of the god An,
When he (Akka) comes, will he inspire fear?
Its (Kish's) troops are small (in number), its rear guard is
   in disarray,
Its men will be unable to oppose you.

Then Gilgamesh, lord of Kulaba,   40
His heart rejoiced at the words of his city's able-bodied men,
   he was in a buoyant mood.
He said to his servant Enkidu:

Now, let the tools and arms of war be made ready,
Let the battle club return to your side.
May they create a fearsome radiance,   45
So that when he comes the terror of me might envelop him,
His judgment will become confused and he will become
   disoriented.

[*The siege of Uruk.*]

3. The young men seem to suggest that there is another solution to Uruk's dilemma besides
   submission or fighting.

Not five days, not ten days, had gone by,
When Akka, son of Enmebaragesi, laid siege to (the city wall)
   of Uruk.
It was Uruk's judgment that became confused!   50
Gilgamesh, lord of Kulaba,
Spoke to his warriors:

    O my hand-picked warriors,
    Let one stouthearted man volunteer, "I will go to Akka."

Birhurture, his royal steward,   55
Praised his king (and said):

    I will go to Akka
    That his judgment will become confused and he will
      become disoriented.

Birhurture went out through the city gate.
When Birhurture went out through the city gate,   60
They snared him at the entrance to the city gate,
They pummeled Birhurture, knocking off his headgear.
They brought him before Akka.
He (Birhurture) spoke to Akka.
Before he had finished speaking, the cupbearer of Uruk went up
    onto the city wall   65
And peered out over the wall.
Akka saw the cupbearer
And he said to Birhurture:

    Slave, is that man your king?

(Birhurture replied):   70

    That man is not my king!
    If that man were my king,
    He would have a terrifying scowl,
    He would have eyes like a bison,
    He would have a beard of lapis,   75
    He would have magnificent fingers.
    But no multitude has been overwhelmed, no multitude has
      been stirred up,
    No multitude has rolled in the dust,
    No foreign lands have been overcome,
    No mouths of the land have been filled with dust,   80
    No prows of ships have been broken,

Akka, king of Kish, has not been taken prisoner amidst
   his troops.

(When he had said this) they thrashed him, they struck him,
They pummeled Birhurture, knocking off his headgear.

[*Gilgamesh appears on the walls.*]

Following the cupbearer, Gilgamesh mounted the city wall.   85
His fearsome radiance enveloped Kulaba, both young and old.
The able-bodied young men of Uruk grasped the battle club
And stood in the street at the doorway of the city gate.
Enkidu went out alone through the city gate.

[*Gilgamesh and Akka spy each other.*]

Gilgamesh peered out over the wall.   90
Looking on, Akka spied (Gilgamesh).

   (Akka to Enkidu): "Slave, is that man your king?"

   (Enkidu): "That man is indeed my king."

Even as Enkidu spoke,
The multitude was overwhelmed, the multitude was stirred up,   95
The multitude rolled in the dust,
All the foreign lands were overcome,
The mouths of the land were filled with dust,
The prows of the ships were broken,
And Akka, king of Kish, was taken prisoner amidst his troops.   100

[*Gilgamesh addresses Akka.*]

Gilgamesh, lord of Kulaba,
Said to Akka:

   O Akka, my lieutenant, Akka, my captain,
   Akka, my general,
   Akka, you gave me breath, Akka, you gave me life,   105
   Akka, you sheltered the refugee,
   Akka, you nourished the fleeing bird with grain.[4]

[*Akka replies.*]

4. Akka apparently sheltered Gilgamesh at some point.

Uruk, the handiwork of the gods—
Its mighty city wall is a cloud touching the earth,
Its lofty seat was established by the god An.   110
They are entrusted to you (Gilgamesh). [Repay me my]
    previous favor!

[*Gilgamesh frees Akka.*]

(Gilgamesh): "By the god Utu, I now repay you the previous
    favor."

He freed Akka (to go) to Kish.

[*Invocation.*]

Gilgamesh, lord of Kulaba,
How sweet it is to praise you!   115

Gilgamesh and Huwawa A

The Sumerian epic poem "Gilgamesh and Huwawa A" describes an
expedition undertaken by Gilgamesh, Enkidu, and a party of warriors
from Uruk to the Cedar Forest, almost certainly in the eastern mountains, to cut down cedar trees needed to provide timber for the roof
beams for the temples of the gods. During the course of their expedition, they encounter the guardian of the Cedar Forest, the monster
Huwawa, and slay him.
    The story of "Gilgamesh and Huwawa A" finds a counterpart in the
second half of Tablet II and Tablets III–V of the Akkadian *Epic of
Gilgamesh.*

[*Gilgamesh ponders man's mortality and proposes a quest.*]

The lord was pondering the realm of mortal man,
The lord Gilgamesh was pondering the realm of mortal man.
Gilgamesh declared to his servant Enkidu:

    O Enkidu, no man can avoid life's end.
    I would enter the mountain land and set up my name,   5
    Where a name is set up, I would set up my name,
    Where a name is not set up, I would set up the names of
        the gods.

His servant Enkidu answered him:

My lord, if you are to enter the mountain land, the god
    Utu should be informed,
The god Utu, youthful Utu, should be informed.   10
Whatever concerns the mountain land is the god Utu's affair,
Whatever concerns the mountain land, where cedars are
    felled, is the god Utu's affair, Utu should be informed.

[*Gilgamesh requests permission in an oracle from the god Utu to enter the
mountain land.*]

Gilgamesh prepared a white kid (for sacrifice),
He clasped a brown kid to his breast as an offering,
He grasped a glistening scepter in his hand and held it to his
    nose.   15
He declared to the god Utu in heaven:

    O Utu, I would enter the mountain land, may you be my
        helper,
    I would enter the mountain land, where cedars are felled,
        may you be my helper!

The god Utu answered from heaven:

    Young man, you are a noble in your own right, but in the
        mountain land, what would you be there?   20

[*Gilgamesh bewails the god Utu's refusal to grant a favorable oracle.*]

    O Utu, I would speak a word to you, may you be mindful
        of my word,
    I would have (my word) reach you, may you heed it.
    In my city a person dies, and the heart grieves,
    A person is no more, and the heart breaks.
    I have peered over the city wall,   25
    I have seen the corpses floating in the river's water.
    So too it will come to pass for me, so it will happen to me.
    A man, no matter how tall, cannot reach heaven,
    A man, no matter how far-reaching, cannot compass
        the netherworld.
    Since no man can avoid life's end,   30
    I would enter the mountain land and set up my name.
    Where a name is set up, I would set up my name,
    Where a name is not set up, I would set up the names of the
        gods.

The god Utu accepted (Gilgamesh's) tears as a gift.
As a merciful one, he showed him mercy.   35

[*The preparations for the quest.*]

Then came "The Warriors," all sons of one mother—they were
    seven in number.
The first, their eldest brother, had the paws of a lion and the
    claws of an eagle,
The second was a slithering snake,
The third was a dragon-snake,
The fourth rained down fire,   40
The fifth was a noble snake that . . . in the upland,
The sixth was like a spring flood that buffets the flanks of the
    mountains,
The seventh flashed like lightning, none could withstand his
    power.
The seven of them the warrior, youthful Utu, gave to Gilgamesh.
[. . .]   45
[. . .] . . . kingship.
[. . .] the goddess Nissaba added [. . .]
[In heaven they sp]arkle, on earth they know the path,
[. . .] may they show him the way.
He brought them into the mountain valley.   50
The warrior, youthful Utu, gave these seven to lord Gilgamesh.
That put the "Cedar-Smiter" in a jubilant mood,
That put Gilgamesh in a jubilant mood.
In his city (Gilgamesh) had the bugle sound for one and all,
He made two act as one.   55

[*Gilgamesh's proclamation.*]

    He who has a house, to his house! He who has a mother,
        to his mother!
    Young spirits such as I, may fifty fall in by my side.

He who had a house went to his house, he who had a mother went
    to his mother.
Young spirits such as Gilgamesh, fifty fell in by his side.
(Gilgamesh) set out for the forge,   60
He had cast there a . . . and a battle-axe, the "Weapon of Bravery."
(Gilgamesh) set out for the shadowy grove,
He felled there hardwood, poplar, apple, and boxwood,
He gave them to the men of his city who accompanied him.

The first, their eldest brother, had the paws of a lion and the
    claws of an eagle,   65
The second was a slithering snake,
The third was a dragon-snake,
The fourth rained down fire,
The fifth was a noble snake that . . . in the upland,
The sixth was like a spring flood that buffets the flanks of the
    mountains,   70
The seventh flashed like lightning, none could withstand his
    power.
The seven of them the warrior, youthful Utu, gave to Gilgamesh.
[. . .]
[. . .] . . . kingship.
[. . .] the goddess Nissaba added [. . .]   75
[In heaven they sp]arkle, on earth they know the path,
[. . .] may they show him the way.
He brought them into the mountain valley.

[*The quest to the mountain land.*]

He traversed the first mountain range, but did not come upon the
    cedar he desired.
He traversed the second mountain range, but did not come upon
    the cedar he desired.   80
He traversed the third mountain range, but did not come upon
    the cedar he desired.
He traversed the fourth mountain range, but did not come upon
    the cedar he desired.
He traversed the fifth mountain range, but did not come upon the
    cedar he desired.
He traversed the sixth mountain range, but did not come upon
    the cedar he desired.
When he traversed the seventh mountain range, he came upon
    the cedar he desired.   85

[*Gilgamesh cuts down the cedar.*]

He inquired no further, sought no other place.
Lord Gilgamesh felled the cedar,
Enkidu cut off the branches and gave them to the men of his
    city who accompanied him,
They piled them up in bundles.

[*Huwawa is disturbed.*]

By all this hubbub Gilgamesh disturbed Huwawa in his den,   90
(Huwawa) let loose his terrifying radiance against him.

[Gilgamesh falls down dazed.]

Gilgamesh [. . .] was held as if in deep sleep,
[Enkidu] was in a stupor,
The men of his city who accompanied him
   cowered at his feet like puppies.
Enkidu awoke as if from a dream, he was bewildered, as if from
   deep sleep,   95
He rubbed his eyes, all was deathly still.
(Enkidu) nudged Gilgamesh but could not rouse him.
He spoke to (Gilgamesh), but he made no reply:

> You who sleep, you who sleep,
> Gilgamesh, son of Kulaba, how long will you sleep?   100
> The mountain land has turned dark, shadows lie over it,
> The glimmer of twilight has descended upon it.
> The god Utu has gone majestically to the lap of his mother,
>   the goddess Ningal.
> Gilgamesh, how long will you sleep?
> The men of your city who accompany you
>   should not be kept waiting in the mountain valley,   105
> Their mothers should not be twisting yarn in your city
>   square.[1]

So he spoke into (Gilgamesh's) right ear.

[Gilgamesh is roused to action.]

(Enkidu's) call to battle enveloped (Gilgamesh) like a woolen
   garment.
(Gilgamesh) took thirty shekels of oil and rubbed it on his chest.
He stood like a bull on a pedestal,   110
He lowered his neck to the ground and bellowed:

> By the life of the mother who bore me, the goddess
>   Ninsun, and my father, the divine pure Lugalbanda,
> Shall I be such a baby as to want to sit on my mother
>   Ninsun's lap?

A second time (Gilgamesh) said to (Enkidu):

1. This may refer to an activity carried out while the women await their sons' return.

By the life of the mother who bore me, the goddess
    Ninsun, and my father, the divine pure Lugalbanda,   115
Until I find out whether he is man or god,
I will not turn my foot from the mountain land, towards
    the city.

The servant who gladdens spirits, who sweetens life,
(Enkidu) answered his lord (Gilgamesh):

My lord, since you have not seen him, he does not
    frighten you.   120
But I have seen him and he scared me witless.
The teeth of that warrior are dragon teeth,
His face is the face of a lion,
His chest is a raging torrent,
His forehead a fire that consumes a reed thicket, none
    can approach it.   125
My lord, you enter the mountain land, I will go back
    to the city.
To your mother I will say, "He is alive"—and she will beam.
But afterwards I will say to her, "He is dead"—and she will
    weep bitterly.

[Gilgamesh] answered [Enkidu]:

O Enkidu, a team of two will not perish. He who is lashed
    to a boat will not sink,   130
No one can tear asunder a three-ply cloth,
Water can wash away no one from a (high) city wall,
An indoor fire cannot be extinguished.
You help me and I will help you, what harm can befall us?
When a boat sinks, when a boat sinks,   135
When a seafaring boat headed for Magan sinks,
When a cargo ship of bundled reeds sinks,
The boat that is strongly lashed to another, the lifeboat, holds
    fast.
Come now, let us go to him and see him face to face.
If when we go to him,   140
There is something frightful, then turn it away,
If there is a ruse, then turn it away.
Whatever your thoughts, come now, let us go to him.

[*Huwawa confronts Gilgamesh and Enkidu.*]

No closer than sixty times sixty paces,[2]
Huwawa sat in his cedar den.   145
He glared at Gilgamesh and Enkidu, it was the look of death,
He shook his head, it was the sign of utter doom,
When he spoke, his words were few:

> You, young man, will never return to your native city.

As for Gilgamesh, fear and dread surged in his muscles and limbs, 150
His feet stayed rooted to the ground.
He dragged the nail of his big toe behind his foot,
. . . his side.

[*Enkidu encourages Gilgamesh.*]

> Hey there, lusty one, anointed with glistening oil,
> Noble one, delight of the gods,   155
> Spirited bull rampant in battle,
> Your mother was the best at bearing a son,
> Your wet nurse was the best at nursing a son.
> Do not be afraid, plant your hands on the earth.

[*Gilgamesh pretends that he has come to Huwawa as a prospective brother-in-law and asks for his protective radiances as engagement gifts.*]

He planted his hands on the earth, he said to Huwawa: 160

> By the life of the mother who bore me, the goddess
>   Ninsun, and my father, the divine pure Lugalbanda,
> Nobody knows where you dwell in the mountain land,
> People should know where you dwell in the mountain land.
> Let me introduce to you Enmebaragesi, my older sister, that
>   she might become your wife in the mountain land,[3]
> Give me one of your terrifying radiances, I want to join your
>   family.   165

Huwawa gave him his first terrifying radiance.
The men of his city who accompanied him
    cut off its branches and bundled them up,
They laid them at the foot of the mountain.

2. Gilgamesh and Enkidu can get no closer to Huwawa without getting through his protective radiances.
3. See "Gilgamesh and Akka," line 1. Since Emmebaragesi was a famous king, this was probably a joke to a Sumerian audience.

A second time Gilgamesh said to Huwawa:

> By the life of the mother who bore me, the goddess
>   Ninsun, and my father, the divine pure Lugalbanda,   170
> Nobody knows where you dwell in the mountain land,
> People should know where you dwell in the mountain land.
> Let me introduce to you Peshtur, my younger sister, that
>   she might become your concubine in the mountain land.
> Give me one of your terrifying radiances, I want to join your
>   family.

Huwawa gave him his second terrifying radiance.   175
The men of his city who accompanied him
    cut off its branches and bundled them up,
They laid them at the foot of the mountain.

A third time Gilgamesh said to Huwawa:

> By the life of the mother who bore me, the goddess
>   Ninsun, and my father, the divine pure Lugalbanda,
> Nobody knows where you dwell in the mountain land,   180
> People should know where you dwell in the mountain land.
> Let me bring to you in the mountain land good flour, the
>   food of the gods, and a waterskin with cool water.
> Give me one of your terrifying radiances, I want to join your
>   family.

Huwawa gave him his third terrifying radiance.
The men of his city who accompanied him
    cut off its branches and bundled them up,   185
They laid them at the foot of the mountain.

A fourth time Gilgamesh said to Huwawa:

> By the life of the mother who bore me, the goddess
>   Ninsun, and my father, the divine pure Lugalbanda,
> Nobody knows where you dwell in the mountain land,
> People should know where you dwell in the mountain land.   190
> Let me bring to you in the mountain land big shoes for your
>   big feet.
> Give me one of your terrifying radiances, I want to join your
>   family.

Huwawa gave him his fourth terrifying radiance.
The men of his city who accompanied him
    cut off its branches and bundled them up,
They laid them at the foot of the mountain.   195

A fifth time Gilgamesh said to Huwawa:

> By the life of the mother who bore me, the goddess
>   Ninsun, and my father, the divine pure Lugalbanda,
> Nobody knows where you dwell in the mountain land,
> People should know where you dwell in the mountain land.
> Let me bring to you in the mountain land little shoes for
>   your little feet.   200
> Give me one of your terrifying radiances, I want to join your
>   family.

Huwawa gave him his fifth terrifying radiance.
The men of his city who accompanied him
    cut off its branches and bundled them up,
They laid them at the foot of the mountain.

A sixth time Gilgamesh said to Huwawa: 205

> By the life of the mother who bore me, the goddess
>   Ninsun, and my father, the divine pure Lugalbanda,
> Nobody knows where you dwell in the mountain land,
> People should know where you dwell in the mountain land.
> Let me bring to you in the mountain land rock crystal,
>   chalcedony, and lapis lazuli.
> Give me one of your terrifying radiances, I want to join your
>   family.   210

Huwawa gave him his sixth terrifying radiance.
The men of his city who accompanied him
    cut off its branches and bundled them up,
They laid them at the foot of the mountain.

A seventh time Gilgamesh said to Huwawa:

> By the life of the mother who bore me, the goddess
>   Ninsun, and my father, the divine pure Lugalbanda,   215
> Nobody knows where you dwell in the mountain land,
> People should know where you dwell in the mountain land.
> Let me bring to you in the mountain [. . .]
> Give me one of your terrifying radiances, I want to join your
>   family.

Huwawa gave him his seventh terrifying radiance.   220
The men of his city who accompanied him
    cut off its branches and bundled them up,
They laid them at the foot of the mountain.

[*Gilgamesh captures Huwawa.*]

When Huwawa had used up his seventh and last terrifying
    radiance, he (Gilgamesh) had come close to his den,[4]
He crept up toward him, as if he were a groggy snake.
Feigning to kiss him, Gilgamesh struck Huwawa on the cheek
    with his fist.   225
Huwawa bared his glistening teeth and wrinkled his brow.
He clutched Gilgamesh by the hand.

[*Huwawa prays to the god Utu.*]

    To you, O Utu, I would speak!
    O Utu, I have known neither mother who bore me nor
        father who raised me.
    I was born in the mountain land, it was you who raised me.   230

[*Gilgamesh finds mercy for Huwawa.*]

Gilgamesh gave his word by heaven, by earth, and by the
    netherworld.
Huwawa clutched Gilgamesh's hand, and threw himself down
    before him.
Then Gilgamesh, being a nobleman, found mercy.
He said to his servant Enkidu:

    Enkidu, should I not let the captured bird return
        to its home?   235
    Should I not let the captured youth return to the lap
        of his mother?

Enkidu answered Gilgamesh:

    Hey there, lusty one, anointed with glistening oil,
    Noble one, delight of the gods,
    Spirited bull rampant in battle,   240
    Lord, prince Gilgamesh, honored in Uruk.
    Your mother was the best at bearing a son,
    Your wet nurse was the best at nursing a son.
    Is there one so high that he can be imprudent?
    Fate consumes all, fate makes no distinctions.   245
    If the captured bird returns to its home,
    If the captured youth returns to the lap of his mother,

---

4. See line 145. As he takes each protective radiance, Gilgamesh moves closer to the den, taking
giant steps.

You will never return to your native city!
To set a captured warrior free,
To return a captured priestess to her residence,   250
To return a captured priest to his bewigged finery, who has
    ever seen the like?
Huwawa will mislead us on the road to the mountain land,
He will confound us on the path to the mountain land.

The warrior Gilgamesh heeded what had been spoken to him.
Huwawa spoke to Enkidu: 255

Against me, Enkidu, you have uttered harmful words.
You hireling, secure with your dole of chow, tagging behind
    your chief, why have you slandered me?

Even as he was speaking,
Enkidu cut off his head in a frenzied rage,
They stashed it in a leather sack.   260

[*Gilgamesh and Enkidu proceed to the city of Nippur.*]

Gilgamesh and Enkidu presented it to the gods Enlil and Ninlil.
Kissing the ground before the god Enlil,
He set the sack down and took out the head,
They presented it to the god Enlil.
When the god Enlil saw Huwawa's head,   265
He spoke angrily to Gilgamesh:

Why have you acted so?
Has it been decreed that his name be obliterated from the
    earth?
He should have sat before you.
He should have eaten the bread that you ate.   270
He should have drunk the water that you drank.
He should have been treated in a fitting manner.

[*Enlil apportions the terrifying radiances.*]

His first terrifying radiance he gave to the field,
His second terrifying radiance he gave to the river,
His third terrifying radiance he gave to the mountain,   275
His fourth terrifying radiance he gave to the lion,
His fifth terrifying radiance he gave to the reed thicket,
His sixth terrifying radiance he gave to the palace,
His seventh terrifying radiance he gave to the goddess Nungal.
Terrifying radiances that remained he took for himself.   280

[*Invocation.*]

Mighty Gilgamesh, may you be honored!
Goddess Nissaba, may you be praised!

Gilgamesh and Huwawa B

"Gilgamesh and Huwawa B" is a shorter, variant version of the composition "Gilgamesh and Huwawa A" and likewise describes an expedition undertaken by Gilgamesh, Enkidu, and a party of warriors from
Uruk to the mountain land.

[*Opening hymn.*]

Hey there, lusty one, anointed with glistening oil,
Noble one, delight of the gods,
Spirited bull rampant in battle,
Lord, prince Gilgamesh, honored in Uruk.

[*Gilgamesh ponders man's mortality and proposes a quest.*]

In Uruk a person dies, and the heart grieves,   5
A person is no more, and the heart breaks.
I have peered over the city wall,
I have seen the corpses floating in the river's water.
My spirit is crushed, my heart is aggrieved.
The end of life is the one sure thing.   10
The grave, the omnipotent netherworld, no man can escape.
No matter how tall, none can straddle the netherworld,
No matter how broad, none can compass the netherworld,
No youth can go beyond life's limits.
By the life of the mother who bore me, the goddess Ninsun,
     and my father, the divine pure Lugalbanda,   15
And my personal god Enki, Nudimmud!

[*gap*]

I would fell [. . .]
I would . . . to its branches.
I would bring in [the felled cedar].

[His servant Enkidu] answered him: 20

My lord, if you are to enter the mountain land,
The god Utu should be informed,
If you are to enter the mountain land, where cedars are
    felled,
The god Utu should be informed.
Whatever concerns the mountain land is the god
    Utu's affair,   25
Whatever concerns the mountain land, where cedars are
    felled, is the youthful god Utu's affair.

[*Gilgamesh requests permission in an oracle from the god Utu to enter the
mountain land.*]

The god Utu of heaven put on his lapis tiara,
He advanced with head held high.
Gilgamesh, lord of Kulaba, grasped a glistening scepter in his
    hand and held it to his nose:

    I would enter the mountain land, may you be my helper.   30
    I would enter the mountain land where cedars are felled,
        may you be my helper.

[*gap*]

[*The preparations for the quest.*]

Then came "The Warriors," all sons of one mother—they were
    seven in number.
The first, their eldest brother, had the paws of a lion and
    the claws of an eagle,
The second was a slithering snake,
The third was a dragon-snake,   35
The fourth rained down fire,
The fifth was a noble snake that . . . in the upland,
The sixth was like a spring flood that buffets the flanks
    of the mountains,
The seventh flashed like lightning, none could withstand his
    power.
In heaven they sparkle, on earth they know the path.   40
In heaven they shine, stars . . . on high,
On earth they know the road to Aratta,
Like merchants they know the trade routes,
Like pigeons they know the mountain clefts.
May they bring us through the mountain valleys.   45

[*Gilgamesh's proclamation.*]

In his city Gilgamesh issued a proclamation,
In Kulaba the bugle sounded:

> O city! He who has a wife, to your wife!
> He who has a child, to your child!
> Warrior or not, 50
> He who has no wife, he who has no child,
> Let such men fall in by my side, Gilgamesh!

The king went out from the city,
Gilgamesh went out from Kulaba.

[*The quest to the mountain land.*]

He took the road to the mountain land, where cedars are felled, 55
He traversed the first mountain range, but did not come
   upon the cedar he desired.
He traversed the second mountain range, but did not come
   upon the cedar he desired.
He traversed the third mountain range, but did not come
   upon the cedar he desired.
He traversed the fourth mountain range, but did not come
   upon the cedar he desired.
He traversed the fifth mountain range, but did not come
   upon the cedar he desired. 60
He traversed the sixth mountain range, but did not come
   upon the cedar he desired
When he traversed the seventh mountain range, he came
   upon the cedar he desired.

[*Gilgamesh cuts down the cedar.*]

Gilgamesh felled the cedar,
His servant Enkidu trimmed the branches for him,
The men of his city who accompanied him piled them
   up in bundles. 65

[*Huwawa is disturbed.*]

Then as one warrior drew near the other,
Huwawa's terrifying radiance flew towards him like a spear.

[*Gilgamesh falls down dazed.*]

Gilgamesh . . . slept peacefully,
He slept and did not wake.

Enkidu nudged Gilgamesh, but could not rouse him,   70
He spoke to Gilgamesh, but he made no reply:

> You who sleep, you who sleep,
> O young lord Gilgamesh, son of Kulaba, how long will you
>   sleep?
> The mountain land has turned dark, shadows lie over it,
> The glimmer of twilight has descended upon it.   75

Gilgamesh awoke as from a dream,
He was bewildered, as from deep sleep.
He rubbed his eyes,
All was deathly still.

> By the life of the mother who bore me, the goddess Ninsun,
>   and my father, the divine pure Lugalbanda,   80
> And my personal god Enki, Nudimmud!

[*Enkidu warns Gilgamesh.*]

> My lord, since you have not yet seen him,
> He does not frighten you.
> But I have seen him and he scared me witless.
> As for that warrior, his face is the face of a lion,   85
> His chest is a raging torrent,
> His forehead, a fire that consumes a reed thicket, none
>   can approach it,
> His tongue, a man-eating lion that . . . blood.
> That warrior, his strength is beyond yours, who can stand
>   against him?

[*gap*]

[*Gilgamesh makes his offers to Huwawa.*]

> By the life of the mother who bore me, the goddess Ninsun,
>   and my father, the divine pure Lugalbanda,   90
> And my personal god Enki, Nudimmud,
> O warrior! People should know where in the mountain land
>   you dwell.
> For your little feet let little shoes be made,
> For your big feet let big shoes be made,

[*gap*]

By the life of the mother who bore me, the goddess Ninsun,
    and my father, the divine pure Lugalbanda,   95
And my personal god Enki, Nudimmud,
O warrior! People should know where in the mountain land
    you dwell.
For your little feet let little shoes be made,
For your big feet let big shoes be made,

[gap]

[Huwawa gives Gilgamesh his terrifying radiances.]

He gave him his first terrifying radiance,   100
The men of his city who accompanied him piled them
    up in bundles.

[gap]

[Gilgamesh captures Huwawa.]

When Huwawa had used up his seventh and last terrifying
    radiance, (Gilgamesh) had come close to his den.
He struck him on the ear with his fist.
(Huwawa) wrinkled his brow and bared his glistening teeth.
He threw a halter over him, like a captured wild bull.   105
He trussed him up at the elbows, like a captured warrior.

[Huwawa begs for mercy.]

The warrior began to weep, he wept long,
Huwawa began to weep, he wept long:

    Warrior! You lied to me. You struck me, you broke your
        oath!
    By the life of your mother who bore you, the goddess
        Ninsun, and your father, the divine pure Lugalbanda,   110
    And your personal god Enki, Nudimmud, you have
        betrayed me,
    You have thrown a halter over me, like a captured wild bull.
    You have trussed me up at the elbows, like a captured
        warrior.

[Gilgamesh finds mercy for Huwawa.]

Then Gilgamesh, being a nobleman, found mercy.
He said to his servant Enkidu: 115

> Come now, let us release the warrior.
> May he be our scout—may he show us the way through
>   the mountains—may he be our scout.
> May he be my [porter], may he carry my pack.

His servant Enkidu answered Gilgamesh:

> Is there one so high that he can be imprudent?   120
> Is there one so . . . that he has no [. . .]?
> To set a captured warrior free,
> To return a captured priestess to her residence,
> To return a captured priest to his bewigged finery,
> Who has ever seen the like?   125
> Huwawa will mislead us on the road to the mountain land,
> He will confound us on the path to the mountain land.
> We will never return to our native city!

[gap]

[Huwawa] answered him:

> The mother who bore me is the mountain cavern,   130
> The father who begot me is the highland cavern,
> O Utu, you made me dwell alone in the mountain!

[Remainder missing.]

Gilgamesh and the Bull of Heaven

The story of "Gilgamesh and the Bull of Heaven" finds a counterpart in the narrative of Tablet VI of the Akkadian *Epic of Gilgamesh.* The Sumerian text, which contains many gaps and obscurities, opens with a short hymn of praise to Gilgamesh. The narrative begins with Gilgamesh's mother, the goddess Ninsun, giving instructions to her son. Following her advice, Gilgamesh enters the courtyard of the goddess Inanna's temple, where he attracts the attention of Inanna herself. Inanna entreats Gilgamesh to stay with her as her lover, forgoing his usual kingly duties. Gilgamesh relates to his mother what Inanna offered, then on her instructions refuses Inanna's blandishments, apparently saying he will manage his own affairs.

In a rage, Inanna goes to her father, the god An, to demand the Bull of Heaven to kill Gilgamesh. An initially refuses to hand over the bull, describing the dangerous consequences of doing so, but gives in when Inanna lets loose a world-shaking scream. In Uruk, the bull devours the green plants and drinks the water in the canal, overwhelming the populace. The royal minstrel composes a song about the bull, singing it as Gilgamesh eats and drinks with seeming unconcern.

Gilgamesh prepares to meet the bull, equipping himself with heroic weapons and issuing instructions to his mother and sister. Enkidu joins him in killing the bull, as Inanna looks on. When he starts to butcher it, the goddess rushes off, leaving him frustrated that he cannot kill her too. Gilgamesh distributes the hide to the tanner, the meat to the poor, and the horns to Inanna herself for holding oil in her temple.

[*Opening paean.*]

The song of the hero of battle, the hero of battle, let me sing,
The song of the lord Gilgamesh, the hero of battle, let me sing,
The song of the dark-bearded one, the hero of battle, let me sing,
The song of the fair-limbed one, the hero of battle, let me sing,
The song of the mighty one(?), the hero of battle, let me sing,   5
The song of the champion(?) boxer and wrestler, the hero
   of battle, let me sing,
The song of the smiter of evil, the hero of battle, let me sing!

[*Gilgamesh's mother, the goddess Ninsun, gives him instructions.*]

O lord, go down to the river . . . , bathe in the river,
O lord, you can enter the juniper garden,[1]
O king, be shorn like a noble sheep in the lordly palace.   10
Sit on a plank at the prow of the boat, it is moored in the
   marsh,
O lord, it is moored in the marsh, bend the oars
   in the water,
Dip the oars in the water like lush reeds,
May you . . .

The lord went down to the river . . . , bathed in the river,   15
The lord, who could enter the juniper garden,
The king was shorn like a noble sheep in the lordly palace.
He sat on a plank at the prow of the boat, it was moored in the
   marsh,
The lord . . . it in the marsh,

1. One manuscript has Zabala, the name of a cult center of Inanna, in place of juniper; the
   two words sounded similar in Sumerian.

The lord dipped the oars in the water like lush reeds,   20
He . . .
He hastened for her sake, for his mother who bore him.

In the wide courtyard of the goddess Inanna's temple
Gilgamesh took his spike in hand,[2]
He . . . to destroy the . . .   25
In the wide courtyard, without opposition.

[*The goddess Inanna spies Gilgamesh.*]

Then did she look upon him, a seductive . . . ,
Then did Inanna look upon him, a seductive . . . ,
From the temple "Source of Sweet Water," she looked upon
    him, a seductive . . . :

>   My bull, my man, I will not let you go,   30
>   Lord Gilgamesh, my bull, my man, I will not let you go,
>   I will not let you go to decide legal cases in my Eanna temple,
>   I will not let you go to render decisions in the sacred lordly
>   palace,
>   I will not let you go to decide legal cases in the god An's
>   beloved Eanna temple,
>   O Gilgamesh, you be the herdsman, I will be the ox!   35

[*Gilgamesh reports back to his mother, the goddess Ninsun.*]

The king listened to her words,
The lord told his mother who bore him,
Gilgamesh [said] to the goddess Ninsun:

>   O mother who bore me,
>   She [. . .] at the portal of the city gate,   40
>   At the crest of the city wall she . . . :

>   My bull, my man, I will not let you go,
>   Lord Gilgamesh, my bull, my man, I will not let you go,
>   I will not let you go to decide legal cases in my Eanna temple,
>   I will not let you go to render decisions in the sacred lordly
>   palace,   45
>   I will not let you go to decide legal cases in the god An's
>   beloved Eanna temple,
>   O Gilgamesh, you be the herdsman, I will be the ox!

2. The tool referred to here was pointed, like a chisel, needle, or pin. A pun may underlie the
use of this particular word.

When he told this to the mother who bore him,
The mother who bore him replied [to Gilgamesh]:

> Gifts of Inanna must not enter your lordly palace,   50
> The goddess Ninegal[3] must not smother your heroic
>   might,
> The goddess Inanna must not block your way!

[gap]

[*Gilgamesh replies to the goddess Inanna.*]

> I will let no gifts of Inanna enter my lordly palace,
> The goddess Ninegal must not smother my heroic
>   might,
> O goddess Inanna, you must not block my way!   55
> I myself will call the cattle of foreign lands and bring them
>   into pens,
> I myself will call the sheep of foreign lands and bring them
>   into folds,
> I myself will make silver and carnelian abundant,
> I myself will fill [the storehouse(?)] with them.

The young woman cried out to him, snorting with rage,   60
The goddess Inanna cried out to him, snorting with rage:

> O Gilgamesh, why have you said this to me?
> O Gilgamesh, why have you said this to me?
> Like . . . is the . . . of Gilgamesh!

[gap]

[*Inanna has gone to her father, the god An, demanding his monstrous bull,
the Bull of Heaven, to kill Gilgamesh. An remonstrates.*]

> [The Bull of Heaven will devour] (the people's) innards,   65
> [It will drink] their blood,
> [It will drink] their blood, as if from a water jar.

The goddess Inanna wept and sobbed,
The god An tried to [comfort] his beloved.
He had her hold the tether(?), the god An said to her: 70

> My little one, why are you weeping and sobbing?

3. Literally, "Lady of the Palace," apparently here another name for Inanna.

Because of that great bull let loose in Uruk,
Because of that great bull Gilgamesh let loose and . . . Uruk,
Because he did not give me what was mine,
That is why I am weeping and sobbing!   75
O my father, give me the Bull of Heaven,
I will kill that lord, I will kill that lord,
The lord Gilgamesh, I will kill that lord!

The great god An replied to the radiant goddess Inanna:

My little one, the Bull of Heaven would have no food, it
    grazes at the horizon,   80
O young woman, goddess Inanna, it grazes at the eastern
    horizon.
I will not give you the Bull of Heaven.

The radiant goddess Inanna replied:

Then I will let loose a scream, it will reach both heaven
    and earth!

[*The goddess Inanna screams and gets her way.*]

Her scream reached heaven, her scream reached earth,   85
[The goddess] Inanna's scream reached heaven, her scream
    reached earth,
It covered [heaven and earth] like a woolen cloak, like a linen
    cloth it spread over them!
Who ever let loose such a scream?
Who ever let loose such a scream?
She spread terror, she spread terror,   90
The goddess Inanna spread terror over the earth!

The great god An replied to the radiant goddess Inanna:

I will give you the Bull of Heaven.

[*The Bull of Heaven attacks Uruk.*]

The young woman, the goddess Inanna, took the tether in hand
    like an ox-driver,
The goddess Inanna brought down the Bull of Heaven from
    the sky.   95
The bull ate up the green plants of Uruk,
The bull drank up the water of the Agilu canal.
Though the Agilu canal reaches a double league in length, its
    thirst was not quenched.

It ate the green plants and stripped the earth bare,
It crushed with its teeth the felled date palms of Uruk.   100
As the bull stood there, it filled Uruk,
The fearsomeness of the Bull of Heaven filled Kulaba.

[*Gilgamesh's minstrel, Lugal-gaba-gal, composes a song about the bull.*]

His minstrel, [Lugal-gaba-gal . . .],
When he saw [the Bull of Heaven],
He bent over [his lyre, singing]:   105

> The goddess Inanna has brought down the Bull of Heaven
>   from the sky,
> It eats up the green plants of Uruk,
> It drinks up the water of the Agilu canal.
> Though the Agilu canal reaches a double league in length,
>   its thirst is not quenched.
> It eats the green plants and strips the earth bare,   110
> It crushes with its teeth the felled date palms of Uruk.
> As the bull stands there, it fills Uruk,
> The fearsomeness of the Bull of Heaven fills Kulaba.

Gilgamesh [said] to his minstrel, Lugal-gaba-gal:

> O my minstrel, sing a song, tune your strings,   115
> I will have a drink, [fill] the bronze goblet.

His minstrel, Lugal-gaba-gal, replied to Gilgamesh his lord:

> O my lord, you may eat, you may drink,
> But have you no care for the words (of my song)?
>
> I? What care [should I have for the words (of your song)]?   120

[*Gilgamesh prepares to kill the bull.*]

For him to slay the bull,
For Gilgamesh to slay the bull,
[He tied around his waist] his belt weighing fifty minas,
[He wore at his side] his dagger of seven talents and a half,
[He took up] his bronze battle-axe [weighing seven talents].   125

[*Gilgamesh tells his mother and sister to look after(?) the cattle and sheep.*]

His mother who bore him [. . .],
His sister [. . .],

[To] the mother who bore him, the goddess Ninsun,
[To] Peshtur, his little sister [. . .],
Gilgamesh [said]:   130

> O my mother . . . [. . .],
> O my little sister Peshtur [. . .],
> The . . . cattle . . . ,
> The . . . sheep . . . ,

[*His mother, Ninsun, asks what he will do.*]

> The Bull of Heaven, what will there be for you [if you
>   slay it]?   135
> What will there be for you if you do not slay it?
> As for me, what will there be if you slay it?

Gilgamesh [replied to her]:

> If I slay it,
> I will throw its carcass in the alley,   140
> I will set its enormous entrails in the main street,
> I will give its hide to the tanner,
> I will dole out its meat by the bushel to the orphans of
>   the city,
> I will give its two horns as oil vessels before the goddess
>   Inanna in the Eanna temple.

[*Gilgamesh challenges the Bull of Heaven.*]

> I will throw your carcass in the alley,   145
> I will set your enormous entrails in the main street,
> I will give your hide to the tanner,
> I will dole out your meat by the bushel to the orphans of
>   the city,
> I will give your two horns as oil vessels before the goddess
>   Inanna in the Eanna temple!

[*Gilgamesh and Enkidu attack the Bull of Heaven.*]

The goddess Inanna watched from the wall,   150
The bull bellowed in the dust.
Lord Gilgamesh stood at its front,
Enkidu went around towards its rear.
The men of his city who accompanied him,
It covered with dust like a calf not trained to the yoke.   155
When Enkidu got behind the bull, he seized its tail,
He shouted to his king, Gilgamesh:

Hey there, lusty one, anointed with glistening oil,
Noble one, delight of the gods,
Spirited bull rampant in battle,   160
Lord, prince Gilgamesh, honored in Uruk,
Your mother was the best at bearing a son,
Your wet nurse was the best at nursing a son.
Lord, noble one of the gods,
Have no fear, a warrior has no strength on his own,   165
Where the ground is firm [. . .],
The people [. . .],
The people of the city [. . .].

No sooner had Enkidu shouted to Gilgamesh,
[Then Gilgamesh] smote the bull on the head with his axe
   weighing seven talents.   170
The bull, tossing its head up and down, collapsed, dissolved
   like clay, spread out like a heap of grain.
The king, as if he were a chief cook, wielded a knife,
He hacked off a shoulder piece, Inanna flew off like a pigeon
   whose wall he had destroyed.
The king wept (in frustration) at the bull's head:

    Just as I destroyed this, so too I would do with you!   175

[*Gilgamesh fulfills his promises to his mother and sister.*]

That which he spoke came true:
He threw its carcass in the alley,
He set its enormous entrails in the main street,
He gave its hide to the tanner,
He doled out its meat by the bushel to the orphans of the city,   180
He gave its two horns as oil vessels before the goddess Inanna
   in the Eanna temple.

[*Invocation.*]

    The Bull of Heaven is dead!
    Radiant Inanna, how sweet it is to praise you!

The Gudam Epic

"The Gudam Epic" may be a variant version of the story "Gilgamesh
and the Bull of Heaven."

[*The beginning of the text is missing.*]

The . . . bull [. . .],
The . . . bull [. . .],
The goddess Inanna [. . .].
The . . . bull in Uruk [. . .].
[The people of Uruk brought beer and wine from] the storehouse,   5
The bull [drank] the beer, he [drank] the wine,
He licked clean the bronze vessels,
He made the vessels shine like gleaming cargo ships,
[He ate] the finest flour and carp fish with dangling barbels,[1]
He [plucked] fish from the fish-laden canals like dates.   10
A mob pursued the bull in the streets of Uruk,
A mob waited with its weapons against him.
His (Gilgamesh's) minstrel, Lugal-gaba-gal-di,[2] stood up,
    came out, and saw the mob.
The minstrel responded to them in song, taking (?) a drum in
    hand:

>   What have you fed him, what have you fed him?   15
>   You have not fed him bread, you fed him with your own
>   flesh.
>   What have you given him to drink, what have you given him
>   to drink?
>   You have not given him beer to drink, you gave him to drink
>   of your own blood!
>   O . . . bull! In the streets of Uruk a mob has pursued you,
>   A mob waits with weapons against you.   20
>   Go! You must not do these things.
>   O people! He will obey what Inanna orders.

The . . . bull heard this and smote his thigh with the flat of his
    hand,
Fear overwhelmed him.

>   Oh, I will lose my heroic might that flattens all!   25
>   Would that I could flee behind the door bolt of the temple
>   of Zabala,
>   Would that I could [. . .] under the branches of the roof
>   beams(?) of the temple of Eanna![3]

The . . . bull came out into the streets of Uruk,
The . . . bull slaughtered the mob in the streets of Uruk,
He killed the mob with its weapons,   30
He blocked the portal of the city gate,

1. "Barbels" refers to the beard and mustachelike projections around the mouth of a fish.
2. The minstrel is called Lugal-gaba-gal in "Gilgamesh and the Bull of Heaven."
3. The exact meaning of this passage is uncertain. The bull evidently wants to seek refuge in one of Inanna's temples.

He stood alone.
The young fisherman, son of the fisherman of the goddess Inanna,
Struck him with his double axe,
He flattened(?) him.   35
The bull began to weep, he wept long:

    O goddess Inanna, grant me my life!
    Let me give you cattle of foreign lands, let me make
        them flourish in your pens,
    Let me give you sheep of foreign lands, let me make
        them flourish in your folds!

Radiant Inanna replied: 40

    [Give me(?)] cattle of foreign lands,
    [Give me(?)] sheep of foreign lands,

    . . .
    Lie down in the fields of Zabala, where you formerly dwelt,
    Stay in the wide plain, . . . the yoke.   45

[*Invocation.*]

    O goddess Inanna, let me proclaim your heroism,
    How sweet it is to praise you!

Gilgamesh, Enkidu, and the Netherworld

Part of the Sumerian epic poem "Gilgamesh, Enkidu, and the Nether
world," beginning at line 161, was translated into Akkadian and appended to *The Epic of Gilgamesh* as Tablet XII (omitted in this Norton
Critical Edition). Parts of it are also related to the story of Enkidu's
death and Gilgamesh's mourning in Tablets VII and VIII.

    Beginning with primeval times when the universe was created, the
poem describes a journey the god Enki takes in his boat. He is battered
by a storm that also buffets a poplar tree growing by the Euphrates
River. The goddess Inanna finds the tree and plants it in her grove in
Uruk. She plans to use its wood to make a chair and bed for herself.
After ten years the tree is ready to be cut, but a snake, a bird, and a
demoness have made their homes in it. When Inanna's brother, the
god Utu, refuses to help her, Inanna turns to Gilgamesh, and he drives
away the creatures and cuts down the tree. Taking part of the wood for
himself, he has a ball and stick made. Gilgamesh plays incessantly with
them in the city square, riding piggyback on the orphans of Uruk as

part of the game. They cry out to the gods for relief and the ball and
stick drop down into the netherworld.

    Enkidu volunteers to bring them back. He ignores Gilgamesh's ad-
vice as to how to act in the netherworld and so is trapped there. Gilgamesh, distraught at the loss of his friend, asks the gods Enlil and Sin
for help, but in vain. The god Enki, however, arranges for Enkidu's
spirit to come back. Gilgamesh questions him about what happens to
people after they die, and Enkidu describes the grim lot in store for
them. Gilgamesh, moved by the misery of the dead, goes to Uruk and
makes offerings to his dead ancestors.

[*Preamble.*]

In those days, in those far-off days,
In those nights, in those distant nights,
In those years, in those far-off years,
In most ancient times, when what was needful had first come forth,
In most ancient times, when what was needful was properly cared for, 5
When bread was enjoyed in the shrines of the land,
When ovens of the land were fired with bellows,
When heaven had been separated from earth,
When earth had been parted from heaven,
When the name of mankind had been determined,   10
When the god An had carried off the heavens for himself,
And the god Enlil had carried off the earth for himself,
And the goddess Ereshkigal had been given the netherworld as a gift,
When he had embarked, when he had embarked,
When the father had embarked for the netherworld,   15
When the god Enki had embarked for the netherworld,
Small ones rained down on the lord,
Large ones rained down on the god Enki:
The small ones were pounding stones,
The large ones were millstones(?),   20
They poured down on the deck of the god Enki's boat like
    bobbing turtles.
Against the lord, the water devoured the prow of the boat like a wolf,
Against the god Enki, the water sprang at the stern of the boat
    like a lion.

[*The goddess Inanna and the poplar tree.*]

At that time, there was a solitary tree, a solitary poplar tree, a
    solitary tree,
Growing on the bank of the glistening Euphrates,   25
Drinking Euphrates water.
The south wind tore out its roots and broke its branches,

The Euphrates battered it with water.
The woman who reverenced the word of the god An was walking
    along,
She who reverenced the word of the god Enlil was walking along.   30
She picked up the tree and brought it into Uruk,
She brought it into Inanna's sacred grove.
The woman did not plant the tree with her hand, she planted it
    with her foot.
The woman did not water the tree with her hand, she watered it
    with her foot.

    How long till there is a shining chair for me to sit on?   35
    How long till there is a shining bed for me to lie on?

Five, then ten years passed.
The tree had grown massive, its bark had not split.
In its base, a snake which fears no spell made its nest,
In its branches, the Anzu bird raised its young,   40
In its trunk, a young demoness made her home.

The young lady, who usually laughs with a happy heart,
Radiant Inanna, burst into tears.

[*The goddess Inanna speaks to the god Utu.*]

As dawn broke and the horizon brightened,
When the birds twittered at dawn,   45
When the god Utu left his sleeping chamber,
His sister, radiant Inanna,
Said to the warrior, youthful Utu:

    My brother, in those far-off days when destiny was
        determined,
    When abundance overflowed in the land,   50
    When the god An had carried off the heavens for himself,
    And the god Enlil had carried off the earth for himself,
    And the goddess Ereshkigal had been given the
        netherworld as a gift,
    When he had embarked, when he had embarked,
    When the father had embarked for the netherworld,   55
    When the god Enki had embarked for the netherworld,
    Small ones rained down on the lord,
    Large ones rained down on the god Enki:
    The small ones were pounding stones,
    The large ones were millstones(?),   60

They poured down on the deck of the god Enki's boat like
  bobbing turtles.
Against the lord, the water devoured the prow of the boat
  like a wolf,
Against the god Enki, the water sprang at the stern of the
  boat like a lion.
At that time, there was a solitary tree, a solitary poplar tree,
  a solitary tree,
Growing on the bank of the glistening Euphrates,   65
Drinking Euphrates water.
The south wind tore out its roots and broke its branches,
The Euphrates battered it with water.
I, the woman who reverenced the word of the god An, was
  walking along,
I, who reverenced the word of the god Enlil, was walking along.   70
I picked up the tree and brought it into Uruk,
I brought it into Inanna's sacred grove.
I, the woman, did not plant the tree with my hand, I
  planted it with my foot.
I, the woman, did not water the tree with my hand, I
  watered it with my foot.

How long till there is a shining chair for me to sit on?   75
How long till there is a shining bed for me to lie on?

Five, then ten years passed.
The tree had grown massive, its bark had not split.
In its base, a snake which fears no spell made its nest,
In its branches, the Anzu bird raised its young,   80
In its trunk, a young demoness made her home.

The young lady, who usually laughs with a happy heart,
Radiant Inanna, burst into tears.
Her brother, the warrior, youthful Utu, did not support her
  in that matter.

[*The goddess Inanna speaks to Gilgamesh.*]

As dawn broke and the horizon brightened,   85
When the birds twittered at dawn,
When the god Utu left his sleeping chamber,
His sister, radiant Inanna,
Spoke to the warrior Gilgamesh:

    My brother, in those far-off days when destiny was determined, 90
    When abundance overflowed in the land,
    When the god An had carried off the heavens for himself,

And the god Enlil had carried off the earth for himself,
And the goddess Ereshkigal had been given the netherworld
    as a gift,
When he had embarked, when he had embarked,   95
When the father had embarked for the netherworld,
When the god Enki had embarked for the netherworld,
Small ones rained down on the lord,
Large ones rained down on the god Enki:
The small ones were pounding stones,   100
The large ones were millstones(?),
They poured down on the deck of the god Enki's boat like
    bobbing turtles.
Against the lord, the water devoured the prow of the boat
    like a wolf,
Against the god Enki, the water sprang at the stern of the
    boat like a lion.
At that time, there was a solitary tree, a solitary poplar tree,
    a solitary tree,   105
Growing on the bank of the glistening Euphrates,
Drinking Euphrates water.
The south wind tore out its roots and broke its branches,
The Euphrates battered it with water.
I, the woman who reverenced the word of the god An, was
    walking along,   110
I, who reverenced the word of the god Enlil, was walking
    along.
I picked up the tree and brought it into Uruk,
I brought it into Inanna's sacred grove.
I, the woman, did not plant the tree with my hand, I
    planted it with my foot,
I, the woman, did not water the tree with my hand, I
    watered it with my foot.   115

How long till there is a shining chair for me to sit on?
How long till there is a shining bed for me to lie on?

Five, then ten years passed.
The tree had grown massive, its bark had not split.
In its base, a snake which fears no spell made its nest,   120
In its branches, the Anzu bird raised its young,
In its trunk, a young demoness made her home.

The young lady, who usually laughs with a happy heart,
Radiant Inanna burst into tears.
In that matter about which his sister had spoken,   125
Her brother, Gilgamesh, did support her in that matter.

[*Gilgamesh expels the creatures from the tree.*]

He tied around his waist his belt weighing fifty minas.
He hefted its fifty-mina weight as if it were thirty shekels.
He took up his bronze battle-axe weighing seven talents and
    seven minas.
In its base, he smote the snake which fears no spell,   130
In its branches, the Anzu bird took its young and brought
    them into the highland.
In its trunk, the young demoness forsook her dwelling
And fled to the wilderness.
As for the tree, he tore out its roots and broke its
    branches,
The men of his city who accompanied him cut off its branches
    and bundled them up.   135
He gave wood to the goddess, radiant Inanna, for her chair,
He gave wood to her for her bed.

[*Gilgamesh makes a ball and stick, plays with them, and loses them.*]

For himself, he had its base made into his ball,
He had its branches made into his stick.
Playing with the ball, he brought it into the city square,   140
Playing with the . . . , he brought it into the city square.
The young men of the city who were playing with the ball,
    rode piggyback on a team of orphans.
"Oh, my neck, oh, my hips!" the orphans moaned.
The son who had a mother, she brought him bread,
The brother who had a sister, she poured him water.   145
As dusk was approaching,
He marked the place where the ball had stopped,
He took it up and carried it home.
At dawn, where he had made the mark, he again rode
    piggyback.
But because of the plaints of the widows,   150
And the pleas of the young girls,
His ball and his stick fell down to the floor of the netherworld.
He used his [. . .], but could not reach it,
He used his hand, but could not reach it,
He used his foot, but could not reach it.   155
At the gate of hell, the entrance to the netherworld,
    he sat down.
Gilgamesh burst into tears and wept long:

> Oh, my ball, oh, my stick!
> My ball which I had not finished enjoying,
> My stick which I had not finished playing with!   160

Today I wish my ball had stayed in the carpenter's shop.
Oh carpenter's wife, like my own mother, I wish that it had
    stayed in the carpenter's shop.
Oh carpenter's daughter, like my own little sister, I wish
    that it had stayed in the carpenter's shop.
My ball has fallen down into the netherworld, who will
    bring it back up to me?
My stick has fallen down into hell, who will bring it back
    up to me?   165

[*Enkidu offers to get them back and Gilgamesh gives advice.*]

His servant Enkidu replied:

My king, why do you weep so? Why are you heartsick?
Today I myself will bring the ball back up from the
    netherworld,
I myself will bring the stick back up from hell.

Gilgamesh said to Enkidu: 170

If today you descend to the netherworld,
Let me give you advice, may you heed my advice,
I will have a word with you, may you pay attention to it.
Do not put on clean clothes,
They would surely see it as the sign of a stranger.   175
Do not anoint yourself with fine oil from a jar,
They would surely encircle you when they smell it.
Do not hurl your throw stick in the netherworld,[1]
Those killed by a throw stick would surely encircle you.
Do not take up your staff in the netherworld,   180
The ghosts would surely hover around you.
Do not put shoes on your feet,
The netherworld would surely raise a clamor.
Do not kiss your wife you loved,
Do not strike your wife you hated,   185
Do not kiss your son you loved,
Do not strike your son you hated,
The pleas of the netherworld would surely seize you.
The one who lies there, the one who lies there,
The mother of the god Ninazu who lies there,   190
Her radiant shoulders are not clothed,
On her radiant bosom no linen garment is spread.
She clatters her fingernails like a drum,
She rips out her hair like leeks.

1. A throw stick was a curved wooden weapon used in hunting and warfare.

[*Enkidu ignores Gilgamesh's advice.*]

Enkidu ignored the words of his master.   195
He put on clean clothes,
They saw it as the sign of a stranger.
He anointed himself with fine oil from a jar,
They encircled him when they smelled it.
He hurled his throw stick in the netherworld,   200
Those who had been killed by a throw stick encircled him.
He took up his staff in the netherworld,
The ghosts hovered around him.
He put shoes on his feet,
The netherworld raised a clamor.   205
He kissed his wife he loved,
He struck his wife he hated,
He kissed his son he loved,
He struck his son he hated.
The pleas of the netherworld seized him.   210
The one who lay there, the one who lay there,
The mother of the god Ninazu who lay there,
Her radiant shoulders were not clothed,
On her radiant bosom no linen garment was spread.
She clattered her fingernails like a drum,   215
She ripped out her hair like leeks.

[*Gilgamesh mourns Enkidu.*]

From that ill-omened day to the seventh day thereafter,
Enkidu did not ascend from the netherworld.
The king sobbed and wept bitterly:

My beloved servant, my faithful companion, the one who
    advised me, the netherworld has seized him.   220
The messenger of death did not seize him, the demon of
    disease did not seize him, the netherworld seized him.
The merciless agent of the plague god Nergal did not
    seize him, the netherworld seized him.
He did not fall in the place of manly battle, the netherworld
    seized him.

[*Gilgamesh seeks help from the god Enlil in the city of Nippur.*]

All alone the warrior Gilgamesh, son of the goddess Ninsun,
Made his way to Ekur, the house of the god Enlil.   225
Before the god Enlil he wept:

O father Enlil, my ball has fallen into the netherworld,
   my stick has fallen into hell.
Enkidu went to bring them back up and the netherworld
   seized him.
My beloved servant, my faithful companion, the one who
   advised me, the netherworld seized him.
The messenger of death did not seize him, the demon of
   disease did not seize him, the netherworld seized him.   230
The merciless agent of the plague god Nergal did not
   seize him, the netherworld seized him.
He did not fall in the place of manly battle, the netherworld
   seized him.

Father Enlil did not support him in that matter, he went to Ur.

[*Gilgamesh seeks help from the god Sin in the city of Ur.*][2]

All alone he made his way to the city of Ur, to the god Sin.
Before the god Sin he wept: 235

O father Sin, my ball has fallen into the netherworld, my
   stick has fallen into hell.
Enkidu went to bring them back up and the netherworld
   seized him.
My beloved servant, my faithful companion, the one who
   advised me, the netherworld seized him.
The messenger of death did not seize him, the demon of
   disease did not seize him, the netherworld seized him.
The merciless agent of the plague god Nergal did not
   seize him, the netherworld seized him.   240
He did not fall in the place of manly battle, the
   netherworld seized him.

Father Sin did not support him in that matter, he went to Eridu.

[*Gilgamesh seeks help from the god Enki in the city of Eridu.*]

All alone he made his way to Eridu, to the god Enki.
Before the god Enki he wept:

O father Enki, my ball has fallen into the netherworld, my
   stick has fallen into hell.   245
Enkidu went to bring them back up and the netherworld
   seized him.

2. This passage, lines 234–42, which is not found in the Sumerian version of the composition,
is restored according to the Akkadian translation.

My beloved servant, my faithful companion, the one who
    advised me, the netherworld seized him.
The messenger of death did not seize him, the demon of
    disease did not seize him, the netherworld seized him.
The merciless agent of the plague god Nergal did not
    seize him, the netherworld seized him.
He did not fall in the place of manly battle, the
    netherworld seized him.   250

Father Enki did support him in that matter.

[*Enkidu returns from the netherworld.*]

The god Enki spoke to Utu, the son of the goddess Ningal, the
    warrior, the youthful god:

    If you would just open a hole in the netherworld,
    You could bring his servant back up.

He opened a hole in the netherworld,   255
The spirit of Enkidu, like a phantom, he brought up out of the
    netherworld.
They embraced and kissed each other,
They wore each other out with questions.

[*Gilgamesh (G.) questions Enkidu (E.) about the netherworld.*]

    (G.) Did you see the way things are in the netherworld?
    (E.) If I tell you, my friend, if I tell you,   260
    If I tell you the way things are in the netherworld,
    You would sit down and weep, I would sit down and
        weep too.
    My body you once touched, in which you rejoiced,
    It will [never] come [back].
    It is infested with lice, like an old garment,   265
    It is filled with dust, like a crack (in parched ground).

"Woe is me!" cried the lord, and sat down in the dust.

    (G.) Did you see him who had one son?
    (E.) I saw him.
    (G.) How does he fare?   270
    (E.) He weeps bitterly at the peg driven into his wall.[3]

3. This shows his house has been sold.

(G.) Did you see him who had two sons?
(E.) I saw him.
(G.) How does he fare?
(E.) He sits on two bricks and eats bread.[4]   275

(G.) Did you see him who had three sons?
(E.) I saw him.
(G.) How does he fare?
(E.) He drinks water from a waterskin kept filled by a youth.

(G.) Did you see him who had four sons?   280
(E.) I saw him.
(G.) How does he fare?
(E.) He rejoices like a man hitching up a team of four asses.

(G.) Did you see him who had five sons?
(E.) I saw him.   285
(G.) How does he fare?
(E.) His hand is deft as a master scribe's, he enters the
    palace directly.

(G.) Did you see him who had six sons?
(E.) I saw him.
(G.) How does he fare?   290
(E.) He rejoices like a man hitching up his plow.

(G.) Did you see him who had seven sons?
(E.) I saw him.
(G.) How does he fare?
(E.) He sits on a throne with the lesser gods to hear legal
    proceedings.   295

(G.) Did you see him who has no heir?
(E.) I saw him.
(G.) How does he fare?
(E.) He eats bread hard as a kiln-baked brick.

(G.) Did you see the royal courtier?   300
(E.) I saw him.
(G.) How does he fare?
(E.) He leans in a corner, like a worn-out staff.

(G.) Did you see the woman who never gave birth?
(E.) I saw her.   305
(G.) How does she fare?

4. His two sons, symbolized by the bricks, maintain his funerary offerings.

(E.) She is discarded like a defective pot, no man takes pleasure in her.

(G.) Did you see the able-bodied young man who did not bare his wife's loins?
(E.) I saw him.
(G.) How does he fare?   310
(E.) He endlessly knots rope and you see him blubbering over it.[5]

(G.) Did you see the able-bodied young woman who did not bare her husband's loins?
(E.) I saw her.
(G.) How does she fare?
(E.) She endlessly plaits reeds and you see her blubbering over it.   315

[gap]

(G.) Did you see the leper?
(E.) I saw him.
(G.) How does he fare?
(E.) His food is separate, his drink is separate. He eats weeds he can snatch and drinks water he can snatch, he resides outside the city.

(G.) Did you see him who suffered from . . . ?   320
(E.) I saw him.
(E.) How does he fare?
(E.) He twitches like an ox as vermin bite him.

(G.) Did you see him who was devoured by a lion?
(E.) I saw him.   325
(E.) How does he fare?
(G.) Sorrowfully he wails, "Oh my hand! Oh my foot!"

(G.) Did you see him who fell from a roof?
(E.) I saw him.
(G.) How does he fare?   330
(E.) His shattered bones cannot . . .

(G.) Did you see him who was drowned by the storm god?
(E.) I saw him.
(G.) How does he fare?
(E.) He twitches like an ox as vermin bite him.   335

5. Because he never untied his wife's clothes, he is doomed to tie knots forever.

(G.) Did you see him who did not heed the words of his
   mother and father?
(E.) I saw him.
(G.) How does he fare?
(E.) He drinks water . . . but is never satiated.

(G.) Did you see him who was cursed by his mother and
   father?   340
(E.) I saw him.
(G.) How does he fare?
(E.) He has no heir. His spirit wanders.

(G.) Did you see him who fell in battle?
(E.) I saw him.   345
(G.) How does he fare?
(E.) His father and mother hold his head, while his wife
   weeps.

(G.) Did you see the ghost of him who has no one to
   make funerary offerings?
(E.) I saw him.
(G.) How does he fare?   350
(E.) He eats table scraps and bread crusts thrown into
   the street.

(G.) Did you seen him whom a ship's spar fell on(?)?
(E.) I saw him.
(G.) How does he fare?
(E.) "Alas!" he cries to his mother, as the pegs . . .   355

(G.) Did you see the little stillborn babies who knew not
   their own names?
(E.) I saw them.
(G.) How do they fare?
(E.) They play with honey and butter at tables of silver
   and gold.

(G.) Did you see him who was cut off in his prime?   360
(E.) I saw him.
(G.) How does he fare?
(E.) He lies on the bed of the gods.

(G.) Did you see him who died by fire?
(E.) I saw him.   365
(G.) How does he fare?
(E.) His ghost does not exist, it went up in smoke to
   the sky.

(G.) Did you see him who deceived a god and swore
        falsely?
(E.) I saw him.
(G.) How does he fare?   370
(E.) At the libation places for the dead in the
        netherworld . . .

(G.) Did you see the man of Girsu at the mourning
        place for his mother and father?
(E.) I saw him.
(G.) How does he fare?
(E.) He faces alone a thousand Amorites, his ghost cannot
        strike them, nor can he oppose them.   375
     The Amorite grabs a place ahead of him at the libation
     places for the dead in the netherworld.

(G.) Did you see the Sumerians and Akkadians?
(E.) I saw them.
(G.) How do they fare?
(E.) They drink filthy water at the field of carnage.   380

(G.) Did you see my mother and my father, wherever they
        dwelt there?
(E.) I saw them.
(G.) How do they fare?
(E.) The two of them drink filthy water at the field of
        carnage.

[gap]

[*Gilgamesh returns to Uruk.*]

. . .   385
They were returning to [Uruk],
They were returning to their city.
They put their equipment, armor, and war clubs in storage,
He celebrated in his palace.
The young men and women of Uruk, the patricians and
        gentlewomen of Kulaba,   390
Beheld their statues and rejoiced.[6]
When the god Utu came from his bedchamber, he turned
        towards him(?),
He said the ritual words(?):

     O my father, O my mother, drink this clear water!

6. These are apparently funerary statues of his parents.

The day was not half over and . . . , he removed his crown, 395
Gilgamesh prostrated himself at the place of mourning,
For seven days he prostrated himself at the place of mourning.
The young men and women of Uruk, the patricians and
gentlewomen of Kulaba wept.
He did what he said he would.
The man of Girsu followed his example: 400

O my father, O my mother, drink this clear water!

[Invocation.]

O warrior Gilgamesh, son of the goddess Ninsun, how
sweet it is to praise you!

The Death of Gilgamesh

Although the events related in the Sumerian poem "The Death of Gilgamesh" do not occur in the Akkadian epic, certain elements may be found in the account of the death of Enkidu in Tablets VII–VIII. The Sumerian poem begins with Gilgamesh lying mortally ill. He dreams that he is taken before the gods. There he learns that despite his heroic deeds and his mother's divinity, he cannot escape death. Once in the netherworld, Gilgamesh will enjoy special status as governor and will be numbered among the lesser gods. After he awakens, Gilgamesh tells his counselors what he dreamed.

In a vision, Gilgamesh then receives enigmatic instructions on where and how he should build his tomb. The royal dog solves the mystery. Gilgamesh calls up a work crew to divert the Euphrates in order to construct his tomb in the riverbed. His royal court assembles in the tomb, a practice attested in graves excavated at Ur, dating to the mid–third millennium B.C.E. After setting out gifts for the gods, Gilgamesh dies, perhaps by drinking poison. The people of Uruk let the river flow over the tomb so not a trace of it is visible. The poem ends with reflections on commemoration of the dead.

[Opening lament.]

The great bull has lain down, he will never get up again,
Lord Gilgamesh has lain down, he will never get up again,
He who was perfect has lain down, he will never get up again,
The warrior adorned with a shoulder belt has lain down, he will
never get up again,
He who was consummate in strength has lain down, he will
never get up again. 5

He who smote(?) evil has lain down, he will never get up again,
He who was champion boxer and wrestler has [lain down, he
    will never get up again],
He who spoke much wisdom has lain down, he will never get
    up again,
The raider of foreign lands has lain down, he will never get
    up again,
He who knew the way up into the mountain lands has lain
    down, he will never get up again,   10
The lord of Kulaba has lain down, he will never get up again,
He has lain down on his deathbed, he will never get up again,
He has lain down on a bed of sorrow, he will never get up
    again!

[*The narrative begins.*]

He could not stand, he could not sit, he whiled away the time
    in sighs,
He could not eat, he could not drink, he whiled away the time
    in sobs,   15
The demon Fate's door bolt had locked him in, he could not
    get up.
Like a fish harpooned in a pond, he lay immobile,
Like a gazelle caught in a snare, he tossed in bed.
The demon Fate, who has no hands, who has no feet, who
    kidnaps a man in the night,
The demon Fate has seized him.   20

[*gap*]

He lay [. . .],
The physician took [. . .] in hand,
Before heaven he held [. . .] the holy first-fruit offerings.
For six days Gilgamesh lay ill like a shattered pot,
Tears(?) flowed in rivulets over his body.   25
As lord Gilgamesh lay ill,
Uruk and Kulaba were agitated,
Report of his illness spread like a bitter . . . in the land.
As the young lord [lay] on his deathbed,
The king fell into a deep sleep (and dreamed):   30

[*The dream of Gilgamesh begins, with the gods talking about his exploits.*]

In that dream, the god, the lord Nudimmud, was bringing
    him(?) before them (the gods).
In the assembly, the ritual place of the gods,
As the lord Gilgamesh came near,

They were speaking about him, the lord Gilgamesh, about his
    fame,
They were talking of the campaigns he had waged: 35

> Bringing down that cedar, like no other, from the mountain,
> Smiting Huwawa in his forest,
> Erecting steles for now and forever,[1]
> Establishing the temples of the gods,
> Reaching Ziusudra in his abode,   40
> Resurrecting the forgotten, archaic and ancient rites of
>   Sumer,
> The ordinances and rituals of the land,
> Executing perfectly the rites of purification,
> Understanding everything of what was needful for the land,
>   from before the flood,

[gap]

[In his dream, the gods discuss Gilgamesh's fate.]

Then Gilgamesh was brought before them (the gods),   45
They relayed the god Enlil's counsel to the god Enki.
The god Enki replied to the gods An and Enlil:

> In those days, in those far-off days,
> In those nights, in those far-off nights,
> In those years, in those far-off years,   50
> After the assembly of gods let the flood sweep over the land
> To cause the human race to disappear,
> Among us a single solitary creature remained alive,
> Ziusudra, a human being, remained alive.
> From that day forth, we swore by the life of heaven and
>   the life of earth,   55
> From that day forth, we swore that no one of the human race
>   would live forever.
> Now Gilgamesh is brought before us.
> Despite the standing of his mother, we cannot spare
>   him (from death).

[Enki pronounces the destiny of Gilgamesh, in the dream.]

> Gilgamesh, as a ghost among the dead in the netherworld,
> Will act as governor of the netherworld, he will be the chief
>   of the shades,   60

---

1. A stele was an upright sculptured stone slab normally inscribed with a depiction of the king
and a god (or gods) on the top and a commemorative inscription on the bottom.

He will render decisions, he will decide legal cases,
His verdict will be as weighty as that of the gods Ningishzida
    and Dumuzi.

[*Gilgamesh's reaction, in his dream.*]

Then was the heart of the young lord, the lord Gilgamesh,
    troubled, realizing that human life must end.
His spirit was crushed, his heart was aggrieved.
When, in the future, the living commemorate the dead,   65
When the heroes and youths, at the appearance of the new
    moon . . . ,
For him, no longer there, there would be no light.
The dream god Sissig, son of the god Utu,
Would be his only light in the netherworld, the place of
    darkness.
Men, those who are remembered by name,   70
When, in the future, their mortuary statues are made,
When the heroes and youths "jump the threshold(?)"[2] at the
    appearance of the new moon,
Box and wrestle before them (the mortuary statues),
In the month of Ab, the festival of shades,
For him, no longer there, there would be no light.   75

[*The god Enlil addresses Gilgamesh, in his dream.*]

Great Mountain Enlil, father of the gods,
Spoke to lord Gilgamesh in the dream:

>   Gilgamesh, your fate was destined for kingship, it was not
>   destined for eternal life,
>   May your heart not sorrow that human life must end,
>   May your spirit not be crushed, may your heart not be
>   aggrieved.   80
>   The misfortune of mankind has come for you, so I have
>   decreed.
>   What was set at the cutting of your umbilical cord has come
>   for you, so I have decreed.
>   The darkest day of mankind has overtaken you,
>   The loneliest place of mankind has overtaken you,
>   The inexorable flood has overtaken you,   85
>   The struggle with no escape has overtaken you,
>   The unequal clash has overtaken you,
>   The fight with no reprieve has overtaken you.

2. Obscure, possibly an athletic event such as the broad or high jump.

Do not descend to the "Great City"[3] with your heart tied in
    knots,
May you call out, "Help me, Utu!"   90
May the knots unravel like the strands of a rope, may they
    be peeled away like an onion.
Go to the head of the funerary banquet where the Anunna
    gods, the great gods, are seated,
There where the high priest lies, there where the assistant
    priest lies,
There where the men and women lie who officiated for the
    gods,
There where the anointed priest lies, there where the
    linen-clad priestess lies,   95
There where the "god's sister" lies, there where the "faithful
    one" lies,
There where your father is, where your grandfather is,
There where your mother, sister, and favorite are,
There where your friend, confidant, and companion are,
There where your friend Enkidu, your comrade in battle, is,   100
In the "Great City" where governors and kings are
    summoned,
There where commanders of armies lie,
There where heads of battalions lie.
In the "Great City" of hell a man . . .
He who enters there . . .   105
From your sister's house, your sister will come towards you,
From your favorite's house, your favorite will come
    towards you,
Your confidant will come towards you, your most valued
    friend will come towards you,
The elders of your city will come towards you.
May your spirit not be crushed, may your heart not be
    aggrieved,   110
Now you will be reckoned as one of the Anunna gods,
You will be counted as one of the lesser gods.
You will act as governor of the netherworld,
You will render decisions, you will decide cases,
Your verdict will be as weighty as that of the gods
    Ningishzida and Dumuzi.   115

[*Gilgamesh wakes up and accepts his destiny.*]

Then the young lord, lord Gilgamesh, woke up, it had been a
    dream!
He shuddered, it had been a deep sleep!

3. A term for the netherworld.

He rubbed his eyes, all was deathly still.
The dream . . .
The dream . . .   120
[Gilgamesh, lord of] Kulaba,
[. . .], hero of the shining mountain,
[. . .] Uruk, the handiwork of the gods:

> By the life of the mother who bore me, the goddess Ninsun,
> And the father who begot me, the divine pure Lugalbanda,   125
> By my personal god Nudimmud,
> Shall I be such a baby as to want to sit on my mother
>   Ninsun's lap?
> My destiny Great Mountain Enlil has decreed,
> The demon Fate, who has no hands, who has no feet, who
>   kidnaps a man in the night, [has seized me].

[*Gilgamesh recounts his dream to his counselors.*]

The king recounted (the dream):   130

> In that dream, the god, the lord Nudimmud, was bringing
>   me before them (the gods).
> In the assembly, the ritual place of the gods,
> When I, the lord Gilgamesh, came near,
> They were speaking about me, the lord Gilgamesh, about
>   my fame,
> They were talking of the campaigns I had waged: 135
> "Bringing down that cedar, like no other, from the mountain,
> Smiting Huwawa in his forest,
> Erecting steles for now and forever,
> Establishing the temples of the gods,
> Reaching Ziusudra in his abode,   140
> Resurrecting the forgotten, archaic and ancient rites of
>   Sumer,
> The ordinances and rituals of the land,
> Executing perfectly the rites of purification,
> Understanding everything of what was needful for the land,
>   from before the flood,"

[*gap*]

[*Gilgamesh reports what he dreamed the great gods ordained for him.*]

> Then I, Gilgamesh, was brought before them (the gods),   145
> They relayed the god Enlil's counsel to the god Enki.

The god Enki replied to the gods An and Enlil:
"In those days, in those far-off days,
In those nights, in those far-off nights,
In those years, in those far-off years,   150
After the assembly of gods let the flood sweep over the land
To cause the human race to disappear,
Among us a single solitary creature remained alive,
Ziusudra, a human being, remained alive.
From that day forth, we swore by the life of heaven and the
    life of earth,   155
From that day forth, we swore that no one of the human
    race would live forever.
Now Gilgamesh is brought before us.
Despite the standing of his mother, we cannot spare him
    (from death).
Gilgamesh, as a ghost among the dead in the netherworld,
Will act as governor of the netherworld, he will be the
    chief of the shades,   160
He will render decisions, he will decide legal cases,
His verdict will be as weighty as that of the gods Ningishzida
    and Dumuzi."

[*Gilgamesh tells how he reacted in his dream.*]

Then was the heart of the young lord, of me, the lord
    Gilgamesh, troubled, realizing that human life must end.
My spirit was crushed, my heart was aggrieved.
When, in the future, the living commemorate the dead,   165
When the heroes and youths, at the appearance of the new
    moon . . . ,
For me, no longer there, there would be no light.
The dream god Sissig, son of the god Utu,
Would be my only light in the netherworld, the place of
    darkness.
Men, those who are remembered by name,   170
When, in the future, their mortuary statues are made,
When the heroes and youths "jump the threshold(?)" at the
    appearance of the new moon,
Box and wrestle before them (the mortuary statues),
In the month of Ab, the festival of shades,
For me, no longer there, there would be no light.   175

[*Gilgamesh reports what Enlil said to him, in his dream.*]

Great Mountain Enlil, father of the gods,
Spoke to me, the lord Gilgamesh, in the dream:

"Gilgamesh, your fate was destined for kingship, it was not
    destined for eternal life,
May your heart not sorrow that human life must end,
May your spirit not be crushed, may your heart not be
    aggrieved.   180
The misfortune of mankind has come for you, so I have
    decreed,
What was set at the cutting of your umbilical cord has come
    for you, so I have decreed.
The darkest day of mankind has overtaken you,
The loneliest place of mankind has overtaken you,
The inexorable flood has overtaken you,   185
The struggle with no escape has overtaken you,
The unequal clash has overtaken you,
The fight with no reprieve has overtaken you.
Do not descend to the 'Great City' with your heart tied in
    knots,
May you call out, 'Help me, Utu!'   190
May the knots unravel like the strands of a rope, may they
    be peeled away like an onion.
Go to the head of the funerary banquet where the Anunna
    gods, the great gods, are seated,
There where the high priest lies, there where the assistant
    priest lies,
There where the men and women lie who officiated for the
    gods,
There where the anointed priest lies, there where the
    linen-clad priestess lies,   195
There where the 'god's sister' lies, there where the 'faithful
    one' lies,
There where your father is, where your grandfather is,
There where your mother, sister, and favorite are,
There where your friend, confidant, and companion are,
There where your friend Enkidu, your comrade in battle, is,   200
In the 'Great City' where governors and kings are
    summoned,
There where commanders of armies lie,
There where heads of battalions lie,
In the 'Great City' of hell a man . . . ,
He who enters there . . .   205
From your sister's house, your sister will come towards you,
From your favorite's house, your favorite will come towards you,
Your confidant will come towards you, your most valued
    friend will come towards you,
The elders of your city will come towards you.
May your spirit not be crushed, may your heart not be
    aggrieved,   210

Now you will be reckoned as one of the Anunna gods,
You will be counted as one of the lesser gods,
You will act as governor of the netherworld,
You will render decisions, you will decide cases,
Your verdict will be as weighty as that of the gods
  Ningishzida and Dumuzi."   215

[*His counselors respond to Gilgamesh's report of his dream.*]

[After the young lord, the lord] Gilgamesh,
[The lord of Kulaba], had related that [dream],
[The counselors] to whom he had related it
Replied to him:

  [O Gilgamesh, why] do you weep?   220
  [. . .] and why . . .
  The birth goddess Nintu has never borne [a man
    whom the demon Fate has not] seized.
  Since the human race began,
  No [such man] has ever existed.
  A mighty man may be caught in a battle net,   225
  A bird of the sky, snared in a trap, cannot escape,
  A fish of the depths, seeing no reed haven,
  The young fisherman casts his net and catches it.
  No man whatsoever can go down to the netherworld and
    come back up again.
  From days of old, who ever saw the like?   230
  No other king has ever been decreed a fate like yours.
  Of men, those who are remembered by name,
  Where is he that . . . like you?
  You will act as governor of the netherworld,
  You will be chief of the shades.   235
  You will render decisions, [you will decide legal cases],
  [Your verdict will be as weighty as that of the gods
    Ningishzida and Dumuzi].

                          [*gap*]

[*Gilgamesh has had an enigmatic vision of where and how to build his tomb,
which the royal dog clarifies for him.*]

The solution of that vision was revealed,
As for that vision, it was the king's dog who explained it,
No human being explained it.   240

[*Gilgamesh diverts the Euphrates.*]

The lord issued a proclamation in his city,
The herald sounded the bugle in the land:

    O Uruk, mobilize! Open the Euphrates!
    O Kulaba, mobilize! Let the Euphrates flood![4]

Uruk mobilized like a torrent,   245
Kulaba mobilized like a persistent fog.
Not one month passed,
Not five, not ten days passed,
When the Euphrates was opened, its flood poured out,
So the shells in its bed gazed in wonder at the sun.   250
Then the Euphrates' main channel lay dry and cracked.

[*Gilgamesh builds his tomb in the riverbed.*]

He built that tomb of stone,
He built its walls of stone,
He set its doors in frames of stone,
The bolt and sill were diorite,   255
The pivot stones were diorite,
The roof beams were cast in gold.
At its . . . he dragged a massive block of stone,
At its . . . he dragged a massive block of stone.
He covered everything with black earth,   260
So that . . . in future days
No one could find it,
No searcher could find its sacred precinct.
[Thus did the young lord, lord] Gilgamesh,
Establish his vault within Uruk.   265

[*Gilgamesh's royal court is buried in his tomb.*]

His beloved wife, his beloved child,
His beloved second wife and concubine,
His beloved minstrel, cupbearer, and . . .
His beloved barber . . . ,
His beloved courtiers and palace retainers,   270
His beloved personal effects,
They were interred, like . . . , within Uruk.

[*Gilgamesh makes various offerings.*]

4. They breach the dikes along the main channel, letting the river flood out, and they block the main channel.

Gilgamesh, son of the goddess Ninsun,
Set out greeting gifts for the goddess Ereshkigal,
Set out presents for the divine demon Fate,   275
Set out marvels for the god Dimpiku,
Set out gifts for the god Bitti,
Set out gifts for the gods Ningishzida and Dumuzi,
For Enki and Ninki, Enmul and Ninmul,
For Endukuga and Nindukuga,   280
For Endashurima and Nindashurima,
For Enutila and Enmeshara,
The maternal and paternal ancestors of the god Enlil,
For Shulpa'e, master of the table,
For Shumuqan and Ninhursag,   285
For the Anunna gods of the Holy Mound,
For the Igigi gods of the Holy Mound,
For the dead high priest, for the dead assistant priest,
For the dead men and women who officiated for the gods,
For the dead anointed priest and the dead linen-clad priestess,   290
He set out greeting gifts.
He set out fine . . . ,
He set out their presents for . . .

[gap]

[Gilgamesh lies down, apparently takes poison, and dies.]

He lay down [on a bed] inlaid with [. . .],
Gilgamesh, son of the goddess Ninsun,   295
Where . . . , he poured out a potion(?) . . .

[gap]

[The people of Uruk return the Euphrates to its channel, covering the tomb, and carry out mourning rites for Gilgamesh.]

Then for the young lord, for the lord Gilgamesh,
They gnashed their teeth,
They tore out their hair.
The people of his city wore no . . . ,   300
They rubbed their . . . with dust.
Then for the young lord, for the lord Gilgamesh,
Their spirits were crushed, their hearts were aggrieved.

[The dead are remembered because of their descendants and their mortuary monuments.]

Men, those who are remembered by name,
Whose mortuary statues have been made since days of old,   305
Placed in shrines in the temples of the gods,
May their names be held in remembrance, never to be forgotten!
The birth goddess Aruru, great sister of the god Enlil,
Gave them children to sustain their names,
Their mortuary statues, made since days of old, proclaim their
    fame in the land.   310

[*Invocation.*]

O goddess Ereshkigal, mother of the god Ninazu, how sweet
    it is to praise you!

The Birth of Gilgamesh According to the Roman Historian Aelian

In his book *On the Characteristics of Animals*, the Roman historian
Aelian (c. 170–235 C.E.) tells a story of Gilgamesh being rescued as a
baby by a flying eagle. Some scholars have suggested that Aelian took
his story from Berossus, supposed to have been a Babylonian priest,
who wrote a history of Babylonia in Greek entitled *Babyloniaca* around
281 B.C.E.

The translation from the Greek given here is by A. Pietersma of the
University of Toronto; the accompanying notes are by D. Frayne.

Now a further characteristic of animals is love of human beings. For
instance an eagle reared a baby. But I want to tell you the whole tale,
in order to furnish evidence for what I have proposed. When Seuechoros was king of the Babylonians, the Chaldeans said that the child born
of his daughter would deprive his grandfather of his kingdom.[1] He was
frightened by this, and if I may put it that way in jest, he played Akrisios
to the girl,[2] for he kept watch over her most strictly, but secretly the
girl bore a child (for fate was more clever than the Babylonian), since
she had become pregnant by some obscure man. So the guards, out of
fear for the king, threw the child from the citadel, for there the afore-
mentioned girl had been imprisoned. Now when an eagle, due to its
keen sight, saw the child while still falling, it went beneath the infant

1. "Seuechoros" may be a corruption of Enmerkar, Gilgamesh's grandfather. "Chaldeans" was
   a general term for Babylonian astrologers in classical sources.
2. Akrisios was an ancient Greek king who, fearing a prophecy that his daughter would bear a
   son who would kill him, placed his daughter and her newborn baby (the hero Perseus) in a
   chest and sent them out to sea to perish.

before he was dashed to the ground, and put its back under him, brought him to some garden and put him down with utmost care. But when the guardian of the place saw the beautiful child, he fell in love with him and reared him. He was called Gilgamos and became king over the Babylonians.

The Hittite Gilgamesh

The tale of Gilgamesh was well known at Hattusha, capital of the Hittite empire, which dominated what is today central Turkey and northern Syria during the latter half of the second millennium B.C.E. Not only have archaeologists recovered from the city's ruins pieces of two different Akkadian-language versions of the epic, one of which has been used in this volume to fill a gap in the Babylonian text, but at least two Hurrian-language tablets dealing with Gilgamesh have also been found. Since these texts are badly preserved and Hurrian remains little understood, it is not yet possible to translate this material. For the most part the sources composed in the Indo-European Hittite language are also fragmentary. The translation from the Hittite that follows is based on a text reconstructed from approximately thirty tablet pieces, some of which are themselves made up of a number of yet smaller scraps. Another fifteen fragments remain unplaced and have not been included here.

The author of the Hittite Gilgamesh cycle has simplified what is known from the Mesopotamian sources, omitting many details. Little attention is paid to the city of Uruk, and none at all to its layout or fortifications. Characters such as Gilgamesh's parents and the father of the hunter have been eliminated. Of primary interest to the Hittite scribes was the expedition to the Cedar Forest, here called "the mountains of Huwawa." This is probably due to the supposed location of this fabled realm within the later Hittite domain. The third tablet treats Gilgamesh's grief at the death of Enkidu and his consequent wanderings in the world's wild regions. We learn that, as in the Babylonian epic, Gilgamesh visits an ancient hero now residing beyond the "waters of death," but neither the motivation for his quest nor its outcome are stated in the preserved lines.

Tablet I

[Although the writer begins by stating his intention to sing of the exploits of his hero, and one of the tablets is labeled "Song of Gilgamesh," the Hittite text is composed in prose, not poetry. In contrast to the Mesopotamian tradition, in which Gilgamesh is the son of a goddess and a king of Uruk, here

157

*he is specially created—not born—and endowed by the gods with great size
and outstanding qualities. Uruk is not his native city, but he takes up residence and rule there after a period of roaming the world. His bullying of the
city's young men and deflowering of its virgins lead the gods to bring Enkidu
into being as a counterweight to Gilgamesh and as a focus for his energies.
Enkidu first comes to the attention of Gilgamesh through the complaint of
a hunter whose activities he has frustrated in the interest of the animals that
had nurtured him in the wilderness.]*

§1 [Of Gilgamesh], the hero, [I will sing his praises . . .]

§2 The hero [Ea(?) fashioned] the frame of the creature Gilgamesh.
[The great gods] fashioned the frame of Gilgamesh. The Sun-god of
Heaven lent him [manliness]. The Storm-god lent him heroic qualities.
The great gods [created] Gilgamesh: His body was eleven yards [in
height]; his breast was nine [spans] in breadth; his . . . was three
[. . .] in length.

§3 He wandered around all the lands. He came to the city of Uruk
and he [settled] down. Then every day he overpowered the [young]
men of Uruk. And the Mother-goddess [. . .] Then she [. . .] in the
winds(?) of Gilgamesh. The Mother-goddess saw [. . .], and she [be-
came angry] in her heart [. . .]

§4 Then all the gods [summoned the Mother-goddess] over to [the
place] of assembly. She entered and [said], "This [Gilgamesh] whom
you created, and [whom] I created [. . .]—he [. . . I(?)] mixed in."
[And] all the [gods . . .] Gilgamesh, [the hero, . . . said, "Gilgamesh
is continually overpowering the young] men [of Uruk." When she]
heard this, then the Mother-[goddess] took the power of growth from
[the river(?)] and went off to create the hero Enkidu in the steppe.

§5 The hero Enkidu was in the steppe, [and] the wild beasts raised
[him. They made . . .] for him [. . .] And in whatever direction the
wild beasts went [for] grazing, Enkidu [went with] them. [In whatever
direction they went] for watering, Enkidu [went] with them.

§6 The [young] man Shangashu, [a hunter], used to prepare pits
[and traps in the steppe] for the wild beasts, [but Enkidu] went out
[before him] and kept stopping up [the pits with earth]. And he [kept
throwing] into the river [the traps which he had set]. Shangashu went
and spoke [to Gilgamesh], "A young man is going around before [me].
He possesses [. . .], and [he knows] the steppe. [He always stops up]
with earth the pits which I [prepare], and he [takes] up and keeps
throwing [into the river] the traps which [I have set]."

§7 Gilgamesh replied to Shangashu, [the hunter], "Lead out a harlot
[to him], so that he might sleep [with the harlot. Let Enkidu] kneel
[. . . !" . . . Then] Shangashu [led] the harlot [out to Enkidu. And he]
slept [with the harlot].

[*short gap*]

[*The prostitute, here named Shanhatu, meaning "whore," dresses Enkidu in fine clothes and suggests that they go into Uruk. She motivates him by telling of Gilgamesh's outrageous conduct.*]

§8 [. . . The harlot] spoke to Enkidu, [". . . to Uruk] let us go, and [. . ." . . .]

[*short gap*]

§9 [. . .] And Enkidu [. . .] had the festive [garments . . .] to him [. . .]

[*gap*]

§10 [Then Enkidu] replied [to Shanhatu], "Have you [. . .]?" And Shanhatu replied [to Enkidu], "Gilgamesh [. . .] they keep taking away. [When a woman] is given in marriage to a young man, before [her husband] has yet drawn near to her, [they] discreetly [take that woman] to Gilgamesh."

§11 [When] Enkidu heard this report, [anger] came over [him]. And Gilgamesh [. . .] back and forth [. . .] he went(?) [. . .] and [Enkidu said, ". . ." . . .] he grabbed [. . .]

[*short gap*]

[*Gilgamesh bests Enkidu in wrestling, and the pair immediately become friends. Sharing a meal, they decide to confront the monstrous Huwawa, whom Enkidu had seen during his time in the steppe. Gilgamesh informs the popular assembly of Uruk of this plan.*]

§12 [. . .] Gilgamesh [and Enkidu] grappled with one another, and Gilgamesh [. . . Enkidu] away. [Then] they [kissed(?)] one another. [And] when they had eaten and drunk, [then Gilgamesh] spoke to Enkidu, "Because the trees(?) have grown tall, [. . .] You wandered about [in the steppe(?) . . .] in the steppe(?)." Then Enkidu spoke [to Gilgamesh, ". . . Huwawa . . ." And Gilgamesh], the king, replied [to Enkidu, ". . .] in the future [. . . let us . . .]"

§13 The fighting men [of Uruk] gathered [to] Gilgamesh [. . .] They [. . .] And he prepared a feast, summoning all [the soldiers to the place of assembly. . . . Gilgamesh] spoke [to] the soldiers, "[. . .] I want to see Huwawa!"

[*gap*]

[*Gilgamesh and Enkidu trek to the mountain of cedars. On the way they cross the Mala River, the upper Euphrates or one of its tributaries. Once in the mountains, they are awestruck at the trees, the dense vegetation, and the forbidding terrain. After Gilgamesh finds evidence of the presence of Hu-wawa, Enkidu must fortify his comrade's resolve to continue their mission. Huwawa observes them secretly and realizes that the pair have come to carry off his cedars.*]

§14 [. . .] Gilgamesh [and Enkidu] went [to . . .] At twenty double leagues [they took a meal. At thirty] double leagues [they . . . And] when they [arrived] at the bank of the Mala River, they made an of-fering [to the gods]. And from there [. . .] in sixteen(?) days they arrived in the heart of the mountains.

§15 [And when] they arrived [. . .] in the heart of the mountains, they [. . .] the mountains and stared at the cedars. [And] Huwawa stared down [at them from . . . , saying to himself], "Seeing that [they have reached] the place of the god, have they finished [cutting down . . .] the god's cedars?" [Then Enkidu] and Gilgamesh said to one another, "[The deity . . . has . . .] these inhospitable mountains and has made the mountains thick [with cedars]. They are covered in bram-bles(?), [so that it is not possible for a mortal] to cross. [. . .] hold the [. . .] limbs of the cedars, and [they are] within the [evil(?)] mountains [. . .]" But [Huwawa] was watching them from [. . .] Huwawa [. . .] They kept striking [the . . .] like musicians.

§16 And when Gilgamesh saw the track [of Huwawa], then he came to [. . .] And [he . . .] it. Then Enkidu [said to Gilgamesh], "Why [. . .], and why against [him do you . . . ?] Won't [you] go down to [Huwawa . . . ? If] Huwawa [. . .] against me, then a man would [. . .] much. And if he [. . .], then he will [. . .] us. [. . .] by means of a heroic spirit [. . .]"

§17 [And] whoever [. . .] to them [. . .] Enkidu [. . .]

[*short gap*]

[*The adventurers begin to harvest timber and are encouraged by the Sun-god to attack the guardian of the forest before he can prepare himself. As battle is joined, Huwawa issues a threat to Gilgamesh and Enkidu but is unable to carry it out. The struggle raises a great cloud of dust, through which Gilgamesh can barely see the Sun-god. He appeals to the deity, pointing out that he is merely fulfilling a fate preordained when the Mother-goddess(?) sent Enkidu to Uruk. Gilgamesh also reminds the Sun-god that he had sought the god's approval before setting out on the quest. The god responds by sending eight winds to disable Huwawa. When the monster begs for mercy, Enkidu dissuades Gilgamesh from granting it.*]

§18 [Then Enkidu] took an axe in his hand [. . .] And when Gilgamesh saw [this], he too took an axe [. . . in his hand, and] he cut down the cedars. [But when Huwawa] heard the noise(?), anger came over him, "Who has come and cut down the cedars [which] have grown up for me [among] the mountains?"

§19 Then down from the sky the Sun-god of Heaven spoke to them, "Proceed! Have no fear! Go [in] while he has not yet entered the house, [has not yet . . .], and has not [yet donned(?)] his cloaks(?)." [When] Enkidu heard [this, rage] came [over him]. Enkidu and Gilgamesh went in against him and fought Huwawa in the mountains. [Huwawa] said to them, "[I will . . .] you up, and I will carry you up to heaven! I will smash you on the skull, and I will bring you [down] to the dark [earth]!" He [. . .] them up, but he [did] not [carry] them [up] to heaven. He [smashed] them on the skull, but he did not bring them down to the dark [earth. They grabbed] Huwawa, and by the hair they [. . .] in the mountains. [. . .] Then he [. . .] away their . . . They stuck the horses in . . . The dust clouds which were raised [were so thick] that heaven was not visible [. . .] Then Gilgamesh looked up at the [. . .] of the Sun-god of Heaven and cried out. He looked into the [. . .] of the Sun-god of Heaven, and his tears [flowed] like canals.

§20 Gilgamesh [said] to the Sun-god of Heaven, "This is the very day that in the city [. . .], because she(?) resettled [Enkidu(?)] in the city.

§21 "But I [prayed(?)] to the Sun-god of Heaven, and then I set out on my journey and fought [him]." The Sun-god] of Heaven heard Gilgamesh's appeal, and raised up(?) the great winds against Huwawa: the Strong Wind, the North Wind, [the . . . Wind, the . . . Wind], the Gale-force Wind, the Freezing Wind, [the Storm Wind], and the Destructive Wind. Eight winds blew up and battered [Huwawa] in the eyes so that he was unable to advance and unable to retreat. Then Huwawa gave up.

§22 Huwawa said to Gilgamesh, "Release me, O Gilgamesh! You shall be my lord and I shall be your slave. [Take(?)] the cedars which I have raised for you. I will fell the mighty [. . .] in [the . . .] And a palace [. . .]" Enkidu [said] to [Gilgamesh], "Don't [listen to the plea] which Huwawa [makes to you! . . .] Don't [release] Huwawa!" [. . . in] the mountains [. . .]

[short gap]

§23 [And] Enkidu answered [Gilgamesh], "[. . .] likewise [. . .] your, [Gilgamesh's, . . .] While [he has] not yet [entered the house(?) . . .]"

[short gap]

§24 [. . . mountains . . .] from the [mountains] of Huwawa
[. . .] they hold him down low.

Tablet II

*[Enkidu suggests that they placate the god Enlil, whom their exploits have
presumably angered, by taking cedar logs to his temple.]*

§1 [Enkidu] replied [to Gilgamesh], "[When(?)] we went [forth . . .]
to the mountains, [we . . .] What will we take back for [Enlil . . .]?
Should we really fell the cedars? Whoever [. . .] the gate of Enlil's
temple from one direction [. . .] They shut you out(?). Let them be
likewise!" [. . .] They felled the cedars and [arrived] at the Mala River.
And when the populace saw them (that is, the cedars), they rejoiced
over them. [. . .] Then Gilgamesh [and] Enkidu threw off their [filthy],
if splendid, garments and cleaned themselves up. [. . .] And to them
[. . . But] when [. . .]

[gap]

*[Gilgamesh offers to construct a fine palace for the goddess Ishtar, who is
more interested in taking the hero as a lover. His rejection of her overtures
has been lost, but an Akkadian text from Hattusha and several fragments
too scanty to be included here mention the Bull of Heaven, which she com-
mandeers to take her revenge.]*

§2 [Then Gilgamesh said] to Ishtar, "[I will build] a palace for you
[. . . It will be] . . . I will lay the threshold [of the gate with lapis
lazuli] and porphyry(?)."[1] [Ishtar] replied [to] Gilgamesh, "[Don't] you
know, O Gilgamesh, [that] there is no [. . .]? And for [it . . .] not
with silver [and gold(?)?" He replied, "I will lay] the threshold [of the
gate . . . with] lapis lazuli [and] porphyry(?)."

§3 [Ishtar replied] to Gilgamesh, "[Come], O Gilgamesh, [be] my
[husband . . . !]" Then Gilgamesh [replied to Ishtar, ". . .] let it
[become(?) . . .]"

Tablet III

*[After their return to Uruk, Enkidu has a troubling dream foretelling his
death as decreed by the gods in retribution for the murders of Huwawa and
the Bull of Heaven. Only the Sun-god, protector of Gilgamesh and Enkidu,*

1. A hard red rock with red and white crystalline inclusions.

speaks against this decision. Gilgamesh is distraught at the thought of losing his friend.]

§1 "[. . .] we will sleep." It dawned, [and] Enkidu said to Gilgamesh, "Oh my brother—the dream which [I saw] last night! Anu, Enlil, Ea, and the Sun-god of Heaven [were seated in council]. And Anu spoke before Enlil, 'Because they have killed the Bull of Heaven, [and because] they have killed Huwawa, who [made] the mountains thick with cedars'—so said Anu—'between them [one must die]!' And Enlil said, 'Enkidu shall die, but Gilgamesh shall not die!'

§2 "Then the Sun-god of Heaven responded to heroic Enlil, 'Didn't they kill them(!) at my(!) behest—the Bull of Heaven and Huwawa? And should innocent Enkidu now die?' Enlil became angry with the Sun-god of Heaven, 'Why do you accompany them daily like a comrade?' " [Enkidu] lay down to sleep before Gilgamesh, and his tears [flowed] forth like canals.

§3 He said, "Oh my brother, you are indeed my dear brother. I will [not] be brought up again to my brother from the netherworld. I will take my seat with the shades. [I will cross] the threshold of [the dead], and I will never [see] my dear brother again with my eyes!"

[*gap*]

§4 [. . .] announces [. . .] Afterwards he [becomes afraid(?)].

§5 But when Gilgamesh heard [the words of Enkidu], then [his tears flowed] forth like [canals . . .] His eyes [. . .]

[*gap*]

[*Reacting to the sight of his dead comrade, Gilgamesh recites a proverb, which seems to mean that it is sometimes necessary to flee a bad situation. Gilgamesh sets out into the wilderness, where he kills many wild beasts, including two lions.*]

§6 While for him the city of Itiha [. . .] he threw off. But when he saw [Enkidu(?) . . .], then Gilgamesh [. . .] He ran off into the mountains, and he [. . .] wailed without cease, "[Whenever] they [must eat(?)] chaff, a woman will [go] forth from the house." [Then] Gilgamesh did likewise. He [abandoned(?)] the land, [and] he departed from the country. He roamed the mountains continually. [No] mortal [knows] the mountains which [he crossed or the rivers] which he forded.

§7 [And] he slew many wild beasts: the wild cow, [the . . .] he [. . .] But when he [arrived] in the heart of the mountains, he [slew] two . . . lions. [And] Gilgamesh arrived in the heart of the mountains [. . .] a bird [. . .]

[*gap*]

[*Gilgamesh arrives at the seashore, where he greets the personified Sea with a blessing upon him and his retainers. For unknown reasons the Sea responds with a curse upon Gilgamesh and the Fates.*]

§8 [And] he wandered around(?) [. . . He didn't say] anything. [. . .] . . . away.

§9 But [when] Gilgamesh [arrived] at the Sea, he bowed down to the Sea, [and said to the Sea], "Long may you live, O Great [Sea, and long may] the minions who belong [to you] live!" The Sea cursed Gilgamesh, [. . .], and the Fate-deities.

§10 [. . .] the sea [. . .] beside [the sea . . .] afterwards [. . .] with his hand(?) [. . .]

[*gap*]

[*The Moon-god demands that Gilgamesh render the lions he had killed earlier into images for his temple. Gilgamesh visits the barmaid Siduri, but the text of their conversation has been lost.*]

§11 [. . .] the hero Moon-god [said to Gilgamesh], "Go and [make] these two [lions] which you slew into two images for me! Transport them into the city! Go and take them to the temple of the Moon-god!"

§12 But at dawn Gilgamesh, like [. . .] . . . When he arrived at [. . .], Siduri the barmaid was seated upon [a golden stool], and a vat of gold [stood before her . . .]

[*short gap*]

[*Gilgamesh argues with Ur-Shanabi about crossing the sea. The boatman informs him that this had been possible only with the aid of the stone images, which according to Mesopotamian sources, Gilgamesh had destroyed. Ur-Shanabi instructs Gilgamesh to cut long punting poles for the voyage. This accomplished, the two of them traverse the sea in a month and a half.*]

§13 [. . .] someone [. . . ". . .] you cross [. . ." Thus said Gilgamesh] to Ur-Shanabi, "[. . .] You are the one who crosses it every day and every night." Thus said Ur-Shanabi, "Those two stone images used to bring me across!" Thus said Gilgamesh, "Why are you quarreling with me?" And Gilgamesh [. . . Ur-Shanabi] replied, "[. . .] your [. . .] up to you [. . .] before [. . .] I planted." [. . .] with wood, down [. . .] they ate. And Ur-Shanabi replied to Gilgamesh the king, "What [is this], O Gilgamesh? Will you go [across] the sea? What will you do when you come to the waters of death? Take an axe in your hand [and cut] poles of forty or fifty yards."

§14 And when Gilgamesh heard the words of Ur-Shanabi, he [took] an axe in his hand and cut poles of fifty yards. He stripped and [trimmed(?)] them and placed them up on the boat. Then both of them, Gilgamesh and Ur-Shanabi, [went] up into the boat. Ur-Shanabi took the rudder(?) in his hand, [while] Gilgamesh <took>² [the poles] in his hand. Their journey lasted one month and fifteen days.

[*The remaining text is too fragmentary for translation. The mutilated final portion of Tablet III mentions Ullu, whose name means literally "the Distant One." This is certainly the same figure as the primordial hero Utanapishtim, who bears the epithet "Distant One" in the Babylonian text. Unfortunately, too little is preserved for us to reconstruct the course of the story here. None of the extant Hittite-language Gilgamesh material deals with the deluge, with the protagonist's contest with sleep, with his receipt and loss of the plant of rejuvenation, or with his final return to Uruk.*]

2. Angle brackets enclose material erroneously omitted by the scribe.

The Gilgamesh Letter

Mesopotamian schoolchildren during the first millennium B.C.E. enjoyed this humorous parody of Tablet VIII of the Gilgamesh epic. The person the letter is addressed to is unknown.

Say to Ti[. . .], king of [. . .]ranunna, thus says [Gilgamesh, k]ing of Ur, the Kulabian, created by Anu, [Enlil], and Ea, favorite of Shamash, beloved of Marduk,[1] who rules all lands from the horizon to the zenith like a cord [. . .], whose feet daised monarchs kiss, the king who has put all lands, from sunrise to sunset, under control, as with a cord, this [according to the com]mand of Enlil-of-Victory:

[I have formed up] and sent you 600 work-troops. I wrote to you concerning the great [blocks] of obsidian and lapis, overlaid with finest gold, to attach to the [stat]ue of my friend, Enkidu, but you said, "There are none."

Now I write to you once again! As soon as you see this letter, [make re]ady and go to the land of Erish, take with you a caravan of horses, send ahead of you(?) [   ] vicious dogs that attack like lions, [. . .] white horses with black stripes, 70,000 black horses with white stripes, 100,000 mares whose bodies have markings like wild tree roots, 40,000 continually gambolling miniature calves, 50,000 teams of dappled mules, 50,000 fine calves with well-turned hooves and horns intact, 20,000 jars of pitch(?), 30,000 jars of ghee, 80,000 jugs of wine, 80,000 bundles of crocuses, 90,000 great tabletops of dark rosewood, 100,000 donkeys laden with cedar and juniper, and then come yourself.

I want to fasten one nugget of red gold, it should weigh 30 minas, to the chest of my friend Enkidu. I want to fashion [. . .] thousand . . . -stones, jasper(?)-stones, lapis, every sort of exotic stone into a necklace for him.

40,000 (ingots) of unalloyed(?) white tin for the treasury of the great lord Marduk, 90,000 talents of iron: pure, excellent, choice, select, scrutinized, precious, first-rate, beaten, flawless, so the smith can make stags.

120,000 talents of pure, good [copper?], with all the goods required, the smith will do work for the temple.

---

1. Marduk was the national god of Babylon and had nothing to do with Gilgamesh.

A new chest, unique, something precious, exotic, such as I have never seen. Look for myriad troops [to bri]ng them, ready or not(?), and gather them together. Fill big new barges(?) with silver and gold and float them down to the Euphrates with the silver and gold. You should send(?) them to the port of Babylon so I can see for myself and be struck dumb with awe.

· If I don't meet you in the gate of my city Ur on the fifteenth day of the seventh month, then I swear by the great gods, whose oath cannot be done away with, and I swear by my gods Lugalbanda, Sin, Shamash, Palil, Lugalgirra, Meslamtaea, Zababa,[2] and (my personal?) god that I will send my lord "Attacker-in-My-Vanguard"(?), whose fame you always hear about, and he will wreck your cities, loot your palaces, uproot your orchards, and put wickets(?) in your canal mouths. I(?) will enter the . . . of your fortified cities, who . . . and speak of its . . . , and I, Gilgamesh, will occupy them. None of this will be my fault.

[I will . . .] your servants, your gener[al], your craftsmen(?), your children, your belongings, and your offspring [. . .] in the gate of Ur. I will bring you and your family(?) into the smithy to . . . talents of copper for twelve . . . I will write an inscription. I will set you up with the (statues of) protective spirits in the thoroughfare, [the citizens] of Ur will lord it over (you) as they go by.

Quickly send me an an[swer to my letter] and come, you will not have to bear anything from me.

Letter of Gilgamesh, the mighty king, who has no rival.

---

2. This list includes little-known Sumerian gods for an antique effect, as well as Gilgamesh's father.

CRITICISM

WILLIAM MORAN

The Gilgamesh Epic: A Masterpiece from Ancient Mesopotamia†

Gilgamesh is overwhelming . . . and I consider it the greatest thing one can experience. From time to time I tell its story to this one and that one, the whole story—and every time I have the most astonished listeners. The synthesis of [G.] Burckhardt [author of a free translation of the epic] is not altogether happy; it doesn't achieve the greatness and significance [of the epic]. I feel I tell the story better. It has meaning for me. It involves me.

(Letter of Rainer Maria Rilke
to Katherine Kippenberg, 11 December 1916)

The Sumerian Background

According to Sumerian tradition, Gilgamesh (originally Bilgamesh)[1] was an early ruler in the city-state of Uruk (Warka, biblical Erech). The evidence, admittedly meager and indirect, puts him there around 2700 BCE, a period of intense intercity rivalries. Nothing is known of his actual achievements in this setting except perhaps what is reflected in the later tradition of Gilgamesh as heroic warrior and the builder of his city's walls. Not very long after his death, Gilgamesh appears in a god-list.

The memory of Gilgamesh lived on in the oral tradition of the Sumerians, especially at the court of Uruk, where he became the subject of heroic tales. How early these tales, and how many of them, may have been committed to writing is not known. The earliest compositions we have probably do not go back beyond the late third millennium. By that time, Gilgamesh had become a very popular figure, especially among the rulers of the Third Dynasty of Ur. As befits a hero, he has a distinguished parentage. His father, Lugalbanda, was another divinized ruler of Uruk, and his mother was the goddess Ninsun.

Gilgamesh is celebrated in a number of works, which in view of their length (115–450 lines) are perhaps better called lays rather than epics.[2] These lays contain themes and tales that would later reappear in the Babylonian epic. In one lay, Gilgamesh, accompanied by Enkidu and other retainers, in order to achieve the immortality that comes with heroic deeds, sets out to confront the monster Khuwawa in the Cedar

---

† From *Civilizations of The Ancient Near East*, Volume IV, pp. 2327–36. Edited by Jack M. Sasson. Reprinted by permission of The Gale Group.
1. Moran refers to a spelling in Sumerian [*Editor*].
2. By "lay" Moran means a simple narrative poem or ballad, less elaborate than an epic [*Editor*].

Forest. In another, Gilgamesh is the oppressor of Uruk, and Enkidu is trapped in, and must remain in, the underworld. In another, for reasons that are not clear, the goddess Inanna (Akkadian Ishtar) sends the Bull of Heaven against Gilgamesh. In yet another version, Gilgamesh protests against his mortality. While these are all independent compositions, they do manifest a certain unity. Death—the fear of death, everlasting fame as victory over death, life after death—is a common theme and distinctive of the late Sumerian Gilgamesh tradition. * * *

The Old Babylonian Version

Sometime early in the second millennium the various Gilgamesh traditions, Sumerian and perhaps Akkadian, oral or written, were sorted out, adapted, and profoundly transformed into either a single composition, which seems more probable, or a two-part cycle. This earlier version of the *Epic of Gilgamesh* has come to be known as the Old Babylonian Version. Though preserved only in fragments, it is clearly a work of great originality. Written in the Babylonian dialect of Akkadian and not a mere translation from the Sumerian, it is poetry of remarkable freshness and simplicity. Its thousand or more lines, like Homer's *Odyssey*, are unified around a central character and a single pervasive theme—the hero's quest for immortality.

With occasional reliance on the later Standard Version, we can reconstruct the narrative line. After a brief hymn in praise of the hero, we are introduced to a Gilgamesh who, driven by his superhuman energies and powerful ambitions, has by his excessive and relentless demands on his people become their oppressor. In answer to the people's prayers, the gods create a match for Gilgamesh, someone of comparable strength, to refocus his energies and ambitions. This is Enkidu. They become friends, and soon Gilgamesh conceives a project that will bring him the immortality of undying fame, a battle with Khuwawa. Thus begins the journey to the Cedar Forest, the confrontation, and the victory.

The characterization of Enkidu here is new, but the Khuwawa adventure, with Enkidu a participant, is based on an earlier, Sumerian tradition. The Old Babylonian Version then goes its own, original way. Enkidu dies, undoubtedly as divine punishment for his part in the slaying of Khuwawa. This is one innovation, and another follows. Gilgamesh, confronted now with death in the person of a beloved friend, becomes consumed with grief and is suddenly riven with fear. Faced with the reality of death, he will now be content only with true immortality, the immortality reserved to the gods. Thus begins another journey, this one to the end of the world to find the lone exception to human mortality—Ut-napishtim (Old Babylonian Uta-napishtim, Sumerian Ziusudra), the Babylonian Noah, the one survivor, along with his family, of the Flood.

After a long journey full of harrowing experiences, Gilgamesh finally reaches Ut-napishtim, at which point the reconstruction of the narrative becomes only partial at best. We still do not know exactly how the Old Babylonian Version ended. Certainly Gilgamesh failed in his quest for divine immortality and learned that his death was inevitable. But how did he react to this discovery? Did he return to Uruk, frustrated and embittered, a broken and tragic figure? Or did he, as in the later Standard Version (see below), recover some sense of purpose, of human goals, and of the satisfaction of human achievements? At present, these are questions for which there are no sure answers.

This long narrative seems to pivot on three seven-day periods, each of which is associated with a profound transformation, first of the non-human into the human, then of the human into the nonhuman, and finally of the nonhuman back into the human. These transformations are associated with corresponding rites of passage, especially those of cleansing and clothing. The underlying theme of evolution is evidently germane to a work that studies someone trying to come to terms with his humanity.

The first transformation is that of Enkidu. The Old Babylonian Enkidu is utterly different from the Sumerian Enkidu. As created by the gods, he is a savage, hairy wild man who lives on the steppe with the animals and acts as their friend. As described, he may ultimately reflect the myth and representations, dating as far back as the early third millennium, of the Bull-Man who fights the Naked Hero. More immediately, however, Enkidu is modeled on a concept of antiprimitivism found elsewhere in Sumerian, Babylonian, and classical sources. According to this notion, the beginning of human existence was neither a golden age nor a period of pristine simplicity. On the contrary, life was savage, and man differed little, if at all, from other animals. Primal man was a beast, and the Babylonian Enkidu was primal man *redivivus*,[3] a figure who introduced into the epic a sharp nature-culture contrast that became a recurrent theme.

The humanization of Enkidu begins with seven days of uninterrupted lovemaking with a harlot sent into the steppe to seduce him. In one of the most amusing and lighthearted passages in Babylonian literature, the humanization proceeds as Enkidu is bathed, anointed, clothed, and then introduced to human fare—bread and beer. He drinks seven kegs of beer and breaks into song. At this point, he is introduced to shepherds, transitional figures who are, by definition, at

---

3. Moran uses here a Christian Latin term that means "who lives again," normally referring to Jesus, but used here in the sense of "revived" or "brought to life again" [*Editor*].

the outer edge of human society and urban life. Enkidu's humanization is complete when, having entered Uruk, he finally kneels in submission before Gilgamesh and acknowledges his kingship, the institution that in the Mesopotamian worldview was the sole guarantee of the guided, the ordered, the fully human life. Now fully human, Enkidu can become the friend of Gilgamesh, and the story can move into what we may call its heroic phase.

The second transformation occurs when, for seven days and seven nights, Gilgamesh grieves over the body of his dead friend, "until a maggot dropped from his nose." His friend gone, Gilgamesh refuses to end his grief or to put away the signs of grief. He does not wash; he puts on no fresh clothes. He will not be reintegrated into human society. Instead, his body covered with grime and wrapped in animal skins, he departs into the steppe. The transformation is radical. He who once voiced so eloquently the heroic ideal—declaring his contempt for death and chiding Enkidu for fearing it as long as there was the prospect of dying gloriously and unforgettably—now utterly rejects that ideal and all the values associated with it. Gilgamesh the hero is dead. Gilgamesh, the anti-man, the would-be god, appears.

The last seven-day period and last transformation, is reconstructed from the Standard Version. In view of the evidence for other, smaller periods of transformation in the Old Babylonian Version, however, it seems virtually certain that the Standard Version reflects the earlier tradition. To prove to Gilgamesh that he does not have the stuff of immortality, Ut-napishtim challenges him to stay awake for seven days. Gilgamesh accepts the challenge and immediately falls asleep—for seven days. Awakened and confronted with the facts, he finally yields, and in evidence of his inner transformation and of his at least grudging acceptance of his mortality, he allows himself to be bathed. His animal skins are cast off and carried away by the sea, and with a new cloak to cover him, Gilgamesh accepts his humanity.

Diffusion, Expansion, and Establishment of the Text

In the centuries that followed, knowledge of the epic spread into Anatolia, Syria, and Palestine. Fragments of the *Epic of Gilgamesh* both in the Babylonian language and in Hittite and Hurrian adaptations have been found, and they date to the fourteenth and thirteenth centuries BCE. They establish the existence of a text that followed the Old Babylonian story at least in broad outline, but they also include what was probably material unknown to the earlier version, most notably Ishtar's sexual advances to Gilgamesh and the slaying of the Bull of Heaven. In other words, almost the entire narrative of the later Standard Version seems to be in place. At times, the language of the text is quite close to that of the older version; at others, it is closer to the language of the

Standard Version; at still others, it goes its own way. A stable story and a fluid text exist well into the late second millennium.

The Standard Version

Late in the second millennium Babylonian literature took on more or less stable forms. The text of the *Epic of Gilgamesh* seems to have been established around this time. Tradition credits this edition to a poet-editor by the name of Sin-leqe-unninni. * * * The text is known mainly from copies of the seventh century in the Nineveh library of the Assyrian king Assurbanipal, but substantial parts have also been found at other sites—Sultantepe, Nimrud (modern Kalkhu), Asshur (modern Qalat Sharqat), Babylon, Uruk—and in copies as late as the first century BCE. Known as the Standard Version—the existence of competing versions is doubtful—it was originally a work of about three thousand lines, traditionally distributed over eleven tablets; a twelfth tablet, a kind of appendix, was a later addition. At present, we possess about three-fifths of the original.

PROLOGUE

The Standard Version begins by repeating and expanding the prologue of the Old Babylonian Version. Line 27 (in the Kovacs translation quoted herein)[4] has been identified as the first line of the latter; thus, lines 1–26 are a later addition, probably from the hand of Sin-leqe-unninni, and are meant to guide our understanding of the narrative that follows.

The earlier prologue, which perhaps contains later additions but certainly nothing dissonant, is a hymn to the unique strength, dignity, and kingship of Gilgamesh. He is first presented as a giant: "He was bigger than (all other) kings, in stature most renowned." (In the Hittite version, he was eleven cubits tall.) The text then goes on, for twenty lines, presenting origins that make him partly divine, his leadership, and his distant journeys. He is mighty, and his deeds are mighty.

How different the Gilgamesh of lines 1–26. In sharp contrast with the earlier hymn, this Gilgamesh suffers and is worn out: "He came back from a long journey and was weary." The feats celebrated in the hymn all become simply "wearying toil," and lest we forget this, just as we are about to begin the celebratory hymn, we are reminded that "Gilgamesh every hardship bore." This is another Gilgamesh, a more human Gilgamesh, a Gilgamesh who, however great his strength and however splendid his achievements, had to pay the price. Behind this expression of admiration are values different from those inspiring the ancient hymn.

4. Maureen Gallery Kovacs, *The Epic of Gilgamesh* (Stanford: Stanford UP, 1989) [*Editor*].

Even more than the hero's sufferings, these opening lines stress his vast experience, knowledge, and wisdom. The very first words introduce Gilgamesh as "The one who saw all." Moreover, he was "possessed (?) of wisdom" and

> Secret things he saw, hidden ones revealed.
> Knowledge brought of days before the Flood.
> (1.5–6)

Here again the later poet-editor complements and refocuses the hymn that follows. The earlier hero's long journeys are seen simply as feats of strength. Here they become sources of knowledge. Here, too, the hero is not only strong but wise, possessed of a quality of mind in the experiential and practical order that is a guide to action in all its manifold forms. This Gilgamesh not only has *emūqān*, physical strength, but *nēmēqu*, wisdom. In short, he is a complete king, something the earlier text did not make clear.

To prove his point and to illustrate this *nēmēqu*, the poet-editor addresses his reader. (It is important to note that the prologue addresses a second participant. The author is not a singer or a reciter but a writer, and his audience is not a group listening to him, but individuals, readers with tablet in hand.) The reader's attention is directed to one of Gilgamesh's most famous achievements, the great walls of Uruk and its renowned temple of the goddess Ishtar, "the like of which no king, no man, will ever build":

> Go up on the walls and walk about.
> Examine the terrace and study the brickwork,
> If its brickwork be not all of baked bricks,
> Its foundations not laid by the Seven Sages.
> One *sar* city, one *sar* orchards, one *sar* pasture and
>   pond—and the fallow fields of Ishtar's house—
> Three *sar* and fallow fields—Uruk you will see [?].
> (1.17–22)

Here is a work of Gilgamesh's *nēmēqu*, conspicuous and resplendent, begun indeed with the assistance of the great and most ancient Seven Sages.

Before turning to the walls of Uruk, the poet-editor tells us two more important things about Gilgamesh. The first is that he is not just weary; he is "weary but at peace." This is a Gilgamesh who contrasts vividly with the Gilgamesh of the older narrative following. The earlier figure is totally unfamiliar with peace. His energies consume him, and he drives everyone around him to exhaustion. His heart is ascribed the wildness of a storm-demon, and even his mother complains of her son's "restless heart." All his projects, whether in Uruk or on his long campaigns and journeys, bespeak anything but peace. Whence, then, this peaceful if weary man?

We are also told that Gilgamesh left a record of his labors: "From a far journey he returned, was weary but at peace. On stone chiseled each wearying toil." The walls having been celebrated, we—still readers, still alone—are told this (some uncertainty attaches to the translation of the beginning of some of these lines):

> Find the copper chest.
> Remove the locks of bronze.
> Open the cover to the treasure there.
> Take up and read diligently the tablet of lapis lazuli,
> How he, Gilgamesh, every hardship bore.
>
> (1.22–26)

There can be little doubt that the inscription chiseled on stone must be identified with the lapis lazuli tablet we are now instructed to read so diligently. In context, it does not seem likely that the two are distinct. Moreover, there is other evidence that kings were supposed to leave records of their labors and deposit them in chests (see below). Note, too, how strongly *kalû mānaḫti*, "each wearying toil," is echoed in sound and sense by what we are now told to read about on the tablet, *kalû marṣāti*, "every hardship" borne by Gilgamesh.

The object on which Gilgamesh writes is called a *narû*, often a "stela," freestanding and on public display, like the Code of Hammurabi stela.[5] * * * But if the *narû* here is identical with the tablet, it is not a stela. Moreover, it lies in a chest, probably in the room of some temple (see below). By implying that the source for the following narrative—and certainly this is implied—was the text inscribed by Gilgamesh himself and by inviting the reader to a comparision with the original, the poet-editor undoubtedly wishes to authenticate his tale. But the text implies more. It implies a particular approach to, and understanding of, the epic.

Babylonian literature possessed a genre known as "pseudo-autobiography," which is characterized by its didacticism. The best-preserved example is very instructive for the interpretation of the prologue. It is called *The Legend of Naram-Sin*, and it is attested in both an Old Babylonian and a later form. * * * In the latter, we find Naram-Sin, the famous king of Akkad, in the broken first line advising the reader to "read diligently the *narû*." It is, moreover, now virtually certain that the break should be restored to read "open the chest." The text that follows is badly broken. Speaking in the first person, Naram-Sin tells about some fabulous bird-men, and the narrative concludes with his

---

5. Moran refers to stone monuments set up by Mesopotamian kings to commemorate their deeds [*Editor*].

reporting an oracle he says he received from Ishtar. The king then addresses the reader:

> Whosoever you may be, whether governor or prince or anyone else,
> Whom the gods shall call to rule over a kingdom,
> I have made for you a chest and inscribed for you a *narû*,
> And in the city of Cuthah, in the temple Emeslam,
> In the chamber of the god Nergal, deposited it for you.
> Find this *narû* and listen to what this *narû* says, and then . . .
>
> (1.147–152)

There follows a long exhortation that reflects the oracle of Ishtar just reported.

The parallels to the prologue are obvious: the address to the reader, the chest, the *narû* within, the command to read it diligently. The parallels from a kind of didactic literature fit perfectly with the Gilgamesh we are first introduced to, the man of *nēmēqu*.[6] Moreover, as most modern interpreters of the epic have stressed, the epic is a kind of bildungsroman,[7] the story of Gilgamesh's education and progress to maturity. It is, in its way, a lesson. In alluding to Gilgamesh's autobiography as his source, the author has thus given us final and formal guidance on how we are to read what follows. We are to read, tablet in hand, quietly, reflectively, intent on learning what the life of Gilgamesh has to teach us. What follows is *narû*-epic, epic in a new key, epic in "the key of wisdom."

TABLETS 1.52–2: GILGAMESH AND ENKIDU

Where preserved, the text follows the Old Babylonian narrative rather closely, but with considerable amplification: Gilgamesh the oppressor; the creation and humanization of Enkidu; his confrontation with Gilgamesh in Uruk; their friendship; Gilgamesh's proposal to fight Khuwawa, now called Khumbaba.

TABLETS 3–4: THE KHUMBABA ADVENTURE

In broad outline, but again with expansions, some now of folkloristic origin, the text follows the old story. The role assigned to Shamash is an innovation, but probably not of the late edition. Counselor and protector in the Old Babylonian Version, he is presented in the Standard Version as the instigator of the whole enterprise. Ninsun charges him with having "touched" her son and set him on his way to Khumbaba, and Khumbaba himself holds Shamash as ultimately responsible

---

6. Akkadian word for "wisdom" [*Editor*].
7. This is a literary term that refers to a novel that shows how a character develops and matures [*Editor*].

for his plight. Later, too, at least according to the Hittite version, when it is decided by the gods that the slaying of Khuwawa and the Bull of Heaven may not go unpunished, Shamash protests, though in vain, that Gilgamesh and Enkidu have only acted on his orders. What may lie behind this apparent conflict between Shamash and the other gods is not clear; a mythic dimension of the text eludes us here.

The Standard Version also enlarges and elevates the purpose of the journey; "Until he [Gilgamesh] slays the fierce Khumbaba. / And makes perish from the land every evil that you [Shamash] hate." No longer is the sole consideration that lasting glory of Gilgamesh. Shamash has his own motive, be it to destroy all moral evil or everything baneful. It seems a loftier view of the whole enterprise and one quite consonant with the didacticism of the late edition. The alleged Old Babylonian parallel is quite uncertain.

Also new and shocking is the manifest hubris of the two companions. As they face Khumbaba, Enkidu speaks of having to contend with the anger of the gods for what they are about to do, but he does not hesitate to urge Gilgamesh to kill. They seem to think that making a great cedar door and bringing it back to Nippur (Nuffar) will placate the gods. As the two heroes head back in apparent triumph, the fifth tablet finishes with a very strong sense of foreboding that the Khumbaba story is not over. The foreboding is only reinforced by the next series of events.

TABLET 6: ISHTAR AND THE BULL OF HEAVEN

Back in Uruk, bathed and decked out in all his finery, Gilgamesh catches the eye of Ishtar, who, smitten by his charms, offers to take him in marriage. Gilgamesh not only rejects her offer but pours out on her a stream of insults. Scorned and enraged, the goddess persuades her father, Anu, to unleash against Gilgamesh the Bull of Heaven only to have Gilgamesh and Enkidu slaughter the Bull, empty its innards, and lay them before Shamash. Ascending the city wall to look down on the scene below, Ishtar "took a stance of mourning, uttered a loud wail, / 'Woe to Gilgamesh, who has insulted me, killed the Bull of Heaven.' " On hearing her, Enkidu tears off the Bull's haunch and hurls it at her as he screams, "Oh that I could reach you and make you just like him."

Whether Tablet 6 serves as a polemic against the ancient institution of the sacred marriage, king and priestess uniting symbolically as god and goddess, remains uncertain, but the context of the Gilgamesh narrative certainly establishes hubris as a quality that makes divine retribution inevitable. There is something undeniably terrifying about the figure of the great goddess standing high on the wall over her city and crying "Woe to Gilgamesh." The gods are not mocked.

TABLETS 7–8: THE DEATH OF ENKIDU

That very night, after a great banquet in celebration of the heroes' return, Enkidu has a dream wherein he learns (here we are briefly dependent on the Hittite version) that the gods have decided he must die while Gilgamesh is to be spared. His resentment is deep and bitter, and he is full of curses for the great door, for the trapper who brought the harlot to him, and for the harlot herself, all of them responsible in some way for his imminent death. Reproached by Shamash for forgetting the blessings of civilized life and the friendship of Gilgamesh that the harlot had led him to, Enkidu relents and blesses her. Thus does the epic celebrate once more culture over nature. Enkidu also has a terrifying dream about life in the underworld. Finally, he falls sick, lingers on for twelve days, and dies. Stricken with grief, Gilgamesh recalls at length their many adventures together, buries his friend after a week of mourning, erects a statue in his honor—and is transformed.

TABLETS 9–10: THE GREAT JOURNEY

The journey to Ut-napishtim leads Gilgamesh through a strange and awesome world. He meets the Scorpion-Man and his wife, who try to dissuade him from going on; but on he goes, on and on under the earth, surrounded by darkness, emerging into a garden of trees loaded with jewels. He has left all that is human, all that is of this world. He reaches a tavern keeper named Siduri, who tries to dissuade him, but eventually she directs him to Urshanabi, Ut-napishtim's boatman, who can bring him across the Waters of Death to his master.

The Ut-napishtim whom he reaches is for Gilgamesh a bitter disappointment. Unlike the superman he had imagined. Ut-napishtim is quite ordinary. But he is also a sage and he chides Gilgamesh with the question "What have you gained?" He is full of brief sayings on the frailty of man "snapped off like a reed," on the transitory nature of whatever man does, and above all, on death—invisible, faceless, silent, certain. And finally he explains that, after the Flood,

> After Ellil had pronounced my blessing [of immortality],
> The Anunnaki gods being assembled,
> Mammetum, creatress of destiny, with them decreed the destinies.
> They established death and life.
> The days of death they did not define.
>
> (10.305–309)

In this meeting, for the first time, the gods made death part of the established order of things. Later—originally, probably in the next line—Ut-napishtim asks rhetorically. "Now who is going to assemble the gods for you?" Obviously, no one. Gilgamesh has journeyed in vain.

TABLET 11: THE FLOOD STORY: CONVERSION AND JOURNEY HOME

It is generally conceded that the Flood was not part of the original epic, which may have referred to it, but only briefly. The long account in Tablet 11 seems to be told for its own sake. It seriously interrupts not only the flow of dialogue between Ut-napishtim and Gilgamesh but the otherwise smooth and natural transition from the end of Tablet 10, where Ut-napishtim tells Gilgamesh about the assembly of the gods after the Flood, to Ut-napishtim's rhetorical question. Finally, the story as told here is not an independent account; it draws on an identifiable source, the myth of Atrakhasis.[8]

It is also generally conceded that the one who added the story was the poet-editor of the prologue. He has a manifest interest in, and esteem for, "the knowledge of days before the Flood" that Gilgamesh brought back. He also speaks in the prologue of the secret things revealed by Gilgamesh but with only two formally identified, one of them the Flood Story. If the poet-editor was not the one who added the story, he certainly directs his reader to it and implies its importance.

In the learned world of Sin-leqe-unninni, the Flood Story is certainly important in that it is knowledge that, were it not for Gilgamesh, would have been lost. And it is not just any knowledge. It is knowledge about the most terrible event in human history. It is knowledge about a terrible truth: the gods can destroy and one may never know why. A wise man, Gilgamesh, should know this.

Another essential truth is revealed in the episode of the Plant of Rejuvenation. Convinced finally by his week-long sleep that he must die, Gilgamesh, as already noted, yields, accepts his mortality, and allows himself to be bathed and clothed in fresh garments. He is ready to return to Uruk. Before he is gone for good, Ut-napishtim and his wife, wishing to give him some reward for his labors, tell him of the Plant of Rejuvenation. It can make him young again, and its existence is identified as the second matter of secret knowledge. Gilgamesh secures the plant, but, returning to Uruk accompanied by Urshanabi, he sets it down as he plunges into the cool waters of a pool, only to watch helplessly as a serpent makes off with it, sloughing off its skin as it goes.

Here Gilgamesh is betrayed simply by his humanity, its frailty and its limitations. Weeping, he delivers his final judgment on his journey across the Waters of Death to the end of the world. He says quite simply, "I should have turned back." He sees now the radical impropriety of the whole enterprise: one should attempt neither to escape death nor even to cheat it. A wise man, Gilgamesh, should know this too.

The story does not end here. Gilgamesh and the boatman push on

---

8. A Babylonian poem about the creation of the human race and the coming of the flood; see *Muses*, pp. 160–85 [*Editor*].

to Uruk, and the language echoes the earlier journey to the Cedar
Forest. We are being drawn back to the memory of earlier events. And,
finally, on their arrival Gilgamesh addresses the boatman:

> Go up on the walls and walk about.
> Examine the terrace and study the brickwork,
> If its brickwork be not all of baked bricks,
> Its foundations not laid by the Seven Sages.
> One *sar* city, one *sar* orchards, one *sar* pasture and pond—
>   and fallow fields of Ishtar's house—
> Three *sar* and fallow fields . . .

(11.314–319)

These are the last words of the epic, and we have come full circle.
We hear again the words of the prologue that were addressed to the
reader, and we have a sense of finality and completeness. We began in
Uruk, and we end there. In this new context, however, after all that has
gone before, the solid, material nature of it all—walls and measure-
ments and topography—tells us, and tells us forcibly, that Gilgamesh is
back from a world of jeweled trees and monsters and regions not meant
for man. He returns to a definable, measurable, human world, a world
indeed made by man. And Gilgamesh, pointing to this man-made
world of Uruk, suggests an intuitive if inarticulate perception that the
work proper to man and his destiny is to build, to create a world of his
own, as well as to die. This perception gives meaning to life and makes
whole the wisdom of Gilgamesh: "From a far journey he returned, was
weary but at peace."

TABLET 12: APPENDIX

Tablet 12 is a literal translation of part of the Sumerian composition
Gilgamesh, Enkidu, and the Netherworld, and it is certainly a later but
not an altogether happy addition, destroying the narrative symmetry of
the earlier eleven-tablet work. Nor are the motives for the addition clear.
Since Enkidu instructs Gilgamesh on the life of various classes of people in the netherworld, it has been suggested that merely by questioning
Enkidu, Gilgamesh implies his readiness to accept his role in the next
life as god and king of the netherworld. And there have been other
proposals, none convincing.

With the end of cuneiform civilization,[9] Gilgamesh was not com-
pletely forgotten. At Qumran, site of the discovery of the famous Dead
Sea Scrolls, in the apocryphal literature associated with the biblical
patriarch Enoch, he appears as one of the giants along with the monster
Khumbaba, who is also found in the Manichaean *Book of the Giants.*

9. Moran means the civilization that used cuneiform writing (writing composed of wedge-shaped
characters), hence, "Mesopotamian" [*Editor*].

Later, in his *On the Characteristics of Animals,* Aelian (circa 175–230 CE) recounts a curious tale about a Gilgamos who became king of Babylon. In the seventh century CE, the scholiast Theodore bar Konai, writing in Syriac, mentions among ancient kings a certain Gmigmos (Gmengos, Glimgos) as a contemporary of Abraham.

Whether (and if so, to what extent) the epic itself may have survived in various transformations remains a matter of discussion. The arguments for influence on works such as the *Alexander Romance,* originally a Greek composition of the fourth century CE, and on the journeys of Buluqiya in the *Arabian Nights* seem the most plausible.

THORKILD JACOBSEN

"And Death the Journey's End": The Gilgamesh Epic†

* * *

Gilgamesh, as far as one can judge, was a historical figure, the ruler of the city of Uruk (the biblical Erekh) around 2600 B.C. It stands to reason that stories about him would have been current long after his death, but they only become graspable to us around 2100 B.C. when they were taken up by the court poets of the Third Dynasty of Ur. The kings of that dynasty counted Gilgamesh as their ancestor. We possess a number of short epical compositions in Sumerian, the originals of which must date to that revival of interest, but the Gilgamesh Epic proper, with which we are here concerned, dates from around 1600 B.C., at the end of the Old Babylonian period, and was composed in Akkadian. Strictly speaking, we should perhaps not say the "epic" but the "contours of the epic," since what we have of Old Babylonian date are fragments, and may represent only separate songs of a loosely-connected Gilgamesh cycle. These fragments do, however, cover all the essential—largely internally dependent—episodes that make up the tale in its later version. This version, made probably toward the end of the second millennium by one Sîn-liqi-unninnî, is preserved for the most part in copies from around 600 B.C. from the famous library of Ashurbanipal in Nineveh.[1] It contains much that is extraneous to the tale, and it lacks the freshness and vigor of the Old Babylonian fragments. In our retelling of the story here we shall therefore quote the older fragments whenever possible.

† From *The Treasures of Darkness: A History of Mesopotamian Religion,* pp. 195–219. Yale University Press, 1976. Reprinted by permission of the publisher. All but one of the author's notes have been omitted.
1. Ashurbanipal was an Assyrian king of the seventh century B.C.E. who caused many Mesopotamian literary and scholarly works to be collected and copied for his library [*Editor*].

The Story

The story begins in the high style of "romantic epic," by introducing the hero to us. As the *Odyssey* begins with a characterization of Odysseus:

> Tell me, Muse, of that man, so ready at need,
> who wandered far and wide, . . .
> and many were the men whose towns he saw and whose minds he learnt.
> yea, and many the woes he suffered in his heart upon the deep,
> striving to win his own life and the return of his company . . .

so the Gilgamesh Epic opens with lines calculated to whet the listener's interest in its hero as a man who has had strange and stirring experiences and who has seen far-off regions:

> He who saw all, throughout the length of the land
> came to know the seas, experienced all things. . . .

But there is a special note to the Gilgamesh Epic introduction not found in the *Odyssey*, a stress on something beyond mere unusual, individual experience, a focus rather on lasting tangible achievements, typified by the walls of Uruk, still extant, still a cause for wonder when the introduction was written:

> He built the town wall of Uruk, (city) of sheepfolds,
> of the sacred precinct Eanna, the holy storehouse.
> Look at its wall with its frieze like bronze!
> Gaze at its bastions, which none can equal!
> Take the stone stairs that are from times of old,
> approach Eanna, the seat of Ishtar,
> the like of which no later king—no man—will ever make.
> Go up on the wall of Uruk, walk around,
> examine the terrace, look closely at the brickwork:
> Is not the base of its brickwork of baked brick?
> Have not seven masters laid its foundations?

From our first meeting with the young Gilgamesh he is characterized by tremendous vigor and energy. As ruler of Uruk he throws himself into his task with zeal. He maintains a constant military alert, calls his companions away from their games, and harasses the young men of the town to the point where it gets black before their eyes and they faint from weariness, and he leaves them no time for their families and sweethearts.

The people of Uruk are understandably not very happy at this, and they begin to pester the gods with complaints and entreaties to do something about it. The gods divine with remarkable insight what is at the root of the trouble: Gilgamesh's superior energy and strength set him apart and make him lonely. He needs a friend, someone who measures up to him and can give him companionship on his own extraordinary level of potential and aspiration. So they call the creator Aruru and ask her to create a counterpart of Gilgamesh:

> You, Aruru, created the wild bull (Gilgamesh)
> now create his image, in stormy heart let it equal Gilgamesh,
> let them vie with each other, and Uruk have peace.

Aruru forms a mental image of the god of heaven as a model, washes her hands, pinches off clay, throws it down in the desert, and thus creates Enkidu.

Enkidu is, as it were, man in a state of nature. He is enormously strong, goes naked, and hair covers all of his body; his locks are long like a woman's and grow as luxuriantly as grain. He knows nothing about the country and people but roams with the gazelles in the desert, eating grass and slaking his thirst in the evening with the animals at the drinking places. As their friend he helps protect them by filling in pits dug to catch them and destroying traps set for them. This brings him into contact with man. A trapper in the neighborhood finds his livelihood severely threatened by Enkidu's actions, but since Enkidu is so big and strong, there is nothing he can do. Dejected, he goes home to his father and tells about the newcomer and how he prevents him from carrying on his trade. The trapper's father advises him to go to Gilgamesh in Uruk and ask for a harlot who will go along and try to seduce Enkidu away from his animals. The trapper makes his way to Uruk and appeals to Gilgamesh. Gilgamesh listens to his story and tells him to take along a harlot to use her wiles on Enkidu.

So the trapper finds a harlot and together they walk out into the desert, until, on the third day they reach the watering place where Enkidu likes to come with the animals, and here they sit down to wait. One day passes, then a second, and on the third Enkidu and the animals appear and go down to drink. The trapper points Enkidu out to the harlot and urges her to take off her clothes and try to attract Enkidu's attention. In this she is eminently successful. For six days and seven nights Enkidu enjoys himself with her, oblivious to everything else. When at last satisfied, after the seventh night, he wants to go back to his animals. But they shy away. He runs after them, only to find that he no longer has his old power and speed and can no longer keep up with them.

In part, of course, that may be simply because he is by then a bit tired; but almost certainly the author of the story saw more in it. Something magical and decisive has happened. The easy, natural sympathy that exists between children and animals had been Enkidu's as long as he was a child, sexually innocent. Once he has known a woman he has made his choice, from then on he belongs to the human race, and the animals fear him and cannot silently communicate with him as they could before. Slowly, Enkidu comprehends some of this. "He grew up," says the author, "and his understanding broadened."

So Enkidu gives up trying to catch up with the animals and returns to the harlot, who is very kind to him, saying:

> I look at you Enkidu, you are like a god!
> Why do you roam
> the desert with animals?
> Come, let me lead you
> into Uruk of the wide streets,
> to the holy temple, the dwelling of Anu,
> Enkidu, rise, let me take you
> to Eanna, the dwelling of Anu,
> where Gilgamesh is administering the rites.
> You could do them too, instead of him, installing yourself!

This speech pleases Enkidu, and he takes her suggestions very much to heart. She then undresses, clothes him in the first of her garments, herself in the second, and, holding him by the hand, leads him through the desert until they come to a shepherd's camp where they are kindly and hospitably received. Here Enkidu has his first meeting with civilization and its complications. The shepherds set food and drink before him, something he has never seen before.

> He was wont to suck
> the milk of the wild beasts only;
> they set bread before him.
> He squirmed, he looked,
> and he stared.
> Enkidu knew not
> how to eat bread,
> had not been taught
> how to drink beer.
> The harlot opened her mouth
> and said to Enkidu:
> "Eat the bread, Enkidu,
> it is the staff of life!
> Drink the beer, it is the custom of the land!"
> Enkidu ate bread,
> until he was full up,
> drank beer—
> seven kegs—
> he relaxed, cheered up,
> his insides felt good,
> his face glowed.
> He washed with water

his hairy body,
rubbed himself with oil,
and became a man.
He put on a garment,
was like a young noble.
He took his weapon
and fought off the lions,
and the shepherds slept at night.

For some days Enkidu stays with the shepherds. One day, however, as he is sitting with the harlot, he sees a man hurrying by and asks the harlot to bring the man to him that he may hear why he has come. The man explains that he is bringing wedding cake to Uruk, where Gilgamesh is about to be married.[2] This upsets Enkidu: he grows pale, and immediately sets out for Uruk with the harlot. Their arrival creates a stir. The people gather around them gaping at Enkidu, noting his tremendous strength and stature. He is slightly shorter than Gilgamesh but equally as strong.

As they admire him, Gilgamesh approaches with his nuptial procession, going to the house of his father-in-law for his wedding, but as he nears the door Enkidu bars the way and does not let him in to his bride. The two seize each other, fighting like young bulls, destroying the threshold and shaking the walls. Eventually, Enkidu gains the upper hand, and Gilgamesh sinks down on one knee; but as the defeated Gilgamesh subsides and turns his back, Enkidu speaks to him—not gloatingly as a victor, but full of admiration and respect:

Matchless your mother
bore you,
the wild cow of the corral
Ninsûna,
raised above men is your head,
kingship over the people
Enlil assigned to you!

Enkidu's magnanimity wins Gilgamesh's heart, and out of their battle grows a lasting friendship. Gilgamesh takes Enkidu by the hand, leads him home to his mother, and she accepts Enkidu as a son, a brother for Gilgamesh.

Thus all problems are solved. Enkidu is happy in Uruk, Gilgamesh has found a friend but—as so often—the happiness does not last. In his new life Enkidu is going soft. The hardness of his muscles is disap-

---

2. In this and other passages, Jacobsen's interpretation and translation of *The Epic of Gilgamesh* differ from those found in this Norton Critical Edition. His proposals have been considered, along with many others, but have not been accepted by the translator for various reasons [*Editor*].

pearing; he feels flabby, out of condition, no longer fit as in the old days in the desert. Gilgamesh comes upon him one day weeping and instantly divines what to do. What they both need is a good strenuous expedition with lots of hardship and high adventure. They ought, he proposes, to set out together to kill a terrible monster called Huwawa, who lives far away in the cedar forest in the west.

Much as Enkidu may deplore the loss of his old hardihood, this way of regaining it seems rather more than he bargained for. For while Gilgamesh has only heard of Huwawa, Enkidu has actually seen him in the days he was roaming the desert, and he has acquired a healthy respect for him:

> Huwawa, his roar is a floodstorm,
> his mouth very fire,
> his breath death.
> Why do you want
> to do this?
> An irresistible onrush
> is the trampling of Huwawa!

But Gilgamesh is not to be dissuaded. He chides Enkidu for lack of courage and shames him into going along. They have mighty weapons forged for them, take leave of the elders of the town, who give them much paternal advice about how to travel, and say goodbye to Gilgamesh's mother.

Their trip is told in great detail, and we especially hear of Gilgamesh's dreams, all of which are terrifying warnings of disaster. But Enkidu is headstrong and with unconscious impiety interprets every one of them to mean that they will overcome Huwawa. The section of the story that deals with their actual encounter with Huwawa is unfortunately badly preserved in all the versions we have, but it seems clear that in one way or other Huwawa loses out, begs for his life, which Gilgamesh is inclined to spare, and is eventually killed at Enkidu's insistence. The most complete account of the episode we have is earlier than the epic, a Sumerian tale which probably was among the sources that the author of the epic had at his disposal. It tells how Gilgamesh at first succumbs to the terror encompassing Huwawa and is unable to move. From that perilous situation he saves himself by pretending to Huwawa that he has not come to fight him but to get to know the mountains where he lives and to offer him his older sister as wife and his younger sister as handmaiden. Huwawa is taken in, divesting himself of his armor of rays of terror. Thus defenseless, he is set upon by Gilgamesh, who smites and subdues him. Huwawa pleads for his life and Gilgamesh—as a gentleman—is inclined to spare him, until Enkidu, with a peasant's distrust, speaks thus:

"The tallest who has no judgment
Namtar (death) swallows up, Namtar who acknowledges no
    (excuses).
Letting the captured bird go home,
the captured lad return to his mother's lap,
you will never make it back to your (own) city and mother who
    bore you."

Huwawa, furious at this interference, cuttingly asks whether Enkidu, "a hireling who, to the detriment of the food supply, walks behind his companions," is thus to put him in the wrong, at which Enkidu, stung by the insult, cuts off Huwawa's head.

When Gilgamesh and Enkidu return to Uruk—we are now back with the epic—Gilgamesh washes the grime of battle and travel off his body and dresses in fresh clothes. Thus arrayed he is so attractive that the goddess of Uruk herself, Ishtar, becomes enamored of him and proposes marriage: If he will become her husband she will give him a chariot of gold and lapis lazuli, kings will kneel before him, his goats will have triplets, his sheep twins. Gilgamesh though, will have none of it and seems to rather panic at the thought. Instead of quietly and calmly refusing, he heaps insults upon her: she is an unfinished door which does not keep out wind and drafts, pitch that dirties the one who carries it, a water skin which leaks on the one who carries it, a shoe that pinches the foot of its owner, and so on. Worse yet, all her previous lovers have come to a bad end. There was Dumuzi, or Tammuz, the love of her youth, for whom she instituted laments year after year. There was the varicolored bird she loved, only to break its wing so that it now runs round in the forests and cries "kappee! kappee!" ("my wing! my wing!"). There was the lion, for which she dug pits, and the war-horse, for which she destined whip and spurs. There was the shepherd whom she loved and then turned into a wolf so that his own dogs set upon him, and there was her father's gardener, Ishullānu, who came to grief at her hand when he refused her advances.

At this catalogue of her shortcomings, Ishtar—never very patient—rushes to her father, Anu, the god of heaven, tells him that Gilgamesh has insulted her, and begs him to let her have the "bull of heaven" to kill him. Anu is not eager to comply, suggesting that probably Ishtar herself has invited the scolding, but Ishtar is so incensed that she threatens to break the gates of the netherworld and let the dead up to eat the living if Anu does not let her have her way. Anu points out that the bull of heaven is such a destructive animal that, if let loose, there will be seven years of famine. But Ishtar assures him that she has stored enough grain and hay for man and beast for seven years, and in the end, Anu gives in to her.

As Ishtar takes the bull of heaven down to Uruk it shows itself a

terrible threat. Its first snort blows a hole in the ground into which fall
a hundred men, its second traps two hundred more. But Gilgamesh
and Enkidu prove old hands at handling cattle. Enkidu gets behind the
bull and twists its tail—an old cowboy trick—while Gilgamesh like a
matador plunges his sword into the neck of the bull.

The death of the bull of heaven shocks Ishtar. She mounts the city
wall, treads a mourning measure,[3] and curses Gilgamesh. At this Enkidu tears off a hind leg of the bull and hurls it up at her, shouting:
"You! Could I but get at you I would make you like unto it." Ishtar
and her women set up a wail over the shank of the bull, while Gilgamesh calls together the craftsmen so that they can admire the size of
the bull's horns before he presents them as a votive offering to his
father, the god Lugalbanda. Then he and Enkidu wash themselves in
the Euphrates and return to Uruk in triumph. The entire population
of the city come out to gaze at them and Gilgamesh exultantly sings
out to the maids of the palace: "Who is noblest of youths? / Who,
most renowned of swains?" and they answer: "Gilgamesh is noblest of
youths! / Enkidu most renowned of swains!"

At this point in the story the two friends stand at the pinnacle of
power and fame. They have killed the terrible Huwawa in the remote
and inaccessible cedar forest, in their arrogance they have treated a
great goddess with disdain, and in killing the bull of heaven they have
proved they could get the better of her. There seems to be nothing they
cannot do.

Now, however, things begin to catch up with them. Huwawa was
appointed guardian of the cedar forest by Enlil, and in killing him
Gilgamesh and Enkidu have incurred Enlil's anger. In a dream that
night Enkidu sees the gods assembled to pass judgment on him and
Gilgamesh for killing Huwawa. Enlil demands the death penalty but
the sun god—god of fairness and moderation—intercedes and is able to
save Gilgamesh. Enkidu, however, perhaps as the more palpably guilty
one, has to die. And so Enkidu falls ill. Horror-stricken at what he
knows is happening to him, he wishes he had never come to Uruk and
curses the trapper and the harlot who brought him. The sun god, again
speaking up for fairness, points out to Enkidu how much he has gained
in his new life of luxury with Gilgamesh for a friend, and Enkidu then
balances the harlot's curse with a long blessing. But, reconciled or not,
Enkidu is doomed and dies.

Up to this point, it will have been noted, Gilgamesh has lived by the
heroic values of his times. Death was a part of the scheme of things,
so, since you had to die anyway, let it be a glorious death in battle with
a worthy foe so that your name and fame would live. Thus, when he

3. Jacobsen thinks that Tablet VI, line 150 refers to a dance of mourning [Editor].

proposed their venturing against Huwawa to Enkidu, and Enkidu
proved reluctant, he sternly upbraided his friend in just such terms:

> Who, my friend, was ever so high (that he could)
> rise up to heaven and lastingly dwell with Shamash?
> Mere man, his days are numbered,
> whatever he may do, he is but wind.
> You are—already now—afraid of death.
> What about the fine strength of your courage?
> Let me lead,
> and you (hanging back) can call out to me: "Close in, fear not!"
> And if I fall I shall have founded fame
> "Gilgamesh fell (they will say) in combat with terrible Huwawa."

He goes on imagining how in later years his children will climb on
Enkidu's knee, and how Enkidu will then tell them how bravely their
father fought and what a glorious death he died.

But all of this was when death was known to Gilgamesh only in the
abstract. Now, with the death of Enkidu, it touches him in all its stark
reality, and Gilgamesh refuses to believe it:

> My friend, the swift mule, the wild ass of the mountain, the
>   panther of the plain.
> Enkidu, my friend, the swift mule, the wild ass of the
>   mountain, the panther of the plain,
> who with me could do all, who climbed the crags,
> seized, killed the bull of heaven,
> undid Huwawa dwelling in the cedar forest,
> now—what sleep is this that seized you?
> You have grown dark and cannot hear me!
> But he was not raising his eyes.
> (Gilgamesh) touched his heart, it was not beating.
> Then he covered the face of his friend, as if he were a
>   bride . . .
> Like an eagle he was circling around him;
> as does a lioness when (returning and) meeting its whelps,
> he kept circling in front and back of his friend;
> tearing the while his hair and scattering the tufts,
> stripping and flinging down the finery off his body.

The loss he has suffered is unbearable. He refuses with all his soul to
accept it as real:

> He who ever went through all hazards with me,
> Enkidu whom I love dearly,
> who ever went through all hazards with me,
> the fate of man has overtaken him.
> All day and night have I wept over him,

and would not have him buried—
as if my friend might yet rise up at my (loud) cries—
for seven days and nights,
until a maggot dropped from his nose.
Since he is gone I can no comfort find,
keep roaming like a hunter in the plains.

Death, fear of death, has become an obsession with Gilgamesh. He can think of nothing else; the thought that he himself must die haunts him day and night and leaves him no peace. He has heard about an ancestor of his, Utanapishtim, who gained eternal life and now lives far away at the ends of the world. He decides to go to him to learn the secret of immortality.

So Gilgamesh sets out on his quest. It takes him through the known world to the mountains where the sun sets in the West. The gate the sun enters is guarded by a huge scorpion man and his wife, but when Gilgamesh tells them of Enkidu's death and his quest for life, they take pity on him and let him enter the tunnel into the mountains through which the sun travels by night. For twelve double miles, then, Gilgamesh makes his way through the dark tunnel: only as he nears the gate of sunrise at the other end does he feel the wind on his face then at last sees the daylight ahead. At the gate of sunrise is a wondrous garden in which the trees bear jewels and precious stones as fruits, but its riches hold no temptation for Gilgamesh whose heart is set on one thing only, not to die. Beyond the gate lie vast deserts over which Gilgamesh roams, supporting himself by killing wild bulls, eating their flesh, and dressing in their skin. To get water he digs wells where wells never were before. Without any goal he follows the prevailing winds. Shamash, the sun god—always the soul of moderation—becomes vexed at seeing him thus, and he reasons with Gilgamesh from the sky. But Gilgamesh will not listen to reason, he just wants to live:

Is it (so) much—after wandering and roaming around in the
    desert—
to lie down to rest in the bowels of the earth?
I have lain down to sleep full many a time all the(se) years!
(No!) Let my eyes see the sun and let me sate myself with
    daylight!
Is darkness far off? How much daylight is there?
When may a dead man ever see the sun's splendor?

Roaming thus, Gilgamesh eventually comes to the shore of the sea that encircles the earth and here he finds an inn kept by an alewife. His unkempt looks and hide clothing frighten the alewife and she hastens to lock her door, thinking him a bandit. As Gilgamesh comes close, however, he tells her who he is and speaks of Enkidu who died and of his own quest for eternal life, the secret of which he hopes to learn from Utanapishtim. The alewife—as had Shamash—sees the hopelessness of his quest and tries to dissuade him:

> Gilgamesh, whither are you roaming?
> Life, which you look for, you shall never find.
> (For) when the gods created man, they set
> death as share for man, and life
> snatched away in their own hands.
> You, Gilgamesh, fill your belly,
> day and night make merry,
> daily hold a festival,
> dance and make music day and night.
> And wear fresh clothes,
> and wash your head and bathe.
> Look at the child that is holding your hand,
> and let your wife delight in your embrace.
> These things alone are the concern of man.

But Gilgamesh cannot be reached:

> Why, my (good) alewife, do you talk thus?
> My heart is sick for my friend.
> Why, my (good) alewife, do you talk thus?
> My heart is sick for Enkidu!

and he asks her to tell him the way to Utanapishtim. She does so. The boatman of Utanapishtim, Urshanabi, happens to be on the mainland to cut timber, perhaps he will let Gilgamesh cross over with him. Gilgamesh finds him, but there are difficulties at first. Gilgamesh, it seems, has broken in anger the stone punting poles that Urshanabi uses to propel his boat across the waters of death, probably because Urshanabi did not immediately grant his request for passage.[4] So now he has to cut a considerable number of wooden (and so perishable) punting poles needed to make up for the durable stone ones. But in the end he is taken across to the island on which Utanapishtim lives.

And so at long last, after incredible hardships, Gilgamesh has reached his goal. There on the shore of the island is his forbear Utanapishtim, and he can ask him how one obtains eternal life.

Yet, the moment Gilgamesh lays eyes on him, he senses that things are not quite what he had thought, something is subtly wrong:

> I look at you Utanapishtim,
> your proportions are not different, you are just like me!
> Nor are you different, you are just like me!
> My heart was all set on doing battle with you,

4. Jacobsen thinks that the words translated in this Norton Critical Edition as "Stone Charms" refer to "stone punting poles." This is contradicted by the Hittite version, so has not been accepted here (see p. 76) [Editor].

but you in idleness lie on your back.
Tell me, how came you to stand in the assembly of gods and
   seek life?

Utanapishtim then tells him the story of the flood, how he alone was
warned by his lord Ea, built an ark and saved his family and pairs of
all animals in it and eventually, after the flood, was granted eternal life
by the gods as a reward for having saved human and animal life. It is
the story of a unique event which will never recur, not a secret recipe
or set of instructions for others to follow. It has no relevance for Gilgamesh and his situation, and so destroys utterly all basis for the hope
that drove him on his quest:

> But for you, now, who will assemble the gods for you,
>   that you might find life, which you seek?

Utanapishtim leaves Gilgamesh no time to answer. Perhaps this is
because he wishes to bring his point home through an object lesson,
the contest with sleep that is to follow, perhaps it is merely an indication
that the flood story was a not too skillful insertion in a shorter tale that
originally had only the object lesson. At any rate, Utanapishtim immediately suggests to Gilgamesh that he try not to sleep for six days
and seven nights. Gilgamesh accepts the challenge—a contest, it would
seem, with Death's younger brother Sleep—but as he sits down Sleep
sends a blast down over him and Utanapishtim sardonically says to his
wife:

> Look at the strong man who craved life!
> Sleep is sending a blast down over him like a rainstorm.

Utanapishtim's wife, however, takes pity on Gilgamesh, knowing that
from this sleep he will never waken by himself, that fighting it is in fact
fighting death; and she begs her husband to wake him, that he may go
back in peace. Utanapishtim is not too keen. He knows only too well
that man is by nature deceitful, and he expects that Gilgamesh will
prove no exception. He therefore tells his wife to prepare food for Gilgamesh each day and to mark the days on the wall behind him. She
does so, and on the seventh day Utanapishtim touches him and he
wakes. His first words—as Utanapishtim had foreseen—are:

> As soon as sleep poured down over me you quickly touched me
>   so that you awakened me.

but the marks on the wall and the food portions in various states of
staleness bear witness to a different truth. There is no hope, then, and
terror holds Gilgamesh in its grip more desperately than ever.

> Gilgamesh said to him, to the faraway Utanapishtim:
> "What can I do, Utanapishtim, where will I go?

The one who followed behind me, the rapacious one,
sits in my bedroom, Death!
And wherever I may turn my face, there he is, Death!"

Utanapishtim has no solace to offer, only tells the boatman Urshanabi to take Gilgamesh to a place where he can wash, and to give him
clean clothes for the return journey. These clothes will stay fresh until
he gets home. Then Gilgamesh and Urshanabi launch the boat once
more, but as they move off, the wife of Utanapishtim again intercedes
for Gilgamesh, asking her husband what he will give Gilgamesh now
that, after so many hardships, he is on his way home. Gilgamesh brings
the boat back to shore and Utanapishtim tells him of a thorny plant
growing in the Apsû, the sweet waters deep under the earth, which has
power to rejuvenate. Its name is "As Oldster Man Becomes Child."
Gilgamesh, overjoyed, makes haste to open the valve down to the Apsû,
ties stones to his feet, as do the pearl divers in Bahrein, to drag him
down, finds the plant and plucks it, though it stings his hand, cuts
loose the stones, and lets the flood carry him up and cast him ashore.
Delighted, he shows the plant to Urshanabi—both, apparently, are now
on the shore of the Persian Gulf rather than at Utanapishtim's island
—and tells him of its qualities and how he is taking it back to Uruk
where he will eat it when he grows old and thus return to childhood.

But the weather is warm and as he travels back Gilgamesh sees an
inviting, cool pond, doffs his clothes, and goes in to bathe. A serpent
smells the odor of the plant which he has left with his clothes, comes
out of its hole, snatches, and eats it. As it disappears again into its hole
it sloughs off its old skin and emerges new and shiny and young.

This spells the end of Gilgamesh's quest. It has come to nothing.
The serpent, not he, has obtained the power of rejuvenation. And so
at last he has to admit defeat, final and utter defeat:

> On that day Gilgamesh sat down and wept,
> tears streaming down his cheeks:
> "For whose sake, Urshanabi, did my arms tire?
> For whose sake has my heart's blood been spent?
> I brought no blessing on myself,
> I did the serpent underground good service!"

The mood in which he meets this final defeat, however, is new and
other than what he has been capable of before; it is one of composure,
one of resignation, even humorous, self-ironical resignation, not of terror and despair. It is a mood not unlike Dryden's:

> Since ev'ry man who lives is born to die,
> And none can boast sincere felicity,
> With equal mind, what happens, let us bear,
> Nor joy nor grieve too much for things beyond our care.

> Like pilgrims to th' appointed place we tend;
> The world's an inn, and death the journey's end.

This late and dearly won resignation, this acceptance of reality, finds symbolic expression in the epic in a return to where we began, to the walls of Uruk which stand for all time as Gilgamesh's lasting achievement. Man may have to die, but what he does lives after him. There is a measure of immortality in achievement, the only immortality man can seek.

And so, when Gilgamesh finally arrives home, his first act is to show the walls to Urshanabi.

> Gilgamesh said to the boatman, Urshanabi:
> "Go up, Urshanabi, on the wall of Uruk, walk around!
> Examine the terrace, look closely at the brickwork!
> Is not the base of its brickwork of baked brick?
> Have not seven masters laid its foundations?
> An acre town and an acre orchards,
> an acre riverbed, also precinct of the Ishtar temple.
> Three acres and the precinct comprises Uruk."

This ends the story.

Sources

To clarify to ourselves what this ancient story is about and what its author was driving at, we may profitably ask two fundamental questions, one about sources and another about the theme. The question about sources asks what the author had to work with or—if the Old Babylonian fragments do not yet represent an epic, merely a cycle of tales—within what frame of reference, within what world of traditional Gilgamesh lore, the telling of these tales moved. The question about theme probes further. It asks what the author (or authors) did with those materials: how they were aimed, what meanings were seen in them or given to them. What made them the stuff of poetry?

The sources—what is known about them or can be surmised—we have tried to present succinctly in a diagram headed "Gilgamesh Tradition." It begins with the "historical Gilgamesh," a ruler of Uruk at circa 2600 B.C., in the period known as Early Dynastic II. The reason we assume that the Gilgamesh traditions cluster around an actual historical figure is that the tradition seems to be remarkably informed about the period with which it deals. Personages encountered in the episodes, such as Enmebaragesi, the father of Agga of Kish, mentioned in the tale "Gilgamesh and Agga,"[5] have been proved to be historical by contemporary inscriptions. The name Gilgamesh itself is composed

5. Included in this Norton Critical Edition as "Gilgamesh and Akka," p. 99 [Editor].

of elements that were current in proper names at that time, but fell out of use later; the custom of burying a ruler's court with him when he died, implied in the tale of "The Death of Gilgamesh," is actually known to us from the only slightly younger Royal Tombs at Ur, after which time it was abandoned.

As ruler of Uruk in the Early Dynastic period the historical Gilgamesh would have had the title often and would have united in his person the two distinct aspects of that office, magical and martial, which we have called on the chart respectively, the Heros and the Hero aspects.

The magical, or Heros, aspect of the office of e n we have touched upon earlier, in our discussion of the yearly rite of the sacred marriage, in which a human e n priest or priestess married a deity.[6] In Uruk, the e n was male and was the ruler of the city. In the rite he took on the identity of Dumuzi-Amaushumgalanna and married the goddess Inanna, or Ishtar. Their union magically ensured fertility and plenty for all. As shown by the famous Uruk Vase on which the rite is pictured, it was celebrated in that city as early as Protoliterate times.[7]

The magic powers of the e n were not limited to his ritual role in the sacred marriage. They belonged to him in his own right and continued to be effective after his death when he dwelt in the underworld, in the earth from which emanated the powers that made trees and plants, orchards, fields, and pasturage all grow and thrive. Notably successful e n priests, in whose time there had been years of plenty, continued, therefore, to be worshiped with funerary offerings after their death to insure that they would continue their blessings. The historical Gilgamesh, we may assume, was such a figure, credited with the power to produce plentiful years and continuing to be worshiped after his death. Our first tangible indication that this was so comes from account texts from Girsu of around 2400 B.C.[8] They show that funerary offerings for successful dead e n priests and other figures credited with fertility powers were made at a sacred locality called "The (River-)Bank of Gilgamesh." Further evidence of Gilgamesh's prominence as a power in the netherworld comes in a composition of about 2100 B.C. dealing with the death of the first king of the Third Dynasty of Ur, Urnammu. Here Gilgamesh appears as a judge in the realm of the dead. He occurs again in that role much later, in magical texts of the first millennium, where he is appealed to for judgment against wayward ghosts and other

---

6. It is the custom of some Sumerologists to set Sumerian words with spaces between the letters. This passage is not reprinted here [Editor].
7. The Uruk Vase is a stone vessel from Uruk, about 3000 B.C.E., that shows a goddess receiving offerings from a man in a distinctive fringed garment. Jacobsen thinks that the goddess is Inanna and the man is an "en," a Sumerian term sometimes understood to be a ruler with priestly, military, and political responsibilities. "Protoliterate times" refers to the period of Mesopotamian civilization between 3500 and 3000 B.C.E. [Editor].
8. Girsu was a Sumerian city important during the last half of the third millennium B.C.E. [Editor].

Gilgamesh Tradition

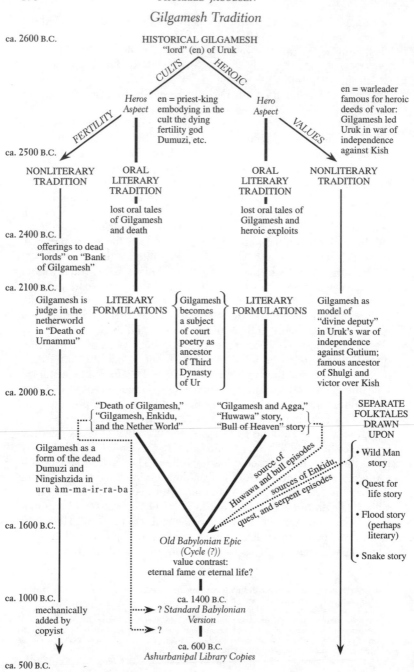

evils. Lastly, copies of laments, which may have been composed in the first half of the second millennium, mention Gilgamesh as a form of the dying god Dumuzi side by side with the god Ningishzida.

It is clear, thus, that there was a vigorous and continuous nonliterary religious tradition arising from the magical aspect of the historical Gilgamesh's office as e n.

The martial aspect of the office of e n implies that the historical Gilgamesh must have headed the army of Uruk; and here again the fact that traditions cluster around his name suggests that he was a military leader of extraordinary stature. Whether the later literary tradition celebrating him as leader in a war of liberation against Kish actually contains a historical kernel is not easy to say, though it is not implausible. At any rate, the role of liberator ascribed to him would seem to be the reason why the god Dumuzi-Amaushumgalanna chose to model himself on Gilgamesh when he served as divine deputy with the army of Uruk in a later war of independence, the one against the hated Gutian mountaineers in about 2100 B.C. Utuhegal, who led that army to victory, tells us in his inscription how he reported this decision of Dumuzi-Amaushumgalanna to his troops in a speech to them when they set out.

The tradition about Gilgamesh's war with Kish is referred to also in a royal hymn written for Shulgi of Ur only a generation or so after Utuhegal, and another military achievement, the building of the city walls of Uruk, is ascribed to him in a tradition attested to around 1800 B.C. in an inscription of the ruler Anam who made repairs on them.

Against the background of these two nonliterary lines of tradition, one about a power for fertility in the netherworld (the Heros line), one about a famed warrior and wall builder of old (the Hero line), we may then set what we might call the literary development. Of its beginnings we know nothing at all, but we may surmise a body of oral tales and songs handed down and lost to us, except as they furnished material for later written compositions.

It seems such written compositions appear first with the accession of the Third Dynasty of Ur around 2100 B.C. The kings of that dynasty not only took great interest in literature and the preservation of old works generally, but considered themselves descendants of Gilgamesh, so that traditions and works about him would have special claim to their attention. What we have preserved (almost all in later copies) are separate short epic compositions in Sumerian, and they divide quite neatly into the Heros and Hero lines of tradition, with works where Gilgamesh confronts the problem of death and works celebrating his martial prowess. Among the former is the tale called "The Death of Gilgamesh,"[9] which tells how death came to him in due time, how he

9. Included in this Norton Critical Edition, p. 143 [Editor].

violently protested, and how Enlil himself personally argued with him
that there was no way for man to avoid it. The story is known to us
only in fragments and its full meaning may only become clear through
future lucky finds. Another Gilgamesh story concerned with death is
called "Gilgamesh, Enkidu, and the Netherworld."[1] It tells how in the
beginning of time the goddess Inanna, wandering along the banks of
the Euphrates, found a tree floating on it, pulled it ashore, and planted
it with the hope that when it grew to maturity she could have a table
and a bed made from its wood. The tree grew apace, and when it had
reached the proper size Inanna wished to fell it but found that the
thunderbird Imdugud[2] had built its nest in the crown, the demoness
Kiskillilla had made her abode in its trunk, and a huge serpent nestled
at its root. Poor Inanna, therefore, could not get to her tree and appealed to her brother Utu, the sun god, for help, but he refused. She
then turned to Gilgamesh, who gallantly took up arms and drove the
intruders away, felled the tree, gave her its wood for a table and a bed,
and made for himself a puck and stick—for a game which seems to
have resembled modern hockey—out of its roots. Uruk played and
feasted, celebrating the victory, and all were happy except a poor waif,
a little girl who had neither father, mother, or brother, and felt left out
and lost. In her anguish she cried out to the sun god, the god of justice
and fairness, with the dread "i - U t u," and he heard her. The earth
opened and the playthings Gilgamesh had made for himself fell down
into the netherworld as a reproof to the thoughtless revelers. Gilgamesh
was disconsolate and Enkidu rashly offered to bring them back up.
Accordingly, Gilgamesh gave him elaborate instructions about how to
conduct himself in the netherworld, to be very quiet, not to call attention to himself by wearing fine clothes and anointing himself, not to
show emotion by kissing the dead child and wife he had loved or striking the dead child or wife he had hated. As it turned out, Enkidu did
all these things and the netherworld held him fast. Gilgamesh appealed
to the gods but all they could do for him was to open a vent to allow
Enkidu's ghost to come up to speak with him. The friends embraced,
and at Gilgamesh's questioning Enkidu told in detail what the netherworld was like. Conditions were dismal, although there were gradations
of misery. Those with large families, those who fell in battle, those who
had lived a good life, were better treated than the rest. But no clear
general principles of a moral or ethical nature seem to have governed
the infernal regions.

   Among the compositions belonging to the Hero line of the tradition
are, first of all, "Gilgamesh and Agga of Kish," a short Sumerian composition which tells how Gilgamesh led Uruk in a war of freedom

1. Included in this Norton Critical Edition, p. 129 [Editor].
2. Imdugud is another way of reading the name of Anzu, a monstrous bird [Editor].

against Kish. After Uruk had refused to do the usual corvée work, Agga's shipborne troops appeared before its walls and began a siege. A first sortie by the warrior Birhurturra proved unsuccessful. A second by Enkidu and Gilgamesh cut its way to Agga's boat and took him captive. The story raises intricate problems of heroic honor and loyalty. Gilgamesh had at one time, it appears, been a fugitive whom Agga received kindly. In fact, it would seem likely that it was Agga who made Gilgamesh his vassal ruler in Uruk, the position from which Gilgamesh now foments a rebellion against him. As a true hero, Gilgamesh cannot bear to owe anything to the largess of another, but must win what he has through his own prowess in battle, must prove himself by defeating Agga. Only after he has taken Agga captive can he acknowledge his debt to him: he sets him free and of his own free will promises to recognize him as overlord. The largess is now his: he is repaying the good turn Agga originally did him and is no more in his debt.

Gilgamesh's Hero aspect also dominates the Sumerian tale about his expedition against Huwawa which we have in two different versions, one elaborate, the other brief. The adventure is undertaken so that Gilgamesh may establish a name for himself, but the tale differs from the one about Agga in its more romantic, almost fairy tale setting. Unlike Agga, who is an entirely human opponent, Huwawa seems more ogre than warrior. Altogether mythical in character, finally, is the Sumerian tale about "Gilgamesh, Inanna, and the Bull of Heaven."[3] Here, as in the corresponding episode in the epic, Gilgamesh's valor is pitted against a deity and a mythical monster.

As will be seen, then, the two lines of the Gilgamesh tradition find literary expression in compositions showing diametrically opposed attitudes toward death. In the Hero tales death is almost recklessly courted by the hero: to repay Agga and no longer feel in his debt, to establish a name by killing Huwawa, to stand up to Inanna. In the Heros tales death is the great unavoidable evil: "the darkness that cannot be resisted has arrived for you," Gilgamesh is told in the "Death of Gilgamesh." "If I instructed you about the netherworld, you sitting down weeping. I would want to sit down and weep," Enkidu tells him in "Gilgamesh, Enkidu, and the Netherworld." These contradictory attitudes united in the person of Gilgamesh prefigure, as it were, what was to become the theme of the later epic: the change from an earlier disdain for death to the obsessive fear of it which drives Gilgamesh on his quest after Enkidu's death.

If we ask more specifically which parts of the Sumerian literary Gilgamesh tradition were used in the epic we would point to the Huwawa story and the "Gilgamesh, Inanna, and the Bull of Heaven" story as

3. Included in this Norton Critical Edition as "Gilgamesh and the Bull of Heaven," p. 120 [Editor].

obvious prototypes of the corresponding episodes in the epic. Both of these episodes are represented in the Old Babylonian materials. No Sumerian prototypes, on the other hand, have been found for the "Coming of Enkidu" and the "Quest for Life" episodes, which also are part of the Old Babylonian materials; and it may in fact be doubted whether these tales ever did form part of the Sumerian Gilgamesh tradition.[4] The likelihood is that they came from elsewhere.

In the case of the "Coming of Enkidu" tale, the motif of the hairy wild man who lives with the animals and is lured into human society by a woman is found in many forms in the folklore of Asia, and has been studied in detail by Charles Allyn Williams in his dissertation, *Oriental Affinities of the Legend of the Hairy Anchorite* (Urbana, 1925–26). His data show that the basis of the story is wonder at the orangutan, which was seen as a "wild man" deliberately shunning the company of other men. Its origin must therefore be looked for in the Far East.

The motif of the "Quest for Life" is also well known outside Mesopotamia. We find it in the story of "The Water of Life" in Grimm's *Hausmärchen*,[5] which tells about a dying king whose three sons set out to find the water of life to revive him. Only the youngest son, helped by animals to whom he has been kind, succeeds in reaching the island where the water of life is and bringing it back. He also, of course, wins a princess and, after further trials, lives happily ever after.

Lastly, there is the motif of the serpent stealing the plant of rejuvenation. This motif has been convincingly traced to Melanesian and Annam folklore by Julian Morgenstern in a study called "On Gilgamesh—Epic XI" in *Zeitschrift für Assyriologie* 29, pp. 284–300.

At what time these Far Eastern folktale motifs spread to Mesopotamia is not easy to determine. The first two must have been there in Old Babylonian times, as shown by the Gilgamesh materials, and there is no reason to assume that they had come in earlier. Why they were drawn into the Gilgamesh tradition is a further puzzle. The simplest answer—which can of course be no more than a surmise—is clearly to assume that the Old Babylonian materials do indeed belong to an epic, the author of which obtained his theme from the contrastive attitudes to death in the Gilgamesh tradition but supplemented his materials with other tales he knew that would serve to develop it. If one would see, rather, the Old Babylonian materials as representing merely a loose cycle of independent tales, it becomes more difficult to imagine what, if anything, about these tales could have made anybody think they referred to Gilgamesh.

If we are right in surmising the existence of an Old Babylonian Epic

---

4. Jacobsen refers here to the story of Enkidu, Tablet I, lines 99–244, and to the story in Tablets IX and X [*Editor*].
5. Fairy tales [*Editor*].

of Gilgamesh, that epic would almost certainly have been shorter than the version credited to Sîn-liqi-unninnī from perhaps the end of the second millennium, and that shorter again than the version in twelve tablets we have from the library of Ashurbanipal.[6] To begin with the latter, the twelfth tablet is a mechanical addition of an Akkadian translation of the last half of "Gilgamesh, Enkidu, and the Netherworld," a tale which has no organic connection with the rest of the epic. The adding on has indeed been done so mechanically that the first lines make no sense and can only be understood in the light of those parts of the original story which were dropped when it was attached to the Gilgamesh Epic. Without this addition—which seems more the work of a copyist than an editor—the epic shows a frame: it begins and ends with the same hymn in praise of the walls of Uruk. Probably this was the form Sîn-liqi-unninnī gave it, and to his version belongs probably also the long account of the flood which is put in the mouth of Utanapishtim and which takes up almost half of the eleventh tablet. That it belongs with the frame is suggested by the stress which the introduction to the epic places upon it, for in a passage omitted in our retelling of the story the introduction lists as one of Gilgamesh's achievements that he brought back information from before the flood. On the other hand the unwieldy length of the flood story, which badly upsets the flow and balance of the quest narrative, and the fact that it duplicates —in fact renders meaningless—the following contest of Gilgamesh with Sleep, strongly suggests that it is an addition and not part of the original story. Its source is obviously the tradition about the flood represented both by the Sumerian flood story and the elaborate account in the Atrahasis Myth.[7] In neither of these settings, of course, does the flood have any relation to the traditional Gilgamesh materials. Probably, therefore, we should imagine the Old Babylonian epic (or story of the quest) as not yet having it—at least not at such length—and assume that it was included because of its intrinsic interest by Sîn-liqi-unninnī in his version.

Structural Analysis: Themes

The question about the sources of the Gilgamesh Epic, which led us back to a historical Gilgamesh, e n of Uruk and point of origin for two lines of tradition with contrasting attitudes toward death, suggests that precisely in this contrast lay, *in nuce*,[8] the central theme of the later epic. The further question about how that theme was developed, what the author did with his materials and how he focused them, is

---

6. Jacobsen refers to a large collection of tablets assembled and copied at the capital city Nineveh by the Assyrian king Ashurbanipal (see p. 183, note 1). Most of the manuscripts of the standard version are from this collection. [Editor].
7. See note 1 on p. 84 and note 8 on p. 181 [Editor].
8. In essence [Editor].

perhaps best asked in terms of Sîn-liqi-unninnî's version. It may be phrased either in positive terms as a quest for achieving immortality or in negative terms, as a flight, an attempt to avoid death. In the accompanying diagram we have indicated progress toward the story goals by upward movement of the story curve, and shown hindrance by a downward turn.

As the story begins Gilgamesh shares the heroic values of his times, and his aspirations to immortality take the form of a quest for immortal fame. Death is not yet truly the enemy; it is unavoidable of course but somehow part of the game: a glorious death against a worthy opponent will cause one's name to live forever. In his pursuit of this goal Gilgamesh is extraordinarily successful and scores one gain after another. He fights Enkidu and gains a friend and helper. Together they are strong enough to overcome the famed Huwawa and to treat with disdain the city goddess of Uruk, Ishtar. At that point they have undoubtedly reached the pinnacle of human fame. And at that point their luck changes. In ruthlessly asserting themselves and seeking ever new ways to prove their prowess they have grievously offended the gods, paying no heed to them whatever. Huwawa was the servant of Enlil, appointed by him to guard the cedar forest; their treatment of Ishtar was the height of arrogance. Now the gods' displeasure catches up with them, and Enkidu dies.

When he loses his friend, Gilgamesh for the first time comprehends death in all its stark reality. And with that new comprehension comes the realization that eventually he himself will die. With that all his previous values collapse: an enduring name and immortal fame suddenly mean nothing to him any more. Dread, inconquerable fear of death holds him in its grip; he is obsessed with its terror and the desirability, nay, the necessity of living forever. Real immortality—an impossible goal—is the only thing Gilgamesh can now see.

Here, then, begins a new quest: not for immortality in fame, but for immortality, literally, in the flesh. As with his former quest for fame Gilgamesh's heroic stature and indomitable purpose take him from one success to another. Setting out to find his ancestor, Utanapishtim, in order to learn how to achieve, like him, eternal life, he gains the help of the scorpion man and his wife, Sidûri, the alewife, and Urshanabi. When after great travail he stands before Utanapishtim it is only to have the whole basis for his hopes collapse. The story of the flood shows that the case of Utanapishtim was unique and can never happen again and—to make his point—Utanapishtim's challenging him to resist sleep, proves how utterly impossible is his hope for vigor strong enough to overcome death.

However, at the point of the seemingly total and irreversible failure of his quest, new hope is unexpectedly held out to Gilgamesh. Moved by pity, Utanapishtim's wife asks her husband to give Gilgamesh a parting gift for his journey home, and Utanapishtim reveals a secret. Down in the fresh watery deep grows a plant that will make an oldster into a

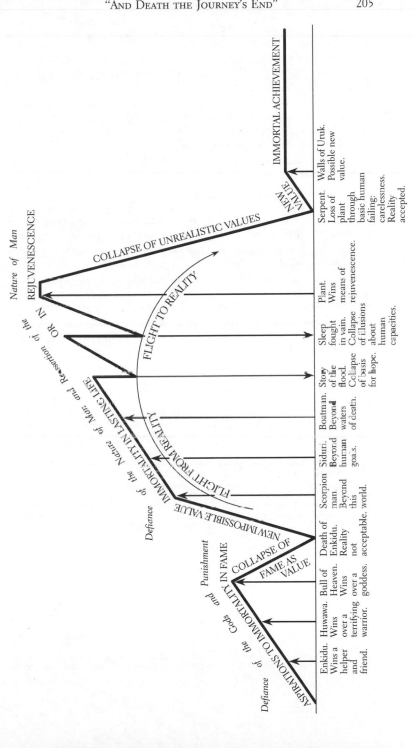

child again. Gilgamesh dives down and plucks the plant. He has his
wish. He holds life in his hand. Any time he grows old he can again
return to childhood and begin life anew. Then on the way back there
is the inviting pool and the serpent who snatches the plant when he
carelessly leaves it on the bank.

Gilgamesh's first quest for immortality in fame defied the gods and
brought their retribution on him; this quest for actual immortality is
even more deeply defiant; it defies human nature itself, the very condition of being human, finite, mortal. And in the end it is Gilgamesh's
own human nature that reasserts itself; it is a basic human weakness, a
moment of carelessness, that defeats him. He has nobody to blame but
himself; he has ingloriously blundered. And it is perhaps this very lack
of heroic stature in his failure that brings him to his senses. The panic
leaves him, he sees himself as pitiful and weeps; then as the irony of the
situation strikes him, he can smile at himself. His superhuman efforts
have produced an almost comical result. This smile, this saving sense of
humor, is the sign that he has, at last, come through. He is finally able to
accept reality and with it a new possible scale of value: the immortality
he now seeks, in which he now takes pride, is the relative immortality of
lasting achievement, as symbolized by the walls of Uruk.

The movement from heroic idealism to the everyday courage of re-
alism illustrated by the Gilgamesh story gains further in depth if one
analyzes it not only positively as a quest, but also negatively as a flight,
an avoidance. A flight from death rather than a quest for life—but a
flight in what terms?

Throughout the epic Gilgamesh appears as young, a mere boy, and
he holds on to that status, refusing to exchange it for adulthood as
represented by marriage and parenthood. Like Barrie's Peter Pan he
will not grow up.[9] His first meeting with Enkidu is a rejection of mar-

---

9. Note Harry Stark Sullivan, *The Interpersonal Theory of Psychiatry* (New York, 1953), p. 245:
"The beginning of preadolescence is equally spectacularly marked, in my scheme of development, by the appearance of a new type of interest in another person. . . . This new interest
in the preadolescent era is . . . a specific new type of interest in a *particular* member of the
same sex who becomes a chum or a close friend. This change represents the beginning of
something very like full-blown, psychiatrically defined *love*. In other words, the other fellow
takes on a perfectly novel relationship with the person concerned: he becomes of practically
equal importance in all fields of value." And ibid., p. 264: ". . . the change from preadolescence to adolescence appears as a growing interest in the possibilities of achieving some
measure of intimacy with a member of the other sex, rather after the pattern of the intimacy
that one has in preadolescence enjoyed with a member of one's own sex."
  The appearance of Enkidu provides Gilgamesh with a "chum" and allows him to remain
in preadolescence rather than moving on to a heterosexual relationship such as is characteristic
of adolescence and adulthood. Note that in explaining Gilgamesh's dream about Enkidu's
arrival his mother says [see Tablet I, lines 291–93 (*Editor*)]: "The axe you saw is a man, you
will love him as (you would) a wife, so that I will make him your compeer" and that at his
arrival Enkidu prevents Gilgamesh's marriage to Ishhara [see Tablet II, lines 98–99 (*Editor*)].
Also when he rejects the adult goal of marriage and children urged by the alewife he does
so in terms of his attachment to Enkidu [see Tablet X, lines 93–96 (*Editor*)]: "Why, my (good)
alewife do you talk thus? / My heart is sick for my friend! / Why, my (good) alewife do you
talk thus? / My heart is sick for Enkidu!" Throughout the epic the relationship with Enkidu
competes with, and replaces, marriage.

riage for a boyhood friendship, and in the episode of the bull of heaven
he refuses—almost unnecessarily violently—Ishtar's proposal of marriage. She spells disaster and death to him. So when Enkidu dies, he
does not move forward seeking a new companionship in marriage, but
backward in an imaginary flight toward the security of childhood. At
the gate of the scorpion man he leaves reality; he passes literally "out
of this world." In the encounter with the alewife he again firmly rejects
marriage and children as an acceptable goal, and eventually, safely
navigating the waters of death, he reaches the ancestors, the father and
mother figures of Utanapishtim and his wife, on their island where, as
in childhood, age and death do not exist. True to his images, Utanapishtim sternly attempts to make Gilgamesh grow up to responsibil-
ity; he proposes an object lesson, the contest with sleep, and is ready
to let Gilgamesh face the consequences. The wife of Utanapishtim, as
mother, is more indulgent, willing for Gilgamesh to remain a child,
and she eventually makes it possible for him to reach his goal with the
plant "As Oldster Man Becomes Child." Gilgamesh is fleeing death by
fleeing old age, even maturity; he is reaching back to security in childhood. The loss of the plant stands thus for the loss of the illusion that
one can go back to being a child. It brings home the necessity for
growing up, for facing and accepting reality. And in the loss Gilgamesh
for the first time can take himself less seriously, even smile ruefully at
himself; he has at last become mature.

> For whose sake, Urshanabi, did my arms tire?
> For whose sake has my heart's blood been spent?
> I brought no blessing on myself,
> I did the serpent underground good service!

The Gilgamesh Epic is a story about growing up.

RIVKAH HARRIS

Images of Women in the Gilgamesh Epic†

Several years ago W. L. Moran urged Assyriologists to adopt "the more
comprehensive critical strategies of the contemporary literary criticism"

† From *Gender and Aging in Mesopotamia: The Gilgamesh Epic and Other Ancient Literature*,
by Rivkah Harris. Copyright © 2000 by the University of Oklahoma Press, Norman. All Rights
Reserved. This material appeared first in *Lingering Over Words: Studies in Ancient Near
Eastern Literature*. Harvard Semitic Studies 37. Scholars Press, 1990. Parenthetical references
to Babylonian words and references to other chapters in this book have been omitted. The
author's notes have been abridged; the footnotes are the author's except where followed by
[*Editor*]. Tablet and line references are to the Akkadian Gilgamesh translation in this Norton
Critical Edition.

and to adapt "to new methods" in studying Mesopotamian texts.[1] This essay is such an attempt, tentative and programmatic, and at this juncture in no way definitive. The complex and multidimensional quality of the *Gilgamesh Epic* is too well known to require documentation. Like all classics that "frame human experience in enduring and universally meaningful forms," it cannot be encompassed in one final interpretation.[2] The many versions of the *Gilgamesh Epic* in ancient languages and the growing number of contemporary studies and translations attest to its enormous, abiding appeal.

Despite the many articles devoted to the *Gilgamesh Epic*, one area —images of women—has received no more than a passing comment or an occasional footnote. For the purposes of this study I will treat the epic as a coherent text, bypassing the many problems of composition and evolution (not that these are irrelevant to the topic). Elucidation of certain issues that pertain to composition and evolution might shed light on changing attitudes, if such there were, toward the roles of women in Mesopotamian society and on differences, if any, between this culture and those others whose scribes translated (and modified) the *Gilgamesh Epic* into their native languages. For example, J. Tigay has noted the different terms used for "wife": *sinništu*, *ḫirītu*, *aššatu*, and *marḫītu*, differences in terminology that relate to the evolution of the epic.[3] Of significance, perhaps, is the expanded role of Ninsun in the Late Version, in the scene preceding Gilgamesh's departure with Enkidu to do battle with Humbaba.[4]

What must be emphasized at the very outset, for it touches on all that follows, is the assumption that the *Gilgamesh Epic*, in whatever version, was composed by men for the edification and entertainment of a presumably male audience who read or to whom the epic was read. The *Gilgamesh Epic* is like the medieval *chanson de geste*,[5] which was "written for a male audience, *to male taste* [my emphasis]."[6] There-

1. In a review of W. Röllig, et al., *Altorientalische Literaturen*, in *Journal of the American Oriental Society* 100 (1980), pp. 189–90.
2. Charles Segal, "Ancient Texts and Modern Literary Criticism," *Arethusa* I/1 (1968), p. 7. Like Moran, Segal pressed for openness to literary-critical analyses of classical texts. Since this article he and other classicists have been highly productive in this direction, especially in treating women in myth and drama.
3. *The Evolution of the Gilgamesh Epic* (Philadelphia: University of Pennsylvania, 1982), pp. 232f. The problem, of course, is whether the contractions and expansions of women's speeches really incorporate changing attitudes or are simply literary structural changes. But I am aware that my not carefully separating the images in the different versions can create some confusion.
4. Ibid., pp. 74–75. There is also more stress put on her wisdom in the Late Version. She is not only *mūdât kalâma* ["one who knows everything" (*Editor*)] but also is wise (*emqet*).
5. Medieval French epic poems composed by troubadours, or wandering minstrels [*Editor*].
6. Penny Schine Gold, *The Lady and the Virgin: Image, Attitude and Experience in Twelfth Century France* (Chicago: University of Chicago, 1985), p. 2. My thinking on images of women was greatly stimulated by Gold's study, especially by her comments in the Preface. Despite the vast differences between Mesopotamian and medieval French society, what Gold has to say about the often uncritical presuppositions of feminist historians in her field has been very helpful to me.

fore, what we find in the epic are essentially male attitudes toward women, both human and divine. Central to the *Gilgamesh Epic* are the concerns and activities of men, with women functioning as supporting and subsidiary characters in the cast.[7] It must, moreover, be underscored that the correlation between the epic's images of women and actual women will not be "a simple unambiguous one of direct reflection or representation. . . . Images can also embody fears, fantasies and wishes."[8] The importance of women in the epic relates to their relationship with Gilgamesh. Their images incorporate the anxieties, longings, fears, and wishes of men, grounded in the realities of human life.[9] These images also reflect the diversity and ambiguity that characterized the lives of real women.

Women are regarded positively only when they assist Gilgamesh (and Enkidu) in those heroes' activities, when they nurture and advise in maternal fashion. The adventures of the heroes preclude a primary role for women. Though Mesopotamians did not live in a sexually dimorphic society like that of ancient Greece,[1] women's domain, nevertheless, did not partake of the political and military arenas that were the masculine domain.

A crucial element in the epic, which I believe is linked to its images of women, is the frequent use of symbolic inversion, especially status and role reversal, in the depiction of women. As B. Babcock notes, "Symbolic inversion may be broadly defined as any act of expressive behavior which inverts, contradicts, abrogates, or in some fashion presents an alternative to commonly held cultural codes, values and norms be they linguistic or artistic, religious or social and political." The term "derives from and conflates several existing discipline-specific uses."[2] Inversion serves more than one function in the *Gilgamesh Epic*; however, in this essay I focus on "the comic switching of expected roles."[3]

---

7. This is even true of Ishtar. Note the brevity of her proposal over against the length of Gilgamesh's refusal of her proposal.
8. Gold, op. cit., p. xviii.
9. Herein lie both the challenges and the pitfalls confronting the modern studying an ancient text. To what extent can ancient fantasies and realities be sorted out without imposing modern western views on an alien culture?
1. Harris refers to an interpretation of ancient Greek society according to which there were two nearly separate spheres of activity for men and women, with little interaction between the sexes outside of the home [*Editor*].
2. Barbara A. Babcock, ed., *The Reversible World: Symbolic Inversion in Art and Society* (Ithaca: Cornell University, 1978), pp. 14–15. In the introduction to this highly stimulating collection of essays, Babcock offers an excellent analysis of the various forms of inversion, their history and functions. She traces inversion back to "Greek parody of the Homeric journey to Hades" (p. 16). In my opinion, and this is at the heart of my essay, the *Gilgamesh Epic* is a far earlier source of inversion.
3. Ian Donaldson, *The World Upside-Down: Comedy from Jonson to Fielding* (Oxford: Oxford University, 1970), p. 6. I am well aware of the need for caution in applying a literary technique common in Western literature to the *Gilgamesh Epic*. But, as Babcock points out in her introduction (see above, n. 2) and as other essays in her book demonstrate, viewing the world as "upside down" and as topsy turvey seems to have universal comic appeal.

The reversal of the expected roles of certain women in the *Gilgamesh Epic* is, in my opinion, an essential feature of the epic's humor and comedy, which must have held great appeal for the ancients.

We now turn to the supporting cast in the *Gilgamesh Epic*, that is, to the women. Though they are not principal actors they are, nevertheless, significant in moving the plot along.

Ninsun, the divine mother of Gilgamesh, is all that a mother should be: caring, nurturing, and assisting her son in his quest, anxious though she is about it. Her name or epithet, Rimat-Ninsun "Wild-Cow Ninsun," incorporates the ubiquitous non-erotic metaphor used to describe tender, loving mother goddesses in Mesopotamia and elsewhere.[4] The all-knowing mother is expert, as are other Mesopotamian women, human and divine, in interpreting dreams.[5] Addressed tenderly by Gilgamesh when he speaks to her, she is the only female with whom there is a loving male/female relationship in the *Gilgamesh Epic*.[6] She laments his restless heart and pleads with Shamash to assist him. In a difficult passage in the Late Version [III, 97–110], Ninsun seems to adopt Enkidu as her son, brother then to Gilgamesh. If this is so, then she, like Siduri, affirms the centrality of family and kin to human life, the importance of the private sphere to men who dominate the public sphere. Ninsun is the only real mother (that is, biological mother) in the epic, but "motherly" also characterizes the other females, except for Ishtar.

The prostitute Shamhat is an intriguing woman.[7] She and Siduri,

---

4. See Wendy Doninger O'Flaherty, *Women, Androgynes and Other Mythical Beasts* (Chicago: University of Chicago, 1980), pp. 33, 42, 91 and passim for the cow as nourishing mother and goddess in Hindu tradition.

5. A. L. Oppenheim, *The Interpretation of Dreams in the Ancient Near East, with a Translation of an Assyrian Dream-book, Transactions of the American Philosophical Society*, New Series 46/III (1956), pp. 221f. The interpretation of dreams by mothers is often an aspect of their reassuring a troubled child.

6. This is an interesting parallel with Achilles and his mother Thetis. With both heroes, the father is very much in the background and there exists an intense relationship with another male.

7. The term *ḫarimtu* in the Enkidu episode is, in my view, a non-judgmental term for a woman who uses her sexuality to support herself. In Enkidu's curse the *ḫarimtu* becomes an object of male control and male violence. Perhaps translating it "harlot" or "whore" in the latter case might more accurately reflect the negative judgment. The feminist historian Gerda Lerner, in her highly speculative and problematic article, "The Origin of Prostitution in Ancient Mesopotamia," *Signs: Journal of Women in Culture and Society* 11 (1986), pp. 236–54, treats the *ḫarimtu*–Enkidu episode as an historical datum. She considers the *ḫarimtu* in the episode as "a temple harlot [who] is an accepted part of society." The *ḫarimtu* of the curse she views as a "commercial" harlot. She goes on to say that "the nature of this curse tells us that the *ḫarimtu* who mated with Enkidu lived an easier and better life than the harlot who has her stand at the town wall and is abused by her drunken customers" (p. 246). Lerner disregards the fact that the *Gilgamesh Epic* is a literary work and therefore historical data must be separated from literary motifs and themes. Among other things, the curse and blessing of Enkidu reflect the ambiguous attitudes toward the prostitute and incorporate the realities of her life. Perhaps the curse of Enkidu describes the life of the poor prostitute whereas the blessing describes the prostitute with something of the status of the Greek *hetaira*, a woman of culture and artistic talents. There is no evidence in the *Gilgamesh Epic* of a "temple" prostitute over against a "commercial" prostitute. Indeed I think the existence and extent of cultic prostitution requires reconsideration and more careful study of the primary sources. It is obvious that prostitution was a social fact. The question is how, when, and where it was transformed into an organized and institutionalized phenomenon of urban life.

the tavernkeeper, are working women who support themselves. Shamhat belongs to a class with low repute in society. Siduri is associated
with a place of low repute. And Ishtar, not incidentally, is associated
with both, as she is in the following hymnic passage: "When I sit at
the entrance of the tavern, I am a loving prostitute."[8]

Both prostitute and tavernkeeper belong to the extradomestic domain; both were important in the leisure activities of Mesopotamian
men. Though the real-life Mesopotamian prostitute had a bad reputa-
tion and was seen as a threat to the stability of the family,[9] her representation in the *Gilgamesh Epic* is quite the reverse. She is depicted,
through her actions and words, as a maternal, beneficent, wise woman
and not as a deceitful, lustful seductress. And significantly, like Siduri,
and unlike Umapishtim's wife, she is named, given individuality and
personhood. The *harimtu*[1] is thus a prime example of role and status
inversion: the lowly, marginal *harimtu* is elevated to the central kin role
of "mother."

The classicist P. Friedrich suggests "the connection between artful,
or sophisticated, sensuousness and civilization" in understanding the
role of Shamhat.[2] But the issue is far more complex. The intermediary
role of the prostitute in transforming Enkidu from one at home with
nature and wild animals into a human being is crucial. Also pertinent
is the Mesopotamian view that among the *mes,* which constitute the
norms of civilized life, are included sexual intercourse and prostitution.[3]
Relevant too is the fact that the prostitute in Mesopotamia, like the
prostitute in ancient Israel, was a prime representative of urban life.[4]
Of special value in appreciating the mediating role of the *harimtu* are
S. Ortner's comments, for she provides a frame of reference in understanding this function. Shamhat serves, as do women in other places
and times, as "one of culture's crucial agencies for the conversion of
nature into culture, especially with reference to the socialization of
children." Shamhat is the primary facilitator of Enkidu's socialization.
What she teaches Enkidu puts "her squarely in the category of culture,"
and "on the basis of her socializing functions alone, she could not be

8. Enkidu's curse also brings "prostitute" and "tavern" together.
9. See, for example, W. G. Lambert, *Babylonian Wisdom Literature* (Oxford: Clarendon Press,
   1960), p. 102, lines 73–79. R. Westbrook in *Journal of the American Oriental Society* 104
   (1984), pp. 753–56, examines evidence suggesting that public authorities might intervene to
   restrain a husband's extra-marital liaison with a prostitute.
1. Harlot [*Editor*].
2. *The Meaning of Aphrodite* (Chicago: University of Chicago, 1978), p. 14.
3. G. Farber-Flügge, *Der Mythos "Inanna und Enki" unter besonderer Berücksichtigung der Liste
   der* me (Studia Pohl 10 [1973]), p. 56:38f. "Me" is a Sumerian word meaning "cultural norm"
   [*Editor*].
4. See N. K. Gottwald, *The Tribes of Yahweh: A Sociology of the Religion of Liberated Israel
   1250–1050 B.C.* (Maryknoll, N.Y.: Orbis, 1979), pp. 557f., where he discusses Rahab's social
   position as a prostitute. Note that she may have "operated an inn," again the common association of prostitute and inn/tavern.

more a representative of culture."⁵ Thus by profession an urban representative and by role (really a role reversed) the domesticator of Enkidu, Shamhat is indeed a fitting intermediary.

Enkidu's break with his former life among wild animals is first achieved through sexual relations and is completed through learning the way of civilized life. Shamhat's is a dual role, as a sexual creature⁶ and as a maternal figure. The first is explicitly spelled out by the hunter: "Show him, the *lullû*-man (your) feminine wiles" [I, 185].⁷ The second is more implicit. Enkidu is untaught, and Shamhat teaches him the basics that every child must learn: eating, drinking, dressing himself.⁸ The predominant image is that of mother, her relationship with Enkidu that of mother and child.⁹ That this is to be the prostitute's function is perhaps already intimated by the hunter even before she meets Enkidu, when he says to her: "Release your hold" [I, 180];¹ the term *kirimmu* is described as "a characteristic and functional position of a mother's arm assumed in order to hold a child safely."² Shamhat later shares her clothing with the naked Enkidu. She takes "hold of him as the gods do" and leads him away from nature to the hut of the shepherds.³ Enkidu's dependence on the *ḫarimtu* is emphasized.

One final point should be noted—one that is, I suggest, an aspect of role reversal—Shamhat speaks in proverbial language and as a woman of wise counsel [I, 213, where an old version has: "the woman's counsel moved him" (*Editor*)].⁴ She thus emulates the wise Ninsun.

5. In Michelle Z. Rosaldo and Louise Lamphere, eds., *Women, Culture, and Society* (Stanford: Stanford University, 1974), pp. 67–87.
6. The masculine (pre)occupation with sexuality can be seen in the uses of *šamḫiš* [lustily, proudly (*Editor*)] and *qašdu* [sacrosanct (*Editor*)] cited by D. O. Edzard, *Orientalia* 54 (1985), pp. 53f. Note, as Edzard does, that Uruk is also described as the city of *kezrēti šamḫāti u ḫarimāti* [cult women, prostitutes, and harlots (*Editor*)] in VI, 156.
7. *Lullû* means "human being" [*Editor*].
8. Here we find perhaps the binary opposition of the raw and the cooked: milk of wild animals over against bread and beer which are cooked and processed. Note too that the hunter and shepherds who live in contact with the wild are also intermediary figures in the *Gilgamesh Epic*.
9. Given the confines of this essay I will only note in passing the consummate artistry with which the author(s) delineate the subtle and significant changes in the relationship, from wordlessness to dialogue; the importance of Enkidu's looking at and listening to Shamhat, beautifully replicating a child's development which ends with leaving mother and home and entering a man's world.
1. In this translation, "Open your embrace" [*Editor*].
2. *The Assyrian Dictionary of the Oriental Institute of the University of Chicago* Volume K (Chicago: The Oriental Institute, 1971), p. 406.
3. Probably "like a god/deity." This too would present a role reversal, the prostitute functioning as a deity and Enkidu as mere mortal! Note that when they eventually go to Uruk roles have changed, Enkidu walks "ahead and Shamhat behind him" [II, 74], in conventional(?) male–female fashion.
4. There may have been the topos of wise woman in Mesopotamia, as Claudia V. Camp, *Catholic Biblical Quarterly* 43 (1981), pp. 14ff., suggests was the case for ancient Israel. What seems to me likely is that the proverbial language of the *ḫarimtu* (and of the *sābītu* [tavern keeper (*Editor*)]) is an important element of inversion: from the mouths of these marginal, and I presume, uneducated, perhaps uncouth, women issue forth words of learning. See S. N. Kramer, *Journal of the American Oriental Society* 89 (1969), p. 10, for the simile "its (the bird's) mouth hurled invectives like a prostitute."

Siduri, the divinized tavernkeeper, is also depicted in ways that are very unlike the actual tavernkeeper.[5] Apart from Ishtar's association with taverns (as noted earlier), Siduri is linked to Ishtar in a problematic way.[6] Like Shamhat, Siduri has a name and is self-employed. Her name has been interpreted as perhaps having a Hurrian origin, meaning "young girl." Yet unlike Shamhat, the *harimtu* who undresses, Siduri is concealed by a veil [X, 4, differently interpreted (*Editor*)], as the modest wife of later Assyrian times would be: she is covered, as the *sābītu* in real life was surely not. Here too is an example of status and role reversal. She too is represented as a supportive figure who assists Gilgamesh in his dangerous journey to find Utnapishtim, after proffering him words of advice. What she has to say deserves special attention: her discourses can be described more accurately, I think, as pragmatic and realistic than as hedonistic or as recommending carpe diem.[7] She speaks practically, and to everyday living.

> Now you, Gilgamesh, let your belly be full!
> Be happy day and night,
> of each day make a party, . . .
> Let your clothes be sparkling clean,
> let your head be clean, wash yourself with water!
> Attend to the little one who holds onto your hand,
> let a wife delight in your embrace.

In contrast to Shamash, she stresses the goodness of food, clean clothing, washing, and bathing, which all belong to woman's domain. She stresses the importance of wife and child and thus of relationship. Siduri, then, like Shamhat, voices and upholds the social norms of Mesopotamian society. She too is depicted as a wise woman, speaking in proverbial language.

The two married women in the *Gilgamesh Epic*—Utnapishtim's wife and Scorpion-man's wife—are unnamed, anonymous creatures.[8] Their position is like that of Mesopotamian wives generally: relational, given definition as wife or daughter. Utnapishtim's wife remains entirely in the background of the flood story. She is passive, acted upon: Enlil

5. I opt for the translation "tavernkeeper" rather than "barmaid," for it seems more in keeping with the economic status of the *sābītu* in the Old Babylonian period. Then too Siduri has the equipment of the brewer (*kannu, namzītu* in X, 3), so she is more than a barmaid. The importance of the *sābītu* in the Old Babylonian period emerges from her mention in Mesopotamian laws. The (*bīt) aštammu* [tavern (*Editor*)] and the *bīt sābīti* [house of the tavern keeper (*Editor*)] were presumably not one and the same place, although there was certainly an overlap in their functions. Both provided drinks, entertainment, and a place to meet prostitutes. Although the *aštammu* probably was also an inn, providing overnight lodging to travellers, there is no such evidence for the *bīt sābīti*. Both appear to have had "bad" reputations. An important aspect of the *aštammu* is its relationship to the cult of Ishtar. Games were "played" in Ishtar's cult, and the *aštammu* and the *bīt sābīti* were places of "games."
6. It seems to me that for both Siduri and the *harimtu* Shamhat, the association with Ishtar is significant. But what its implication is remain unclear.
7. See Tigay, op. cit., pp. 167–69, 211–12, for a discussion of her "philosophy."
8. It is a striking contrast that men are always addressed by name in the Utnapishtim story.

brings her aboard the boat and has her kneel beside her husband [XI, 204]. But she speaks and acts on behalf of Gilgamesh. Hers is an intercessory role, a not-uncommon feminine and maternal role in Mesopotamian literary texts.[9] She beseeches her husband not to let Gilgamesh die when he falls asleep [XI, 220]. Begrudgingly he accedes, adding the jaundiced proverb, "Man is wicked, he will treat you wickedly" [XI, 223].[1] He has her bake breads to prove to Gilgamesh that he has slept for days. When Gilgamesh has failed the sleep test and prepares to return to Uruk, it is she who, mindful of society's rules of hospitality and sensitive to his enormous efforts, sees to it that he does not leave empty-handed.

Unfortunately the passage about the Scorpion-man and his wife is poorly preserved. What may be noteworthy is the specificity of her response when her husband comments that "he who has come to us is of divine flesh" [IX, 45]. She corrects this: "(Only) two thirds of him are divine, one third is human." Whether this specificity was an aspect of real women's rhetoric cannot be ascertained without further study.[2] I would suggest that, in keeping with the pattern described above, the Scorpion-man's wife may have been instrumental in having her husband assist Gilgamesh on his way.[3]

Before turning to Ishtar, the most intriguing and complex of the females in the *Gilgamesh Epic*, note should be taken of the very minor roles of other women characters. Aruru, the mother goddess, is told to create a replica of Gilgamesh [I, 96], and she follows those instructions. The mediating role of the women of Uruk, whose complaints against Gilgamesh are heeded by the gods, should also be noted.[4] As a result, the gods take action, which leads to the creation of Enkidu. Finally, attention should be given to Ninsun's suggesting to Shamash that Aya remind him of Gilgamesh lest he forget him [III, 56].[5]

All of the above-mentioned women (both divine and human) are assisting, nurturing, caring persons. Ishtar alone departs from the paradigmatic feminine role in the *Gilgamesh Epic*. She alone does not fit the mold. And yet even she is depicted as "motherly" in the flood story related to Gilgamesh by Utnapishtim, when she cries out "like a woman giving birth" [XI, 119] at the terrible destruction wrought upon man-

---

9. See the examples noted below of Aya and the women of Uruk.
1. In the *Gilgamesh Epic*, women speaking proverbially are consoling. Note also the harsh proverbial discourse of Gilgamesh with Ishtar.
2. A close study of letters to and by women focusing on women's rhetoric in light of recent analytical methods and comparative studies in this area might yield important results. Siduri's speech might also be described as "specific" in character.
3. If this is indeed the case, it would be strong confirmation of one of the basic theses of this essay.
4. "Anu(?) kept hearing their [the women's] complaints" (I, 89) [*Editor*].
5. This seems to be an echo from everyday life: the wife having to remind the busy, forgetful husband of some family matter or member.

kind by the flood.[6] But her representation in the episode where she proposes to Gilgamesh and he rejects her [VI, 7–79] is ruthlessly negative. What is to be made of this?

T. Jacobsen, in his sensitive analysis of Inanna-Ishtar, justly describes her as "in some respects the most intriguing of all the figures in the pantheon."[7] Although the Ishtar-Gilgamesh episode is open to various interpretations,[8] I suggest that a key to understanding it, if only in part, is the factor of inversion—the reversal of expected roles.[9] One does not expect a mortal (even one who is two-thirds divine) to reject a goddess. And yet Gilgamesh does so, detailing his refusal at length with the sordid features of Ishtar's many love affairs and her previous marriage. He castigates her with a series of metaphors,[1] several of which may provide clues to the reason for his rejection of her: she has behaved like a man in proposing marriage and in offering him gifts. She has thus assumed an active, aggressive posture, an unacceptable role for a female. In the many-faceted and paradoxical aspects of her personality, Ishtar is often depicted as warrior and hence as one who participates in the public domain of males.[2] But in the *Gilgamesh Epic* this aspect of her is rejected. Gilgamesh mocks and scoffs at her, as if she were a man. Enkidu humiliates her later in an unbelievable way [VI, 153–55]. And like a man, she retaliates.

Gilgamesh, in describing Ishtar's many affairs, is illustrating graphically the negative view toward the prostitute, as one with "countless husbands."[3] Ishtar—the prostitute par excellence in religious texts, the patroness of prostitutes—is repulsed by Gilgamesh because she has assumed an intolerable role for a female. Shamhat and Siduri are depicted positively because they act "motherly." There are, then, two inversions in the case of Ishtar: the status inversion, in which a mortal mocks a goddess; and the role (or category) inversion, in which a female behaves like a male.

Scholars have interpreted Ishtar's rejection as having its roots in theo-

6. It is amazing that in the *Gilgamesh Epic*, Ishtar's name has been substituted for Mami and Nintu of the Old Babylonian Atrahasis flood versions (see Tigay, op. cit., p. 224f.), given the antipathy toward her in Gilg. VI 1–79. There was no attempt to reconcile the contradiction. Though never a mother goddess in the Mesopotamian pantheon, Ishtar as the "mother" of kings is well attested. And yet the paradox is so much part of her nature.
7. *The Treasures of Darkness* (New Haven: Yale University, 1976), p. 135.
8. Tzvi Abusch, *History of Religions* 26 [1986], pp. 143–87. It is a comprehensive and in-depth analysis, the focus of which is very different from mine. This, once again, demonstrates the mutivalence of the *Gilgamesh Epic*, surely the touchstone of a classic.
9. Yet even she proposes marriage and not an affair. So despite the inversion she too reinforces the social norms as do other women in the *Gilgamesh Epic*.
1. The *nādu* "waterskin" of line 38 and the *šēnu* "shoe" of line 41, I suggest, are perhaps masculine symbols.
2. For the bisexuality of Ishtar, see H. Hoffner in *Journal of Biblical Literature* 85 (1966), pp. 333f. n. 54. What is an integral part of Ishtar's nature, her "manliness," is rejected in the *Gilgamesh Epic*.
3. W. G. Lambert, *Babylonian Wisdom Literature*, p. 102, line 72.

logical, political, or historical factors. I propose a different interpretive
direction, which I borrow from W. D. O'Flaherty: she writes that "the
gods are often imagined to *be* men, to *be like* men in character, and
here they appear not on the top but rather at the very *bottom* [my
emphasis] of the continuum, as ludicrous."[4] In the episode with Gilgamesh, Ishtar too is at the bottom, not on the top as one would expect
a goddess to be. This is an accurate description of status inversion.

Related to the question of images of women in the *Gilgamesh Epic*
is the nature of the relationship between Gilgamesh and Enkidu. Apart
from his closeness to his mother, Gilgamesh's only other intimate
relationship—demonstrated by kissing, embracing, and the holding of
hands—is with Enkidu.[5] As Jacobsen has so aptly put it, "throughout
the epic the relationship with Enkidu competes with, and replaces marriage."[6] I think that on a subliminal level, if not overtly, the composers
of the epic were critical of so intense a relationship between men.[7] A.
Kilmer has suggested that the word plays *ḫaṣṣinnu: assinnu* and *kiṣru:
kezru*,[8] as well as the sexual symbolism of *pukku* and *mekku*, point to
what may well have been a homosexual relationship between Gilgamesh and Enkidu.[9] She calls attention to what I would more precisely
describe as reverse sexual similes and metaphors: Enkidu's hair is like
a woman's [I, 106], and Gilgamesh veils his dead friend like a bride
[VIII, 58], to mention a few. Several times in his early dreams, Gilgamesh makes love to Enkidu's symbol " * * * as a wife."[1] The relationship between them is not simply that of male and female but that
of husband and wife. Theirs, then, was a reversal of normal societal
relations, which potentially undermined the continuity and stability of
the family. It is an example of category inversion—male acts like female.

4. *Women, Androgynes, and Other Mythical Beasts*, pp. 72ff. There is I think much merit in
looking to other polytheistic traditions and the scholarly work done with these to better understand Mesopotamian attitudes to the gods. This is not to dismiss political or historical issues
which I think must be considered. More questionable is the view that the "immorality" of
Ishtar was rejected. Application of O'Flaherty's "banalization of the gods" deserves far more
space than I devote to it here.
5. See Tigay, op. cit., p. 9 n. 20, p. 274 n.
6. Op. cit., p. 218*. [See p. 206, note 9, above (*Editor*)].
7. Homosexuality is banned only in the Middle Assyrian laws (§20) and so it may well have
been a social reality. However, it seems hardly to have been institutionalized as it was in
classical Athens (see the study by K. Dover, *Greek Homosexuality* [New York: Vintage, 1978]).
Enkidu is often referred to as *ibru* ["comrade," "companion" (*Editor*)] by Gilgamesh and on
occasion Enkidu so refers to Gilgamesh.
8. *Ḫaṣṣinnu* means "axe"; *assinnu*, "male prostitute"; *kiṣru*, "strength"; and *kezru*, "man with
curled hair" (see p. xix) [*Editor*].
9. G. M. Driel, T. J. H. Krispijn, M. Stol, K. Veenhof, ed., *Zikir Šumin, Assyrological Studies
Presented to F. R. Kraus on the Occasion of his Seventieth Birthday* (Leiden: E. J. Brill, 1982),
pp. 130ff. [*Pukku* and *mekku* are the athletic implements of Gilgamesh; see p. 129 (*Editor*)].
1. See also the simile describing the mourning Gilgamesh in VIII, 60–61: *kīma nēšti ša šuddat
mēraniša ittanašḫur ana pānīšu u arkīšu*. This has a maternal association and perhaps is an
extension of the husband/wife motif. Note too that all descriptions of physical beauty in the
Gilgamesh Epic are confined to Gilgamesh and Enkidu.

In view of this, one aspect of Tablet XII needs to be underlined. Along with others, I would contend that Tablet XII is an integral part of the *Gilgamesh Epic*.[2] Central to its theme is the importance of family, the necessity of offspring to mourn the deceased and provide the kispu offering.[3] Enkidu, who has been treated like a woman and wife, voices this view implicitly, if not explicitly. The nonbiological immortality that Gilgamesh sought so mightily is rejected by the author(s) of the epic: the importance of family and kin to a meaningful life is upheld.

Inversion, then, is one of the keys to understanding the *Gilgamesh Epic*. The reversals of the norms detected in the epic (of the *ḫarimtu*, of the *sābītu*, of Ishtar, of Gilgamesh and Enkidu) and thus the inversion of the social pyramid and of expected roles and categories must have made for humor and comedy, which would have had great appeal to ancient audiences. What has been said about inversions in carnival-like festivals may well be applicable to Mesopotamian society. Through inversion "a society with an acute sense of the necessity of everyday social distinctions [might experience] an apparently 'ideal' state of anarchy which it had no wish to bring permanently into being."[4]

Before concluding, we should give brief consideration to the paradigmatic image of "mother" in the *Gilgamesh Epic*. I suspect that this is a common image in other myths and epics in Sumerian and Akkadian. For example, in *Enuma Elish*, Tiamat is the mother regarded negatively. She, like Ishtar, breaks the boundary between male and female, setting up an assembly and doing battle with Marduk, thus participating in male spheres. Damkina by contrast, like Ninsun, acts as a mother should. When Marduk is raised to kingship, her gift to him is singled out.[5]

What is the significance of this mother image? One might suggest that its prevalence in the *Gilgamesh Epic* reflects the wish for the intimacy of the mother-child relationship in infancy, for a time of deep security and ignorance of death and thus distance from the reality of human mortality.

One should also ask whether this pervasive image tells us something about intrafamilial relations in ancient Mesopotamia. Was the mother

2. Kilmer, op. cit., pp. 130f.; B. Alster, *Revue d'Assyriologie* 68 (1974), pp. 55ff.; and Abusch, op. cit., as well.
3. Incredibly, even in the netherworld unexpected mention is made of a mother, "the mother of Ninazu" in Gilg. XII 29, 47 [see "Gilgamesh, Enkidu, and the Netherworld," line 190, above, p. 135 (*Editor*)]. The mention of "her breast" (*iratsa*), with its maternal association, in Gilg. XII 31, 49, should also be noted. [The *kispu* offering is an offering for dead ancestors (*Editor*).]
4. Donaldson, op. cit., p. 15.
5. *Enuma Elish* is the Babylonian "Epic of Creation"; in *Enuma Elish*, Tiamat is the mother of the younger generation of gods, Marduk is the Babylonian hero who kills Tiamat, and Damkina is the mother of the god Marduk. See *Muses*, pp. 350–401 [*Editor*].

RIVKAH HARRIS

the significant female in a man's life even after he had grown up and married, as was and is the case in India and China?[6] Was there an "ascending scale of affection"[7] of wife, sister, and mother, with mother first in importance? Definitive responses to what must at this time remain questions require close and sensitive study of the sources reflecting everyday life: legal and economic texts and especially letters. Perhaps related to the issue is the parricide motif found in Mesopotamian myths such as *Enuma Elish* and the Theogony of Dunnu.[8]

The *Gilgamesh Epic* informs and reveals cultural stereotypes and ideals, perhaps even the irretrievable life experiences of its author(s), but what can it inform us about everyday life?

6. Margery Wolf, "Chinese Women," in Rosaldo and Lamphere, op. cit., p. 168, notes that the Chinese mother made "full use of her husband's isolation from his children to strengthen their bond to her." For the close mother–son relationship and the importance of sons to mothers in the politics of the Indian family, see Sudhir Kakar, *The Inner World: A Psychoanalytic Study of Childhood and Society in India* (New Delhi: Oxford University, 1978), p. 57. The unusual text describing Lú-dingir-ra's message to his mother may have some bearing on the issue of the mother–son relationship in Mesopotamia. For a translation, literature on, and discussion of this text, see S. N. Kramer, "Poets and Psalmists," in D. Schmandt-Besserat, ed., *The Legacy of Sumer* (Bibliotheca Mesopotamica 4; Malibu, 1976), pp. 19–21.
7. This phrase is used by J. Th. Kakrides, *Homeric Researches* (Lund: Gleerup, 1949). On pp. 152ff. he discusses the ascending scale of affection in ancient Indian tales where siblings and parents rank above spouse; in other words, brotherly love is valued more highly than conjugal or filial love. The Inanna/Dumuzi laments might also be reexamined in light of this perspective. Note the comments by S. N. Kramer in his recent review of J. Van Dijk, *LUGAL UD ME-LÁM-bi NIR-GÁL*, in *Journal of the American Oriental Society* 105 (1985), p. 137, where he differs with Van Dijk on the nature of the relationship between Ninurta and his mother. He seems to suggest incestuous overtones. Much, I think, can be learned regarding problems and methods in utilizing myths as sources for rediscovering ancient intrafamilial relations from the critical and balanced review of Philip Slater's *The Glory of Hera: Greek Mythology and the Greek Family* by Helene P. Foley in *Diacritics* 5 (1975), pp. 31–36.
8. The Theogony of Dunnu is a short Babylonian mythological poem; see Stephanie Dalley, *Myths from Mesopotamia* (Oxford: Oxford UP), pp. 278–82. [*Editor*].

HILLARY MAJOR

Gilgamesh Remembers a Dream†

I have not been able to loose
that image,
the rosy root coils
of that nether plant
shining for the first time
in my palm, looping
to my elbows,
damp as I was,
soft in a sodden slimy way
like fish skin,
entrails pumping with blood.
Your lips had no tenderness
like its leaves, clinging on fingertips,
your voice no depth
like the dark places where I found it.
I have sifted through
piles of carnelians
in search of that hue
that holds my eyes like sunspots.
All brightness caught
in water drops,
reflected leaf to root,
beads of sweat on desert skin,
sea to sky, all
one burning opal
out of time.
The sands we crossed together
have slid with our footsteps
into story,
and I cannot recall
the lines of your face,
sitting again behind brick walls;
but every morning I am stunned
by the seconds I held eternity
in helpless arms.

† Hollins University's *Album*, spring 2000. Reprinted by permission of the author.

Glossary of Proper Names

Ab   Sumerian name for the tenth month of the Mesopotamian calendar. In the first millennium B.C.E., it was described as "the month of Gilgamesh. For nine days (or: on the ninth day) young men compete in boxing and wrestling matches by their city gates."

[. . .]-absu   A netherworld deity; the first part of the name is lost in the original, so identification is uncertain.

Adad   God of thunderstorms.

Adapa   Ancient sage of the city Eridu in Sumer who was a favorite of the god Enki but who lost a chance for immortality; see *Muses*, pp. 429–36.

Agilu canal   A canal in the vicinity of Uruk.

Akka   King of the city Kish and a contemporary of Gilgamesh. His siege of Uruk is described in the Sumerian poem "Gilgamesh and Akka."

Akkadian   One of the two major languages spoken in ancient Mesopotamia; the other was Sumerian.

Amorites   A Semitic-speaking people, originally at home in north Syria and the upper Euphrates region, who migrated in large numbers to Mesopotamia at the beginning of the second millennium B.C.E.

An   Sumerian name for the sky god, Akkadian Anu.

Antum   Wife of Anu, the sky god.

Anu   Akkadian name for the sky god, supreme in the pantheon but remote from human affairs.

Anunna gods   Literally "Noble Seed," a class of important gods in heaven and the netherworld, sometimes said to number fifty.

Anzu   Monstrous bird with the head of a lion, subject of a mythological story wherein he steals power from the god Enlil but is defeated in battle by Enlil's son Ninurta; see *Muses*, pp. 458–81.

Apsu   The fresh water under the earth, abode of the god Enki/Ea.

221

Aratta   A city fabled by the Sumerians for its wealth, especially in the precious blue stone lapis lazuli. It lay far to the east of Sumer in present-day Iran; see *Harps*, pp. 275–319.

Aruru   A goddess of birth, here credited with the creation of human beings.

Ashimbabbar   A Sumerian name for Nanna, the moon god.

Atrahasis   Literally "Super-wise," another Akkadian name of the immortal flood hero, Utanapishtim/Ziusudra; see *Muses*, pp. 160–203.

Aya   Goddess of dawn and wife of Shamash, the sun god, often called upon in prayers to intercede with her husband.

Babylonia   The southern half of Mesopotamia, roughly the region from present-day Baghdad to the Gulf.

Belet-ili   A goddess of birth, said in the Atrahasis version of the flood story to have created the human race along with the god Enki.

Belet-seri   Literally "Lady of the Steppe," scribe and bookkeeper in the netherworld.

Bibbu   In the epic, a deity serving as butler in the netherworld.

Birhurture   Hero of the city Uruk, who served as a negotiator during the siege of Uruk in the Sumerian poem "Gilgamesh and Akka."

Bitti   A netherworld deity.

Dilmun   Sometimes said to be the remote home of the immortal hero of the flood story, Utanapishtim/Ziusudra. Actually, Dilmun was the ancient name of the island of Bahrain.

Dimpiku   A netherworld deity, otherwise unknown.

Dumuzi   Shepherd god, youthful lover of Ishtar, who forces him to go to the netherworld; see *Harps*, pp. 1–84, and *Muses*, pp. 402–9.

Ea   Akkadian name for Sumerian Enki, god of wisdom, magic, and fresh water, known for his ingenious solutions to dilemmas and for his beneficence to the human race.

Eanna   Name of the temple of Inanna/Ishtar at Uruk and elsewhere.

Ekur   Name of the temple of Enlil at Nippur, later a generic term for "temple."

Endashurima   Literally "Cow Pen Beside the Lord," husband of the god Nindashurima and paternal ancestor of the god Enlil.

Endukuga   Literally "Lord of the Holy Mound," husband of Nindukuga and paternal ancestor of the god Enlil.

Enki (1) Sumerian name for the god of wisdom, Akkadian Ea. (2) Literally "Lord Earth," husband of Ninki and paternal ancestor of the god Enlil in "The Death of Gilgamesh."

Enkidu Shaggy man from the steppe, Gilgamesh's match and closest friend.

Enlil Chief god on earth, residing at Nippur, usually harsh and inimical to the human race.

Enmebaragesi King of Kish and father of Akka in "Gilgamesh and Akka." In "Gilgamesh and Huwawa A," Gilgamesh names Enmebaragesi as his older sister.

Enmerkar Gilgamesh's grandfather, hero of two Sumerian epic poems; see *Harps*, pp. 275–319.

Enmesharra Literally "Lord of All(?)," paternal ancestor of the god Enlil.

Enmul Literally "Lord Star," husband of Ninmul and paternal ancestor of the god Enlil.

Ennugi Minor deity in charge of water courses.

Enutila Literally "Lord of the Finished Days," paternal ancestor of the god Enlil.

Ereshkigal Queen of the dead and the netherworld, sister of the goddess Ishtar; see *Muses*, pp. 410–18.

Eridu City in southern Sumer with a sanctuary to the god Enki, regarded by the Sumerians as one of the oldest in their land.

Erish City in Sumer with an important temple to the goddess Nissaba.

Errakal A name for Nergal, god of the netherworld.

Etana Ancient Mesopotamian king who was said to have flown up to heaven on an eagle; see *Muses*, pp. 437–57.

Euphrates One of the two major rivers of ancient Mesopotamia, the other being the Tigris. In ancient times, the city Uruk lay on the banks of the Euphrates River.

Fate Netherworld deity (Sumerian name: Namtar), courier of death.

Gilgamesh King of Uruk, hero of this epic.

Great City A euphemism for the netherworld.

Great Mountain Epithet of the god Enlil as overlord of the netherworld.

Gudam   Literally "It is the Bull," a bovine creature, probably winged, that served as the agent of the goddess Inanna/Ishtar in her attack on the city of Uruk, as narrated in "The Gudam Epic."

Hanish   A god of destructive storms.

Hattusha   Capital city of the Hittites in central Anatolia.

Hittite   The language of Indo-European-speaking people who settled in central Anatolia during the first half of the second millennium B.C.E. and created a powerful nation-state in that region.

Holy Mound   Name of a shrine in the temple of Enlil at Nippur; also the name of the ceremonial throne for the chief god presiding in the cosmic assembly of the gods.

Humbaba   Monster appointed by the god Enlil to guard the forest of cedars, famous in Mesopotamian tradition for his hideous face.

Hurrian   Ancient language of northern Syria and Mesopotamia, not related to Sumerian or Akkadian.

Huwawa   Earlier form of the name Humbaba.

Igigi gods   A class of great gods of heaven, sometimes thought to number seven. The Sumerians called them the "Great Princes."

Inanna   Sumerian goddess of fertility and reproduction, equated with the Akkadian goddess Ishtar. One of her main temples was at Uruk.

Irnina   Another name or local form of the goddess Ishtar.

Ishtar   Goddess of sex, love, and warfare; the planet Venus; and the principal female deity in the Mesopotamian pantheon.

Ishullanu   According to a Sumerian myth, Ishtar, while on a journey, seduced a gardener, whom she then sought to kill. In the epic, the gardener is called Ishullanu and is said to have resisted her advances.

Itiha   A city mentioned only in the Hittite Gilgamesh, location unknown.

Kish   City in Babylonia. Kish and Uruk competed for control over Mesopotamia in the time of Gilgamesh.

Kulaba   A city quarter of the greater city Uruk. Gilgamesh is named as the chief priest of Kulaba.

Land of No Return   A name for the netherworld.

Larsa   City in Babylonia with an important temple to the god Shamash.

Lil Sumerian name for a class of demons, male and female, sometimes noted for their sexual appetites.

Lugalbanda Early king of the city Uruk, father of Gilgamesh, and hero of several Sumerian epic poems; see *Harps*, pp. 320–44.

Lugal-gaba-gal Minstrel of Gilgamesh, mentioned in "Gilgamesh and the Bull of Heaven." Appears as Lugal-gabagal-di in "The Gudam Epic."

Magan Mountainous land to the south and east of Sumer, famous for its hard black stone, identified with present-day Oman and the Makran coast of Pakistan.

Mala Hittite name for the upper Euphrates River or one of its tributaries.

Mammetum A name for the mother goddess.

Mashum Mythological mountain where the sun rose and set.

Mount Lebanon Mountain ranges along the Mediterranean coast of present-day Lebanon.

Mount Nimush High peak sometimes identified with Pir Omar Gudrun in Kurdistan. Landing place of the ark in the Gilgamesh epic.

Namtar God of destiny or fate, courier of death and the netherworld.

Nanna Sumerian name for the moon god. His main Sumerian temple was at the city Ur.

Nergal Sumerian name for the chief god of the netherworld.

Ninazu A god of healing and netherworld deity.

Nindashurima Literally "Cow Pen Beside the Lady," wife of Endashurima and maternal ancestor of the god Enlil.

Nindukuga Literally "Lady of the Holy Mound," wife of Endukuga and maternal ancestor of the god Enlil.

Ninegal Literally "Lady of the Palace," a goddess at Nippur sometimes identified with Inanna.

Ningal Literally "Great Lady," wife of the moon god.

Ningishzida Literally "Lord of the True Tree," a netherworld deity, sometimes depicted as a horned snake.

Ninhursag Literally "Lady of the Mountains," Sumerian birth and mother goddess.

Ninki   Literally "Lady Earth," according to some traditions, wife of the god Enki and maternal ancestor of the god Enlil.

Ninlil   Wife of the god Enlil.

Ninmul   Literally "Lady Star," wife of Enmul and maternal ancestor of the god Enlil.

Ninshuluhha   A netherworld deity in charge of ritual washing.

Ninsun   Sumerian goddess, called the "wild cow," wife of Lugalbanda and mother of Gilgamesh.

Nintu   Literally "Lady Who Gives Birth," a name for the Sumerian birth goddess.

Ninurta   Son of the god Enlil, agricultural and warrior god, who defeated the monstrous bird Anzu in battle; see also *Harps*, pp. 233–72.

Nippur   City in Babylonia with an important temple to the god Enlil.

Nissaba   Sumerian goddess of grain and writing.

Nudimmud   Literally "The One Who Fashions and Gives Birth," an epithet of the god Ea/Enki, referring to his creative aspect as patron god of artisans and craftsmen.

Nungal   Sumerian goddess in charge of the household of the temple of Enlil at Nippur.

Peshtur   Literally "Little Fig," named as a younger sister of Gilgamesh in the Sumerian poem "Gilgamesh and the Bull of Heaven."

Puzur-Amurri   Boatbuilder mentioned by Utanapishtim in his account of the flood, otherwise unknown.

Qassa-tabat   Minor netherworld deity, apparently in charge of ritual sweeping before the preparation of offerings.

Sebettu   Literally "The Seven," usually seven malevolent demons, but sometimes beneficent, as in the Sumerian poem "Gilgamesh and Huwawa A."

Shamagan   Another form of the name Shumuqan.

Shamash   God of the sun and of oracles, concerned with justice and honesty.

Shamhat/Shanhatu   Literally "Joy Girl," the harlot who seduces Enkidu.

Shangashu   Literally "Murderer," in the Hittite Gilgamesh the name of a human hunter active in the countryside outside Uruk.

Shulgi Sumerian king of the city Ur (c. 2094–2047 B.C.E.), who claimed kinship with Gilgamesh.

Shullat God of destructive storms.

Shulpa'e Literally "Hero Who Comes Forth Magnificently," god sometimes identified with the planet Jupiter, mentioned in "The Death of Gilgamesh" as a god of the netherworld.

Shumuqan Sumerian name of god of wild beasts and cattle.

Shuruppak City in Babylonia reputed to antedate the flood, long abandoned at the time the epic was written.

Siduri Literally "Maiden" in the Hurrian language, a tavern keeper whose establishment lay at the edge of the world.

Silili Mother of the horse in *The Epic of Gilgamesh*, otherwise unknown.

Sin God of the moon and of oracles, ruler of the sky during the night.

Sissig Sumerian god of dreams, mentioned in "The Death of Gilgamesh" as an illuminating spirit in the netherworld.

Sumer The southern half of Babylonia, especially during the third millennium B.C.E.

Sumerian The major language spoken in Sumer, or the southern half of Babylonia, during the time of Gilgamesh.

Sur Sunabu Another form of the name Ur-Shanabi.

Tigris One of the two major rivers of ancient Mesopotamia, the other being the Euphrates.

Ubar-Tutu Father of Utanapishtim, otherwise unknown.

Ulaya Modern Karun River in southwestern Iran.

Ullu Another name for Utanapishtim in the Hittite Gilgamesh.

Ur City in Babylonia with an important temple to the moon god.

Ur-Shanabi Servant of Utanapishtim, ferryman who crosses the ocean and the waters of death.

Uruaz City to the east of Babylonia, possibly near present-day Ahwaz in Iran.

Uruk Largest city in Mesopotamia in the time of Gilgamesh, with important temples to Anu and Ishtar.

Utanapishtim Literally "He Found Life," Akkadian name for the immortal flood hero, called Ziusudra in Sumerian, Atrahasis in Akkadian, and Ullu in Hittite. Sage and only human being, along with his wife, to survive the flood.

Utu   Sumerian name for the sun god, Akkadian Shamash.

Zabala   City in Babylonia with an important temple to the goddess Inanna/Ishtar.

Ziusudra   Literally "Long-Lived," Sumerian name for the immortal flood hero, Akkadian Utanapishtim.

Selected Bibliography

•indicates works included or excerpted in this Norton Critical Edition.

Bryce, Trevor. *The Kingdom of the Hittites*. Oxford: Clarendon Press, 1998.
Dalley, Stephanie. *Mesopotamian Myths*. Oxford: Oxford UP, 1989.
Foster, Benjamin R. *Before the Muses, An Anthology of Akkadian Literature*, 2nd ed. Bethesda, MD: CDL Press, 1996. Abridged version published as *From Distant Days*. Bethesda, MD: CDL Press, 1995.
George, Andrew. *The Epic of Gilgamesh, A New Translation*. London: Allen Lane, Penguin Press, 1999.
•Harris, Rivkah. "Images of Women in the Gilgamesh Epic." *Lingering over Words, Studies in Ancient Near Eastern Literature in Honor of William L. Moran*. Ed. T. Abusch, J. Huehnergard, and P. Steinkeller. Atlanta: Scholars Press, 1990, pp. 219–30. Also published in *Gender and Aging in Mesopotamia: The Gilgamesh Epic and Other Ancient Literature*. Norman: U of Oklahoma P, 2000, pp. 119–28.
•Jacobsen, T. *The Treasures of Darkness, A History of Mesopotamian Religion*. New Haven: Yale UP, 1976.
Jacobsen, T. *The Harps that Once . . . Sumerian Poetry in Translation*. New Haven: Yale UP, 1987. The major anthology of Sumerian literature.
Kuhrt, Amélie. *The Ancient Near East, c. 3000–330 BC*. London and New York: Routledge, 1995. Concise historical survey, with bibliographies.
Maier, John, ed. *Gilgamesh, A Reader*. Wauconda, IL: Bolchazy-Carducci, 1997. Contains essays on the epic from various viewpoints and an extensive bibliography.
•Moran, William L. "The Gilgamesh Epic: A Masterpiece from Ancient Mesopotamia." *Civilizations of the Ancient Near East*. Ed. Jack M. Sasson, John Baines, Gary Beckman, and Karen S. Rubinson. New York: Scribner's, 1995, pp. 2327–36.
Oppenheim, A. L. *Ancient Mesopotamia, Portrait of a Dead Civilization*, 2nd ed. Revised and completed by Erica Reiner. Chicago: U of Chicago P, 1977. Survey with emphasis on intellectual culture.
Sasson, Jack M., ed. *Civilizations of the Ancient Near East*. New York: Scribner's, 1995. Contains essays on Sumerian, Akkadian, and Hittite literature, as well as many aspects of ancient Near Eastern history and cultures.
Tigay, Jeffrey. *The Evolution of the Gilgamesh Epic*. Philadelphia: U of Pennsylvania P, 1982. Detailed study of differences among different versions of the epic, showing how the epic changed and evolved over time.

229